The Holiday Na
in

ITALY

Christopher O'Toole and Linda Losito

Illustrations by Paula Chasty

THE STEPHEN GREENE PRESS
Lexington, Massachusetts

OTHER BOOKS IN THE HOLIDAY NATURALIST SERIES

The Holiday Naturalist in France
The Holiday Naturalist in Greece (forthcoming)
The Holiday Naturalist in Spain (forthcoming)

First published in Great Britain in 1987
by Christopher Helm Publishers Ltd
First published in the USA in 1987
by The Stephen Greene Press, Inc.
Published simultaneously in Canada
by Penguin Books Canada Ltd
Distributed by Viking Penguin Inc.,
40 West 23rd Street, New York, NY 10010.

CIP DATA available

ISBN 0-8289-0626-2
Produced for Christopher Helm Publishers Ltd by
Curtis Garratt Limited, The Old Vicarage,
Horton cum Studley, Oxford OX9 1BT

Map by Taurus Graphics
Photographic acknowledgements:
Title page Krauskopf/PRISMA: Planet Earth Pictures; *page 8* Breig/
PRISMA: Planet Earth Pictures; *page 11* T C Middleton/Oxford Scientific
Films; *page 15* G I Bernard/Oxford Scientific Films

Filmset in Univers by SX Composing Ltd
Printed in Hong Kong
by Mandarin Offset

Title page
Typical Tuscany, with its cultivated fields, stands of cypress trees, olive groves, and solitary farm houses

CONTENTS

INTRODUCING ITALY

Italy has much to offer the holidaymaker – a warm climate, a wealth of resorts, fine food and wines, and many of Europe's cultural treasures. But it has rather more than this. Among some of the most compelling scenery of Europe, from the Alps in the north, to the sun-baked gorges and coastal hills of the south, there is a rich plant life and a fascinating world of wild animals to explore.

Merely to sit on a sunny hillside overlooking the sea is to experience the exuberance of Mediterranean life. With the sun golden green on the pine tops, with all the aromatic flowers and shrubs, and with the steady hum of insects and the calls of exotic

birds, there comes the sensual realization that, somehow, humankind was meant to live in such parts.

The lie of the land

Italy is a narrow, boot-shaped peninsula with the island of Sicily balanced on the toecap. The peninsula is 560 miles (900 kilometres) long and is never wider than 143 miles (230 kilometres). To the east is the Adriatic Sea and the coasts of Yugoslavia and Albania; to the west lies the Tyrrhenian Sea and Corsica and Sardinia.

While we may think of Italy as primarily a peninsula, at least one-third of its 116367 square miles (301 260 square kilometres) is very much part of the European landmass, though separated from it by the natural barrier of the Alps. This relatively young mountain range forms a wide arc, running for more than 590 miles (950 kilometres), from the high Graian Alps in the west, to the Dolomites in the east. Italy's political borders follow this natural one and, running from west to east, they are with France, Switzerland, Austria, and Yugoslavia.

In the north and west, the Alps comprise a girdle of crystalline rocks – granites, schists, and gneisses – while limestones predominate in the east. The Italian Alps boast some of Europe's most spectacular scenery. In the west, the Gran Paradiso National Park has many peaks of more than 10000 feet (3000 metres), the most notable being La Grivola, at 13056 feet (3969 metres). The Alto Adige in the extreme north was once part of Austria, known then as the South Tyrol (Südtirol), and German is still the major language. Here, peaks such as the Ortler reach 12829 feet (3900 metres). Yet, within sight of the permanent alpine snows and glaciated crags, places, such as Bolzano (Bozen) and Merano (Meran), enjoy a Mediterranean climate.

Further east, the Italian Dolomites get their name from dolomite, a type of limestone rich in magnesium. Mountains, such as Tofano and Sorapis, exceed 10500 feet (3200 metres) but the highest peak in the Dolomites is the Marmolada, at 10993 feet (3342 metres); perversely, however, it consists almost entirely of pure limestone.

Some of the southern valleys of the Alps have fine lakes, each with resorts in the midst of superb scenery. Maggiore, with an area of 82 square miles (212 square kilometres), is the second largest. Its northern end is in Switzerland while the southern, Italian end, enjoys a mild climate, and many Mediterranean crops are grown around its shores. To the east is Lake Lugano [18 square miles (48 square kilometres)], also with its northern tip in Switzerland. Lakes Como [56 square miles (146 square kilometres)] and Garda [143 square miles (370 square kilometres)], further east still, also enjoy a mild, Mediterranean climate. All of the lakes have excellent fisheries.

The wide arc of the Alps is separated from the Apeninnes, Italy's other major mountain range, by the great, triangular Padano-Venetian or Po Plain. This is drained by the greatest of Italy's rivers, the Po and its tributaries, the Orco, Ticino, and Oglio. This massive plain accounts for more than half the total area of lowland Italy and is made up of silts which were washed down by glacial meltwater between two and three million years ago. The plain continues to be built out eastwards by the Po, where it enters the Adriatic in a large delta between Venice and Ravenna.

South of the Po Plain, the Apeninne chain of mountains forms the backbone of peninsular Italy. They extend 870 miles (1400 kilometres) from the Alps of the Ligurian Gulf, to the south-west tip of Calabria. The Apennines vary between 19 and 93 miles (30 and 150 kilometres wide). At 7122 feet (2165 metres), Monte Cimone is the highest point of the northern Apennines. The northern and central Apennines are characterized by continuous summit ridges and regular slopes, and are composed of rocks of Cretaceous and Tertiary age (between 135 and 2.8 million years old); sandstones, schists, and clays predominate.

The wilder scenery of the Abruzzi region of the central Apennines owes its stark grandeur to the weathering of dolomite and limestone. The highest peak is the Gran Sasso d'Italia, at 9586 feet (2914 metres). Further south, the Calabrian Apennines are composed of ancient granites but are of lower altitude, the major peaks being Sila 6349 feet (1930 metres) and Aspromonte 6441 feet (1958 metres).

Across the Strait of Messina, only 1¾ miles (3 kilometres) wide at its narrowest, the island of Sicily is a continuation of the Calabrian Apennines.

The Alps and the Apennines are very young mountain ranges. They can be regarded as wrinkles on the Earth's crust caused by the collision of the African continent with that of Europe as a result of continental drift. This mountain building started in the Triassic period, between 225 and 180 million years ago, but reached its most intense phase in the late Oligocene and Miocene, between twenty-eight and fifteen million years ago. The geological faulting involved in the formation of the Apennines gave rise to intense volcanic activity. The island of Ischia in the Bay of Naples was formed in this way; the volcano of Monte Epomeo 2595 feet (789 metres) last erupted in 1310.

Vesuvius, in the hinterland of the Bay of Naples, is still active, its most recent catastrophic eruption being in AD 79, when the towns of Pompeii and Herculaneum were buried. More recently, a major eruption occurred in 1944. On Sicily, Mount Etna 10941 feet (3326 metres) is the largest active volcano in Europe and marks Italy's highest mountain outside the Alps.

The mountainous island of Sardinia 9270 square miles (24000 square kilometres) is mainly granitic overlain with limestones, with more recent volcanic deposits. Sardinia is separated from the French island of Corsica by the Strait of Bonifacio, which is only 7½ miles (12 kilometres) wide. Both islands were once part of southern France; they broke away and began their southerly drift some time during the Tertiary, between 65 and 2.8 million years ago.

The climate

Italy has a very varied climate, partly because of its great north-south extent and also because the country is divided by great

ountain barriers.
The Alps and the Po Plain have a mainly continental climate. The incipal influence is the East European high-pressure zone. The mmers are warm and the winters very cold, often with many isp, cloudless days. The mountainous regions have snow and infall all year while the plain has most of its rain in spring and tumn; there are often long periods of cold, damp fog in winter.
The Apennines separate the Po Plain from the benign influence the Mediterranean. Just how benign this influence can be is en in the table below. Compare the average January mperatures of San Remo and Rome, bearing in mind that the astal San Remo is some 146 miles (235 kilometres) further north an Rome and that Rome is 20 miles (32 kilometres) inland.
South of the northern Apennines, Italy has a distinct editerranean climate. The winters are mild and the summer are ery hot and dry. Rain falls throughout autumn, winter, and early ring, but irregularly and in short, heavy storms. This is the result Atlantic depressions penetrating the western Mediterranean.
In the summer, Atlantic depressions are deflected by subtropical gh pressure from the Azores and there is virtually no rain. deed, in the south of Italy, there may be more-or-less permanent ought for three or four months. Sunshine records for the south e impressive: there may be as many as 2500 hours a year.
Two kinds of winds have important climatic effects. The *bora* is a old, often very dry wind, which blows from the north-east, across e Adriatic, from Yugoslavia. It is sometimes very destructive and aches speeds of up to 100 mph (160 kilometres an hour). ccasionally, the *bora* may be associated with very heavy rain; it sually occurs between mid-May and mid-October. The *scirocco* is hot wind, which can be either dry *or* moist and rather enervating; blows from North Africa for fifty days of the year on average.

Weather statistics for six Italian cities

	Average temperature °F (°C) January	July	Average annual rainfall in (mm)
ilan	35.6 (2)	75.2 (24)	39.3 (997)
enice	38.3 (3.5)	75.2 (24)	
an Remo	50 (10)	74.3 (23.5)	31.7 (805)
lorence	41 (5)	77 (25)	32.7 (830)
ome	44.6 (7)	77 (25)	32.3 (821)
yracuse	51.8 (11)	78.8 (26)	20.8 (529)

abitats

uman settlement during the last 7000 to 8000 years has had rofound effects on the natural habitats of Italy. With the xceptions of mountainous areas and remote, inaccessible orges, most of the natural, climax forests have either disappeared r have been extensively modified, especially by grazing animals. levertheless, important remnants of natural habitats survive and, in many cases, they are in protected areas such as National Parks or Nature Reserves.

Alpine areas
Coniferous forests interspersed with alpine meadows are the main vegetation types. The meadows are rich in flowering plants and butterflies: swallowtails, Apollos, and Mountain Ringlets fly in the summer, and the air is rent with the cries of Alpine Choughs and the calls of eagle and buzzard.

Interesting plants include Lady's Slipper Orchid, Fire Lily, Peony, Edelweiss, and gentians. In all, nineteen species of flowering plants are protected by law, and there are substantial fines for people caught uprooting or picking flowers.

In the southern Alps, especially the Dolomites, deciduous forests occur as well as conifers. Some of the valleys are well protected from north winds by mountains, and a sub-Mediterranean type of plant life flourishes: Olives, Holm Oak, and Winter Jasmine grow. The animal life reflects the southern influence, too – cicadas, praying mantids, and Green Lizards.

The Po Valley
This is the most intensively farmed region of Italy, with few remnants of natural habitats. Narrow, rectangular fields bounded by irrigation ditches are the dominant landscape features here, interspersed with poplars, pastureland, mulberry trees, and vines. The field pattern is roughly arranged on a north-south axis, a result of the Roman pattern of land division called 'centuriation'. It is, indeed, the oldest surviving system of land division in Europe; it is best seen between Padua and Mestre.

Wetlands
The largest wetland area of Italy, the Pontine Marshes, was drained between 1932 and 1934. Situated just to the south of Rome, they were a breeding place for malaria mosquitoes. The few remaining wetlands of wildlife interest are mentioned in the next section.

The dramatic crags of the Dolomites stand guard over the north-eastern approaches to Italy.

Mediterranean habitats
From the north-west of Italy, to the extreme south, the Mediterranean climatic region is dominated by the Apennines. A typical Mediterranean type of plant life would normally grow at the foot of the Apennines, and remnants survive, especially in coastal regions. Evergreen forest is the climax vegetation, (*see* Glossary), with Holm Oak as the main component, with a shrub layer of Strawberry Tree and Laurestinus. Cork Oak sometimes grows with Holm Oak while, in areas modified by humans, Edible Chestnuts abound.

Much of the coastal lowlands is given over to Olive groves and vineyards. Here, the weeds of disturbed ground flourish, and a wander through such country will be repaid with glimpses of Golden Orioles, with their melodious, fluting calls, while the occasional electric blue-black flash betrays the presence of fast-flying, Violet Carpenter Bees, exploiting the flowers of wayside and field margins.

At higher altitudes, the evergreen forest gives way to open Beech woods and, higher still, the Beech is replaced by Silver Fir.

Coastal sands in the Mediterranean region are often colonized and dominated by Aleppo Pine, the source of the edible pine kernel. It also flourishes in dry limestone areas. The Maritime Pine is also mainly a coastal tree, but forms forests only in granitic areas. Much of the evergreen forest is restricted to coastal fringes. They are replaced by two types of habitat, *maquis* and *garrigue*, both of which have been encouraged to a greater or lesser extent by human interference.

Maquis comprises dense thickets of evergreen shrubs 6½ to 13 feet (2 to 4 metres) high and includes pink- and white-flowered Rock Roses, Brooms, and Tree Heather, together with the ccasional Strawberry Tree. The word *maquis* is a corruption of ıe Corsican word for Rock Rose, *macchia*. When these plants are ı flower, the *maquis* is a blaze of colour; the heady scents of romatic oils are a reminder that we are dealing with plants dapted for hot, arid conditions: the aromatic vapours are trapped ı the tiny air spaces between small, downy hairs on the leaves and tems. This reduces the rate of water loss from the plants.

Similar adaptations are found in plants of the *garrigue*. This is an pen community of plants, no more than 20 inches (0.5 metre) igh, with a fair amount of bare ground or rocks between clumps of egetation. Many of our culinary herbs are *garrigue* plants: Rue, arlic, Lavender, Hyssop, Savoury, Sage, Rosemary, and Thyme.

Mass-flowering occurs in April, and there is a rich community of ulbous plants, such as tulips, crocuses, Grape Hyacinths, orchids, ıd lilies. By the end of May, though, flowering is over and the egetation is burned brown by the fierce Mediterranean sun. With ıch prodigious flowering, albeit short lived, it is not surprising at both *maquis* and *garrigue* support a rich insect population. 'ild bees and wasps abound; lizards, snakes, and tortoises are ɔmmon sights, and the conspicuous webs of the equally ɔnspicuous Golden Orb Web Spiders stretch across openings in e vegetation. The riches of plants and animals in Italy will reward anyone who takes the trouble to wander through its hillsides and woodlands.

The Mediterranean

The almost land-locked Mediterranean connects with the narrow Straits of Gibraltar. The Straits themselves lie across a shallow shelf, which slows down the rate of flow in and out of the Mediterranean. Atlantic water flows inwards in a shallow stream and is relatively cool. The outward flow of Mediterranean water is heavier and this spills out over the Gibraltar sill. The water is heavier because the Mediterranean has a higher salt content than the Atlantic, with 37 to 39 parts per thousand of salt, compared with the Atlantic's 35 parts per thousand. A rate of evaporation as high as 4 million cubic feet (115 000 cubic metres) per second accounts for the high salt concentration. Rivers flowing into the sea contribute salts, too. One effect of this is that swimmers are more buoyant in Mediterranean waters than in those of the Atlantic.

The waters of the Mediterranean flow in a roughly anticlockwise direction and tidal fluctuations are small. Reduced tidal scouring, the land-locked nature of the sea, and the slow rate of interchange with the Atlantic, all conspire to make the Mediterranean very vulnerable to pollution. Many countries discharge untreated sewage, both industrial and domestic, directly into the sea. Many of Italy's beaches are now a serious health hazard. For this reason, it is wise to consult your travel agent or tourist guidebooks to see if your anticipated contact with the Mediterranean is likely to be in a safe area. While the exploration of rockpools for sea life may well be rewarding, remember the hazards of polluted water.

National Parks and Nature Reserves

There are several categories of protected land in Italy. These include National Parks (three established, four proposed), five Natural Parks, two Nature Reserves, and several Wildlife Refuges and Protection Oases. The last two are managed by the Italian World Wildlife Fund, and another private organization, Italia Nostra, is also active in conservation matters. There are also 101 reserves set up in State Forests.

The apparent inability of Italian authorities to enforce hunting laws put a premium on effectively protected wildlife habitats. The Wolf is protected by law, but is continually threatened by illegal poisoning. The Bear, Monk Seal, Ibex, and Chamois are also protected. The protected list includes all birds of prey, owls, storks cranes, the Flamingo, Swallows, Martins, tits, and warblers. However, many migrant birds which are protected in other countries may still be shot in Italy, and twice a year have to run the gauntlet of hunters.

National Parks

1 **Stelvio** *Situation* northern Italy, adjacent to the Swiss National Park. *Area* 530 square miles (1370 square kilometres). *Special features* the largest National Park, containing Italy's most

'he Valle d'Aosta stretches from Mont Blanc to the Gran Paradiso. Here lurks a glacial lake.

ɔxtensive glacier, the Ghiacciaio dei Forni; good alpine pastures, vith several flowering plants that are either rare or restricted to the 'ark; fine forests of Larch, Norway Spruce, and Arolla Pine at ıigher altitudes. The animal life includes 134 bird species, such as Golden Eagle, Alpine Chough, Rock Partridge, Ptarmigan, Black Grouse, Capercaillie; there are Roe Deer and Ibex introduced from he Gran Paradiso. *Information* Direzione del Parco Nazionale, 3órmio (Sondrio). *Access* unrestricted.

Gran Paradiso National Park *Situation* in the Graian Alps, etween 4000 and 13000 feet (1200 and 4000 metres), adjacent to ıe French Vanoise National Park. *Area* 283 square miles (730 quare kilometres). *Special features* former royal hunting reserve, ımous for herds of Ibex which, in Europe, owe their survival to fforts made at Gran Paradiso; Ibex now re-introduced from here ıto French, Swiss, Austrian, and other Italian Alps; Ibex best seen ɔove 10000 feet (3000 metres) at dawn or dusk; superb alpine ıeadows rich in wild flowers and Apollo butterflies; interesting pine botanic garden, 'Paradisia' at the head of the Valnontey ılley; forests of Larch, Arolla Pine, and Norway Spruce; animal e includes Eagle Owl, Golden Eagle, Ptarmigan, and abundant pine Chough; Marmots, Chamois, Brown Hare and Mountain are, and Foxes survive; Lammergeier, Lynx, Brown Bear, and olves are all now extinct. *Information* Ente Autonomo Parco azionale Gran Paradiso, Via Della Rocca, 46, 10123 Torino. *ccess* unrestricted.

Abruzzo National Park *Situation* Central Apennines, between 00 and 7250 feet (700 and 2200 metres). *Area* 155 square miles 00 square kilometres). *Special features* ancient Beech forests, ıs two species of maple, local race of pine, the Black Pine; assland above treeline with interesting plant life, including arberry, Bilberry, and several types restricted to the area, luding a recently discovered species of *Iris*. Animal life includes

Brown Bear, the largest European population outside the Balkans, and the now very rare Apennine subspecies of the Wolf; Foxes, Pine Martens, Squirrels, Snow Voles, and Wild Cats are to be found, as are the recently re-introduced Red and Roe Deer. The Apennine race of the Chamois is present, and in the absence of hunting has become quite tame; birds include Common Chough, Alpine Chough, Raven, Eagle Owl, Rock Partridge, and Golden Eagle as well as the very rare White-backed Woodpecker. *Information* Ente Autonomo Parco Nazionale d'Abruzzo, Via Livorna 15, Roma. *Access* unrestricted.

4 **Circeo National Park** *Situation* on the coast, 56 miles (90 kilometres) south of Rome. *Area* 29 square miles (74.5 square kilometres). *Special features* coastal dunes with interesting plant and insect life; lagoons important for wildfowl, and many migratory species recorded among a total of 220; woods of Hungarian Oak, Caucasian Ash, Common Alder, and English Elm, together with exotics such as False Acacia and Eucalyptus. Animal introductions include the Indian Mongoose, now a major pest; good population of Wild Boar throughout the reserve, together with Foxes, Pine and Beech Martens, Weasels, and Brown Hares. *Information* Ministero dell'Agricoltura e della Foreste, Parco Nazionale del Circeo, Ufficio Amministrazione di Sabaudia, 04016, Sabaudia. *Access* permission to visit must be sought from the park office because most of the forest is a closed Nature Reserve.

5 **Pollino National Park (proposed)** *Situation* the forested massif of Pollino in the southern Apennines. *Area* 194 square miles (500 square kilometres). *Special features* relict population of the Bosnian Pine, otherwise known only from Greece and the southern Balkans; forests, streams, gorges, noted for birds of prey, particularly the gorge of Raganello. Other animals include the Roe Deer, Crested Porcupine, Wild Cat, Otter, Wild Boar, and Wolf. *Information* Ufficio Amministrazione Foreste Demaniali dell Calabria, Via Bagnano, Castrovillari. *Access* unrestricted.

6 **Calabria National Park** *Situation* the Sila Grande, Sila Piccola and Aspromonte mountain ranges in southern Calabria. *Area* 106 square miles (170 square kilometres). *Special features* forests of Corsican Pine, Beech, White Fir, Chestnut, Oak, Aspen, and Maple with interesting wild flowers; animal life includes Spectacled Salamander, confined to Italy, Asp Viper, Red and Black Kites, Eagle Owl, Peregrine Falcon, Sparrowhawk, Goshawk, Egyptian Vulture, Short-toed Eagle, Bonelli's Eagle, Forest Dormouse, Wild Boar, Roe Deer, Appenine Wolves, Southern Red Squirrels, Martens, Otters, and Wild Cats. *Information* Ministero dell'Agricoltura e delle Foreste, Parco Nazionale della Calabria, Ufficio Amministazione di Cosenza, 87100 Cosenza. *Access* unrestricted, except in winter; best visited in autumn or late spring.

7 **Gennargentu National Park (proposed)** *Situation* south of Nuoro and Dorgali on the island of Sardinia. *Area* 388 square miles

(1000 square kilometres). *Special features* the finest wilderness area in all Italy, with cliffs, rolling hills, and rocky crags, with large areas of forest and *maquis*. Holm Oak and plantations of Corsican Pine; interesting plant life on 'islands' of limestone rock, including Thrift and Sea Lavender. Animal life includes native population of wild sheep (Mouflon); birds of prey less numerous than formerly, though Goshawk, Kestrel, Peregrine Falcon, Buzzard, and Golden Eagle still breed, but Lammergeier, Black Vulture, and Griffon Vulture are now seldom seen; Monk Seal no longer breeds. *Information* Ente Provinciale Turismo, Piazza Italia 9, Nuoro. *Access* unrestricted.

8 **Etna National Park (proposed)** *Situation* eastern Sicily. *Area* 194 square miles (500 square kilometres). *Special features* the tenth largest volcano in the world and the largest active one in Europe; lower slopes under cultivation, with Carobs, Olives, and Figs; Oak, Sweet Chestnut, and Black Pine grow above cultivated zones, replaced at 6250 feet (1900 metres) by the Etna Birch; there is a plant life restricted to the lava fields up to 8225 feet (2500 metres); reptiles are of interest, but overshooting has reduced the animal life considerably, so that Rabbits and Rock Partridge are the most conspicuous species; the Golden Eagle is now rare. A Management Plan was devised by Italia Nostra in 1969 but, at the time of writing, it had not been implemented; area under constant threat from building developments and remaining forest is now becoming overexploited. *Information* Ente Provinciale Turismo, Largo Paisiello 5, 95124 Catánia. *Access* unrestricted.

Regional Parks

Maremma Regional Park *Situation* on west coast, near Grosseto. *Area* 27 square miles (70 square kilometres). *Special features* unspoilt rocky outcrops overlooking cattle-grazed, brackish marshes, the cattle being of an unusual white, broad-horned breed; good dunes, and Stone Pine woodland, also Holm Oak, Strawberry Tree, Cork Oak, and a well-developed *maquis*-type vegetation; animals include Crested Porcupine, Wild Boar, Fox, Roe and Fallow Deer, many snakes and lizards; Wild Cat and Pine Martens have been seen. *Information* Conzorzio de Parco Naturale della Maremma, 58010 Alberese. Località Pinacce. *Access* Saturdays, Sundays, Wednesdays, and all public holidays, .00 am until one hour before sunset, 16 June-30 September, 7.00 am-4.00 pm, tickets available from park office, local post office.

Natural Parks

Alpe Veglia Natural Park *Situation* on Swiss frontier, near Simplon Pass. *Area* 15 square miles (39.3 square kilometres). *Special features* typical alpine area with good Larch forests and alpine pasture, with hillsides carpeted with Edelweiss, gentians, saxifrages, orchids, crocuses, primulas, and Creeping Azalea. Birds of prey rarely seen because of overhunting in recent past; typical alpine birds include Ptarmigan, Alpine Chough, Ring Ouzel, and Raven; Squirrel, Fox, Mountain Hare, Polecat, Ermine, Beech

Marten, Chamois, and Marmots can be seen. *Information* Ente Provinciale Turismo, Corso Cavour 2, Novara. *Access* unrestricted.

2 **Adamello-Brenta Natural Park** *Situation* Trentine Alps of northern Italy. *Area* 1½ square miles (4.36 square kilometres). *Special features* steep, forested slopes, with Spruce, Rowan, Birch, and Alder; much of the area is inaccessible; said to contain the only alpine populations of Brown Bear outside Yugoslavia, but recent information is hard to obtain and the current situation concerning the Bears is unknown. *Information* Ente Provinciale Turismo, Corso 3 Novembre 132 Trento. *Access* unrestricted.

3 **Panaveggio-Pale di San Martino Natural Park** *Situation* eastern Italian Alps. *Area* 61 square miles (158 square kilometres). *Special features* magnificent mountain scenery, with pink dolomitic limestones which take on a redder hue in the evening sun; mountain lakes and waterfalls, with three State Forests, all relatively undisturbed, comprising Scots and Arolla Pines, firs, and several flowers confined to the Park; good alpine meadow flowers with Apollo and Mountain Ringlet butterflies; animals include Marmot, Roe Deer, and Chamois, with birds such as Ptarmigan, Black Grouse, Capercaillie, and Golden Eagle. *Information* Ente Provinciale Turismo, Corso 3 Novembre 132, Trento. *Access* unrestricted, but visitors must keep to the marked footpaths.

4 **Fusine Natural Park** *Situation* Julian Alps, close to borders with Austria and Yugoslavia. *Area* ⅕ square mile (0.45 square kilometres). *Special features* very small but beautiful mountain lake area, the lakes occupying a natural amphitheatre carved by ice action during the last Ice Age and later dammed; dwarfed by massive peak of the dolomitic Margant 8806 feet (2677 metres); woodland comprises Scots Pine, Red and White Firs, Larch, Black Pine, Beech, Bird Cherry, and Hazel; animal life includes Martens, Foxes, Chamois, Red Deer, Roe Deer, hares, with birds, including Black Woodpecker, Golden Eagle, Eagle Owl, Black Grouse, and Capercaillie. *Information* Regione Autonoma Fruili Venezia Guilia Azienda delle Foreste, Via Manzini 41, 33100 Udine. *Access* unrestricted.

5 **Monte di Portofino Natural Park** *Situation* on coast, 18½ miles (30 kilometres) east of Genoa. *Area* 4½ square miles (12 square kilometres). *Special features* a rugged peninsula, with a fine rocky coast and well-developed *maquis* plant cover; Aleppo Pine on lower slopes, replaced higher up by Maritime Pine; also, forests of Hornbeam and Chestnut. Interesting animals include the Italian Wall Lizard, and the Park is one of the few localities for the rare Ocellated Lizard. *Information* Ente Provinciale Turismo, Via Rom 11-4, 16121 Genova. *Access* sunrise to sunset.

Wildlife Oases

1 **Punte Alberete Wildlife Oases** *Situation* delta of the River Po. *Area* 1⅕ square miles (3 square kilometres). *Special features*

Little of Tuscany has escaped cultivation but there is still much to attract the visitor seeking quietude.

marshland area, with lagoons, willows, Poplars, and Elms; internationally recognized waterfowl reserve, established by International World Wildlife Fund as one of the last remaining Italian examples of this kind of habitat; breeding birds include Little Egret and Heron, Penduline Tits, Garganey, Mallard, Shoveler, Ferruginous Duck, Glossy Ibis. *Information* WWF Italia, Sezione Emilia-Romagna, Via Cartoleria 17/2, 40124, Bologna. *Access* visitors allowed on perimeter embankments between sunrise and sunset, but ten or more people must get permission to enter from WWF Ravenna, Via Mentana 19, 48100, Ravenna.

Forest Reserves

1 **Val di Farma Forest Reserve** *Situation* 22 miles (35 kilometres) south of Siena. *Area* 17½ square miles (45 square kilometres). *Special features* one of few remaining watercourses in Tuscany in fairly natural state; Mediterranean trees on both sides of valley, including Holm Oak, Strawberry Tree, Cork Oak, and pines; Chestnut, Holly, Hazel, Hornbeam, Oak, Maple, and Poplar grow on the northern slopes of the valley, with one of the few areas in Italy where Yews grow; Alpine Newts occur in small, shaded ponds, their southernmost site. *Information* WWF Italia, Sezione di Siena, Piazza San Agostino 14, 53100 Siena. *Access* unrestricted.

2 **Umbra Forest Reserve** *Situation* Gargano promontory, southern Italy. *Area* 39 square miles (100 square kilometres). *Special features* rich plant life, 2000 species, with several restricted to the area; Beech woodland, with Yew, Flowering Ash, Field Maple, and Hornbeam; animal life includes the Edible Dormouse, Owls, Buzzards, and Red Kites. *Information* Ufficio Amministrazione Foreste Demaniali del Gargano, 71030, Forestra Umbra (Foggia). *Access* unrestricted, except for strict reserve, where visitors must be accompanied.

Nature Reserves

Orbetello Nature Reserve *Situation* 12½ miles (20 kilometres) north of Lago di Burano. *Area* 3 square miles (8 square kilometres). *Special features* series of tidal lagoons, forming the most important wetland reserve for migrant birds in Italy; habitats include freshwater ponds, brackish lakes, and low dunes covered with *maquis*; nesting birds include the Black-winged Stilt, the emblem of the reserve, Montagu's Harrier, Stone Curlew, several duck species and, possibly, the Great Spotted Cuckoo; Bee-eaters nest in sandy areas, and Flamingos, terns of several kinds, Avocet, Collared Pratincole, White Stork, Spoonbill, and Osprey all breed. *Information* WWF Italia, Delagazione per la Toscana, Via San Gallo 32, 50129 Firenze. *Access* Thursdays and Sundays, October-April, 2 hours per day, at 10.00 am and 1.30 pm, guided by duty warden; other times by special arrangement with WWF.

2 **Salina di Margherita Nature Reserve** *Situation* immediately north-west of Barletta, southern Italy. *Area* 14 square miles (37 square kilometres). *Special features* fresh, brackish, and saltwater areas, with good rush plant life, and many sedges, with abundant frogs and toads; extremely important refuge for wildfowl. *Information* Ufficio Amministrazione Forest Demaniali del Gargano, 71030 Foresta Umbra (Foggia). *Access* only when accompanied.

Wildlife Refuges

1 **Bolgheri Wildlife Refuge** *Situation* west-central coast. *Area* 8½ square miles (21.8 square kilometres). *Special features* important marshland for wildfowl, comprising low-lying, cattle-grazed marshy grassland, subject to winter flooding. The reserve is the most southerly nesting area for Lapwing; Night and Purple Herons nest in wooded area, and many wildfowl, including waders and ducks can be seen, undisturbed, by walking along a specially constructed pathway which runs for 1½ miles (2 kilometres) through the reserve; Blyth's Reed Warbler, Western Bluethroat, Crane, Black Stork, Lesser Spotted Eagle, and Osprey can all be seen in favourable conditions. Other animals include, Crested Porcupine, Tortoises, Pine Marten, Roe Deer, and Wild Boar. *Information* WWF Italia, Delagazione per la Toscana, Via San Gallo 32, 50129 Firenze. *Access* Tuesdays and Fridays only, November-March, by arrangement with the WWF.

2 **Lago di Burano Wildlife Refuge.** *Situation* in the extreme south of the Province of Grosseto. *Area* 1⅖ square miles (3 square kilometres). *Special features* coastal lake attracting large numbers of waders and waterfowl, especially during the hunting season, when other areas are decidedly unsafe. Important migrant visitors are Glossy Ibis, Great White Heron, Hoopoe, and Great Spotted Cuckoo; as well as lakeside habitats, there are important areas of *maquis*-covered dunes, with several kinds of oak, Mastic Tree, Myrtle, Juniper, and Broad-leaved Mock Privet. Animals include the terrestrial Tortoise, Crested Porcupine, Polecat, Weasel, and Badger. *Information* WWF Italia, Delagazione per la Toscana, Via San Gallo 32, 50129 Firenze. *Access* Thursdays and Sundays only September-May, at 10.00 am and 1.00 pm, at other times by arrangement with the WWF.

HOW TO USE THIS BOOK

The colour plates are arranged according to groups; for example, mammals, birds, and so on but, for ease of reference, the section on plants is arranged by flower colour.

This is not intended to be an exhaustive or comprehensive identification guide. Instead, we have selected plants and animals on the basis of those which the holidaymaker is likely to see. Our aim is to give a good idea of the commonest kinds of animals and plants, without the threat to baggage allowances posed by a set of more comprehensive field guides. If our book stimulates a special interest in any particular group of animals or plants, then the holidaymaker can explore this in more detail using one or more of the guides listed under 'Further reading'.

Key to the habitat symbols

coniferous and deciduous woodlands and forests

heaths, moors, and dry grasslands

marshes, swamps, and damp meadows

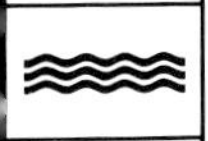
inland fresh water: rivers, streams, ponds, lakes, etc

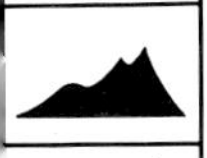
uplands: hills and mountains

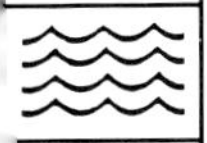
coastal: dunes, saltings, seacliffs, estuaries, sea

farmland and marginal areas

parks, gardens, urban areas

Crested Porcupine *Length* body 22½-26¾ in (57-68 cm), tail 2-4¾ in (5-12 cm). *Call* grunts and growls if disturbed; also rattles quills. *Habitat* wide ranging, but often near cultivated land; nocturnal.

Wild Cat *Length* body 20-31½ in (50-80 cm), tail 11-13¾ in (28-35 cm). *Call* loud wails and miaows. *Colour* some dark forms exist. *Habitat* scrubby hillsides and woodland; nocturnal.

Brown Hare *Length* 19-25½ in (48-65 cm). *Call* occasional grunts and whistles. *Habitat* scrubby woodland, open fields, and farmland; nest above ground, solitary; largely nocturnal except during courtship.

Water Shrew *Length* body 2¾-3½ in (7-9 cm), tail 2-2¾ in (5-7 cm). *Call* high-pitched shrieks and twittering; very noisy. *Habitat* aquatic; hunts under water; nests ir banks of streams; active during night and day.

Black Rat *Length* body 6-9 in (15-23 cm), tail 7-10 in (18-25 cm). *Call* squeaks and squeals. *Habitat* lives near to humans, in barns, sheds, stables, ships; very agile climber; seldom burrows; nocturnal.

Wood Mouse *Length* body 3¼-4¼ in (8-11 cm), tail 2¾ 4¼ in (7-11 cm). *Call* soft squeaks, or sharp chirrups if alarmed. *Habitat* woodland edge, hedges, scrubby areas, gardens; will enter houses; agile climber; nocturnal.

Edible Dormouse *Length* body 5-7½ in (13-19 cm), tail 4¼-6 in (11-15 cm). *Call* series of squeaks, whistles, and grunts. *Habitat* broadleaved woodland, parks, gardens; agile climbers; may overwinter in sheds and houses; nocturnal.

Garden Dormouse *Length* body 4-6¾ in (10-17 cm), t 3½-4¾ in (9-12 cm) *Call* range of grunts, snores, and whistles. *Habitat* broadleaved and coniferous woodland, orchards, and gardens; agile climber; w enter houses; largely nocturnal.

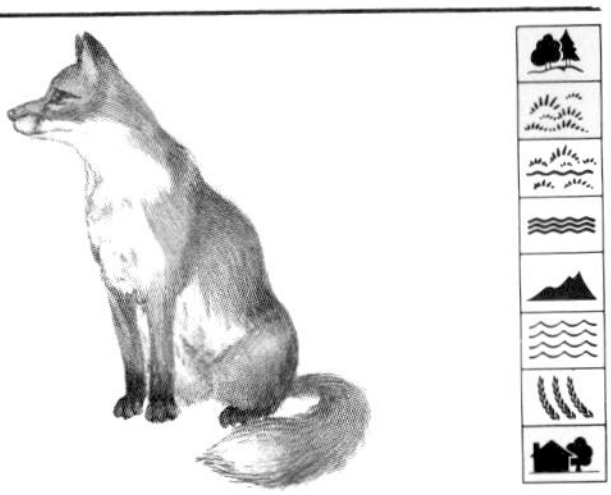

Red Fox *Length* body 22¾-30¼ in (58-77 cm), tail 12½-19 in (32-48 cm). *Call* a range of barks, whimpers, and screams. *Colour* occasional black or white forms occur. *Habitat* woodland, scrub, and in towns; largely nocturnal.

Badger *Length* body 26½-31¾ in (67-81 cm), tail 6-8 in (15-20 cm). *Call* a range of grunts, moans, snorts, and occasional screams. *Habitat* open woodland with well-drained soil; live in groups in large underground burrows or setts; largely nocturnal.

Pine Marten *Length* body 17½-20½ in (42-52 cm), tail 8¾-10 in (22-26 cm). *Call* 'tok-tok-tok', also growls, chatters and wails. *Colour* distinguished from Beech Marten by yellow throat. *Habitat* mainly coniferous woodland; active climber; partly nocturnal.

European Polecat *Length* body 12½-17½ in (32-45 cm), tail 5-7½ in (13-19 cm); females smaller than males. *Call* growling and chattering when disturbed. *Habitat* forested areas; hunt mainly on the ground but will climb trees.

Stone or Beech Marten *Length* body 16½-19 in (42-48 cm), tail 9-10 in (23-26 cm). *Call* a loud 'tok-tok-tok', also growling and chattering. *Habitat* woodland edge in mountainous regions; will nest in outbuildings; nocturnal.

Common Weasel *Length* body 6½-9 in (16-23 cm), tail 1½-2¼ in (4-6 cm); females much smaller than males. *Call* a shrill whistle. *Habitat* woodland, scrub, in low-lying or more mountainous regions; largely nocturnal.

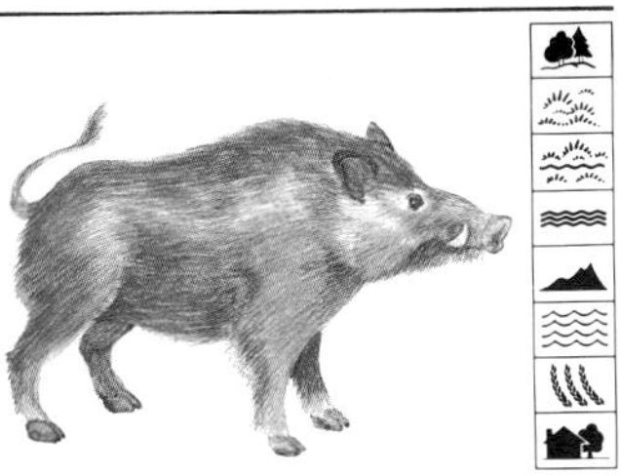

Wild Boar *Length* body 35½-71 in (90-180 cm), tail 6-8 in (15-20 cm). *Call* chatters, barks, and snorts. *Habitat* broadleaved woodland; often wallow in muddy ponds; active during day and evening.

Grey Wolf *Length* body 43¼-55 in (110-140 cm), tail 12-16 in (30-40 cm). *Call* growls, yelps, and long howls. *Habitat* mountains, forests, open plains; very restricted; largely nocturnal.

Great Crested Grebe *Length* 19 in (48 cm). *Call* a shrill 'er-wick' and a barking 'kar-arr'. *Habitat* freshwater lakes; colonial nesting in floating vegetation, wintering in estuaries and coastal waters; resident.

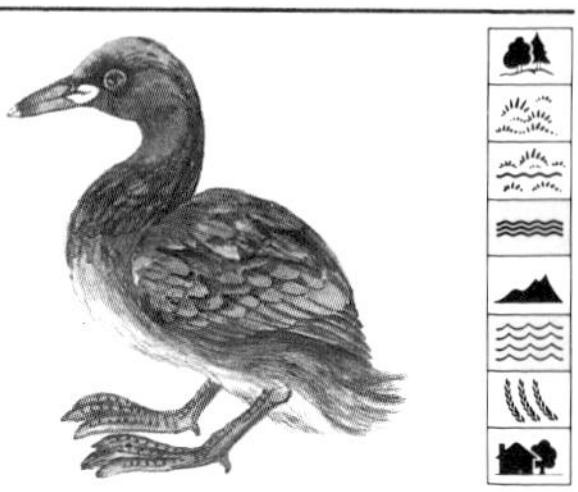

Little Grebe or Dabchick *Length* 10½ in (27 cm). *Call* a loud whinnying trill, also 'whit-whit' when alarmed. *Habitat* ponds, lakes, rivers, reservoirs; breeding resident; winters on estuaries and also inland.

Manx Shearwater *Length* 13¾ in (35 cm). *Call* raucous crowing and crooning sounds, especially at night at breeding sites. *Habitat* open seas; winter visitor.

Cory's Shearwater *Length* 18 in (46 cm). *Call* raucous wailing at nesting colonies. *Habitat* open seas, occasionally coastal waters, nesting in colonies in rock crevices on islands and cliffs.

Shag *Length* 30 in (76 cm). *Call* loud hissing and deep grunts at nest, otherwise a loud rasping croak. *Habitat* strictly marine, nesting on rocky coasts, rarely visiting sandy or muddy shores or inland; winter visitor.

Cormorant *Length* 35½ in (90 cm). *Call* a low, deep 'r-rah'. *Habitat* coasts, estuaries, coastal lagoons, occasionally inland lakes; colonial nests on rock ledges, occasionally trees on inland lakes; winter visitor, breeding on Sicily.

Grey Heron *Length* 35 in (90 cm). *Call* a harsh, deep 'frank'; in breeding season, numerous retching and croaking noises. *Habitat* rivers, lakes, damp meadows, seashore, nesting colonially in tall trees; resident breeder in north, otherwise winter visitor.

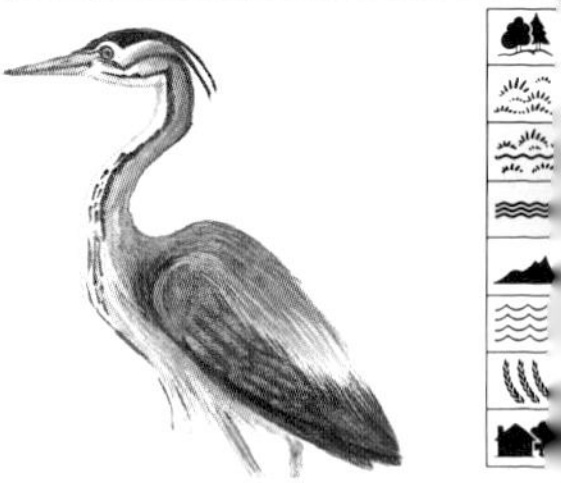

Purple Heron *Length* 31 in (79 cm). *Call* similar to that o Grey Heron, but usually less vocal. *Habitat* dense reedbeds, overgrown ditches and swamps, nesting colonially in reedbeds, sometimes in bushes; residen breeder.

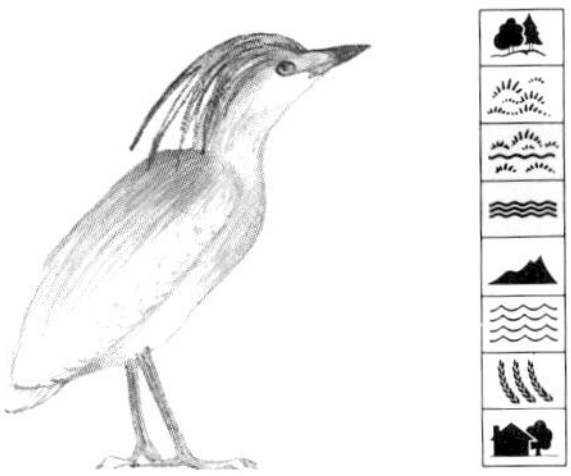

Squacco Heron *Length* 18 in (46 cm). *Call* a harsh, crow-like 'karr', in breeding season, especially at dusk. *Habitat* swamps, lagoons, marshes, but usually not in the open; regular spring and autumn migrant.

Little Bittern *Length* 13¾ in (35 cm). *Call* short croaking notes or a song comprising deep croaks every two seconds, often for hours at a time. *Habitat* reedbeds, wooded swamps, ponds, overgrown rivers; resident, and breeds in summer.

White Stork *Length* 40 in (102 cm). *Call* infrequent hissing and coughing notes; rhythmic bill-clattering during displays. *Habitat* farmland, damp meadows, marshes; spring/autumn migrant.

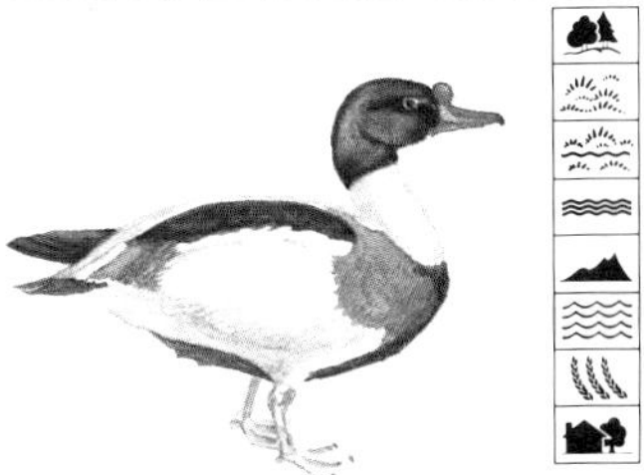

Shelduck *Length* 24 in (61 cm). *Call* rarely vocal outside breeding season, otherwise a nasal 'ak-ak-ak' and a deeper 'ark, ark'. *Habitat* sandy and muddy coasts; breeds along north and south coasts, nesting in rabbit burrows.

allard *Length* 23 in (58 cm). *Call* female, a loud uacking, male a quiet 'yeeb'. *Habitat* almost any water, intering sometimes on seacoasts and estuaries; esident breeder.

Garganey *Length* 15 in (38 cm). *Call* female, a short high quack, male dry rattling noise. *Habitat* reedy pools, marshes, rarely on salt water; summer breeder in north, nests in long waterside vegetation, spring/autumn migrant in south.

ite-headed Duck *Length* 18 in (46 cm). *Call* usually nt, but drakes cluck and squeak in breeding season. *bitat* shallow, reedy, freshwater and brackish pools; ident breeder in south, winter visitor in Sicily.

Ferruginous Duck *Length* 16 in (41 cm). *Call* drakes with a low, wheezy whistle, ducks a harsh 'kurr kurr'. *Habitat* large reedswamps or freshwater to brackish, still or slow-moving water; breeding resident.

Osprey *Length* 20-22¾ in (51-58 cm). *Call* a shrill cheeping. *Habitat* moorland or wooded country with lakes and rivers, wintering near large expanses of fresh, brackish, or salt water; resident breeder in Sicily, otherwise a spring/autumn passage migrant.

Red Kite *Length* 24 in (61 cm). *Call* a high, buzzard-like mewing. *Habitat* wooded hills, open areas with scattered trees, sometimes seen feeding on animals killed by road traffic; resident breeder, nesting in trees, sometimes old crows' nests.

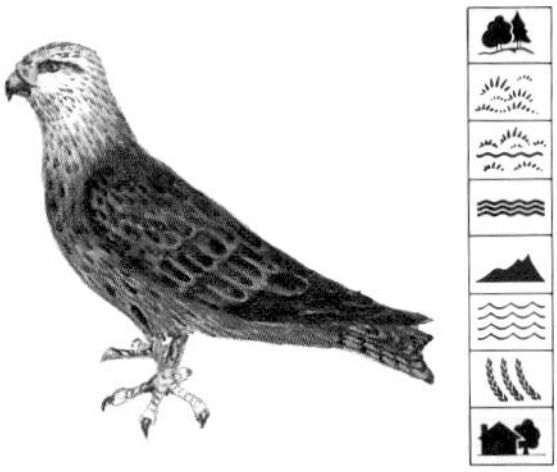

Black Kite *Length* 22 in (56 cm). *Call* high-pitched squealing cries, very noisy in breeding season. *Habitat* open woodland, scattered trees near lakes and rivers, sometimes in towns and villages; summer visitor.

Short-toed or Snake Eagle *Length* 24¾-27¼ in (63-69 cm). *Call* loud, either a harsh 'jee', a buzzard-like 'mew-ok' or a weak 'ok, ok, ok'. *Habitat* open country, both hills and plains, with scattered woods; feeds mainly on snakes in south; breeding summer visitor.

Sparrowhawk *Length* 11-15 in (28-38 cm). *Call* chattering, based on 'kek', 'kew', 'kyow', or 'kiv'. *Habitat* woodland, farmland, coppices, nesting in fir trees in mixed woods; presence often indicated by feathers, fur under perches; resident breeder.

Goshawk *Length* 19-24 in (48-61 cm). *Call* male, a shrill 'ca-ca-ca-ca' or 'qek-qek-qek-qek', from female a screaming 'hi-aa', 'hi-aa'. *Habitat* both broad-leaved and coniferous forests; resident breeder.

Buzzard *Length* 20-22 in (51-56 cm). *Call* sometimes a short, croaking note, more usually a long drawn-out, high mewing 'pee-oo'. *Habitat* forests and areas with scattered woods, rocky coasts; resident breeder, nests on rock ledges, trees.

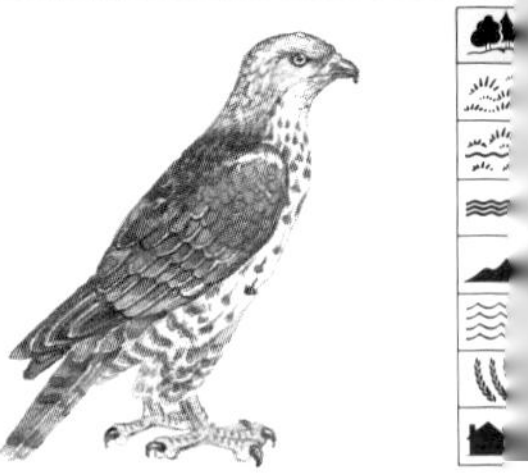

Honey Buzzard *Length* 20-22¾ in (51-58 cm). *Call* a hi squeaky 'kee-er' and a rapid 'kikiki'. *Habitat* open gla and outskirts of deciduous woods; robs wasps' and bees' nests; breeding summer visitor in north, otherwise passage migrant.

Bonelli's Eagle *Length* 26-29 in (66-74 cm). *Call* a Goshawk-like chattering 'kie, kie, kikiki'. *Habitat* rocky mountains, wintering in plains; resident breeder in south, nesting on steep cliff faces, sometimes in trees.

Golden Eagle *Length* 29½-34½ in (75-88 cm). *Call* a few whistling notes, occasionally a yelping 'kya'. *Habitat* open mountain country, sometimes mountain forest; resident breeder, nesting on crags, sometimes in trees.

Egyptian Vulture *Length* 22¾-26 in (58-66 cm). *Call* usually silent. *Habitat* open country in mountains and lowlands; breeding summer visitor, nests on cliffs or in trees.

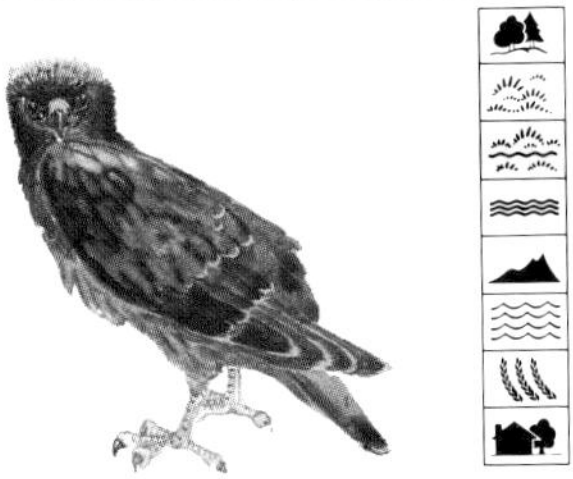

Marsh Harrier *Length* 19-22 in (48-56 cm). *Call* a high, Lapwing-like 'quee-a'. *Habitat* fens, swamps, marshes, and large reedbeds; resident breeder, large nest in reedbed, usually surrounded by water.

lontagu's Harrier *Length* 16-18 in (41-46 cm). *Call* 'kek-ek-kek', shriller than Hen Harrier. *Habitat* fens, arshes, farmland, moors with tree clumps; spring/ ıtumn passage migrant.

Lanner Falcon *Length* 17 in (43 cm). *Call* in breeding season, a shrill 'kri, kri, kri'. *Habitat* rocky, mountain slopes, cliffs, stony plains; resident breeder, nests in rocks, sometimes trees and ruins.

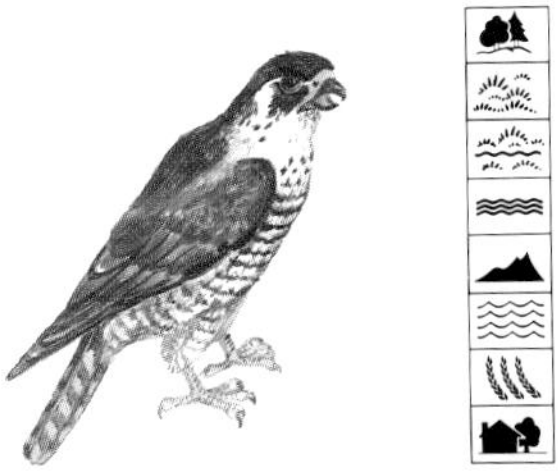

regrine Falcon *Length* 15-19 in (38-48 cm). *Call* mainly arsh chattering note, wide range in breeding season, cluding 'we-chew', 'kek-kek-kek'. *Habitat* wild untains, moors, spires; breeds on crags, cliffs.

Hobby *Length* 11¾-14 in (30-36 cm). *Call* a distinct 'ket' or 'kew', and a rapid 'kikikiki'. *Habitat* open woodland, grassy hills with scattered trees; resident breeder, breeds in trees, often in old crows' nests.

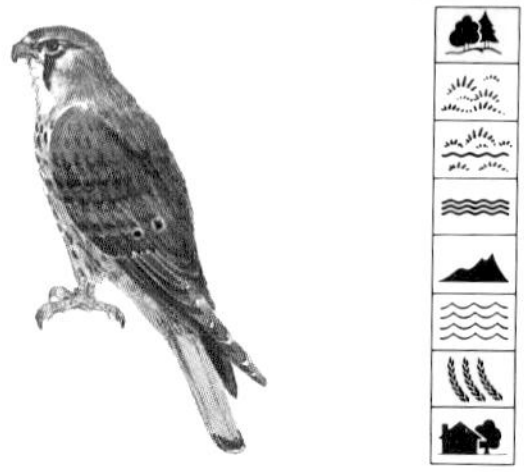

Kestrel *Length* 13½ in (34 cm). *Call* usually silent outside breeding season; shrill, repeated 'kee, kee, kee' and a musical 'kee-lee'. *Habitat* open woodland, farmland with scattered trees; resident breeder, breeds in old crows' nests.

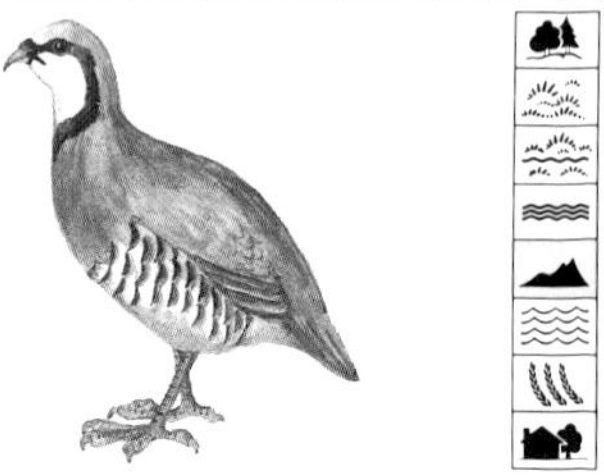

Rock Partridge *Length* 13 in (33 cm). *Call* in spring and autumn, a staccato 'tchertsi-ritt-chi', an explosive 'pitchi-i' when alarmed, usual call a Nuthatch-like 'whit-whit-whit'. *Habitat* rocky hillsides, nests among rocks.

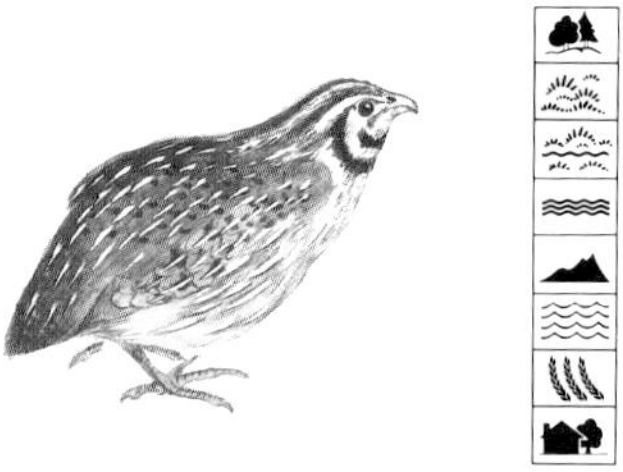

Quail *Length* 7 in (18 cm). *Call* male, a repeated 'quic, quic-ic', female a wheezing 'queep, queep'. *Habitat* open ground with grass tussocks, rough pasture, crops; resident breeder in south, breeding summer visitor in north.

Pheasant *Length* male 26-35 in (66-89 cm), female 21-24¾ in (53-63 cm). *Call* male with strident 'korrk-kok', both sexes also cackle and chuckle. *Habitat* farm and parkland, woodland edges, reeds; resident breeder, nests on ground: INTRODUCED.

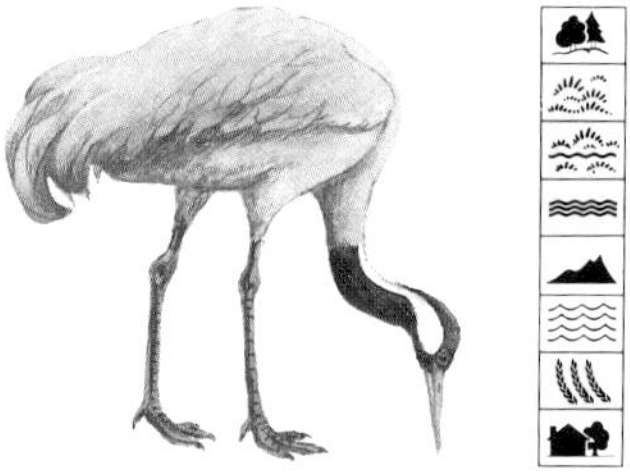

Crane *Length* 45 in (114 cm). *Call* a loud 'krooh' and quieter 'kr-r-r' plus various hissing and grating noises. *Habitat* fields, large marshes, steppes, river banks; winter visitor in south, otherwise spring/autumn passage migrant.

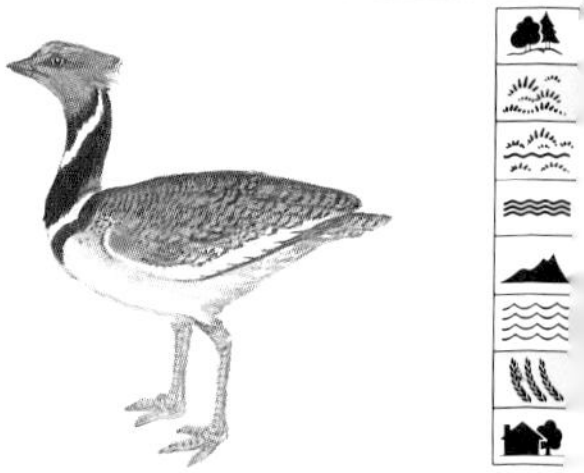

Little Bustard *Length* 17 in (43 cm). *Call* a short 'dahag' c 'kiak' and a snorting 'ptrr' or 'prett'. *Habitat* grassy plains, large fields of grain, clover; resident breeder, nests on ground.

Water Rail *Length* 11 in (28 cm). *Call* a hard, repeated 'gep-gep-gep', also 'krui, krui, krui', other groaning, squeaking notes. *Habitat* dense aquatic vegetation, reedbeds, weedy ditches; resident breeder, nests in reeds.

Spotted Crake *Length* 9 in (23 cm). *Call* male a hard, ticking 'tchich-tchuck', otherwise a high, sharp 'quitt. . . quitt. . . quitt'. *Habitat* swamps, fens, overgrown ditches; resident breeder, nests in boggy areas.

Moorhen *Length* 13 in (33 cm). *Call* a harsh 'kr-r-rk' or 'kittick'. *Habitat* ponds, marshes, slow streams, town parks; resident breeder, nests in bushes, reeds near water, often in trees and in old nests of other species.

Coot *Length* 15 in (38 cm). *Call* a distinctive, high 'kowk', 'kewk', and 'cut'; flocks make a communal roaring when alarmed by predator. *Habitat* as for Moorhen but with more open water; resident breeder, nests in reeds, etc.

ystercatcher *Length* 17 in (43 cm). *Call* a shrill 'kleeep', shorter 'pic, pic, pic', and a loud, piping communal isplay call. *Habitat* coastal waters, estuaries, ometimes inland; resident breeder in north, winter isitor in south.

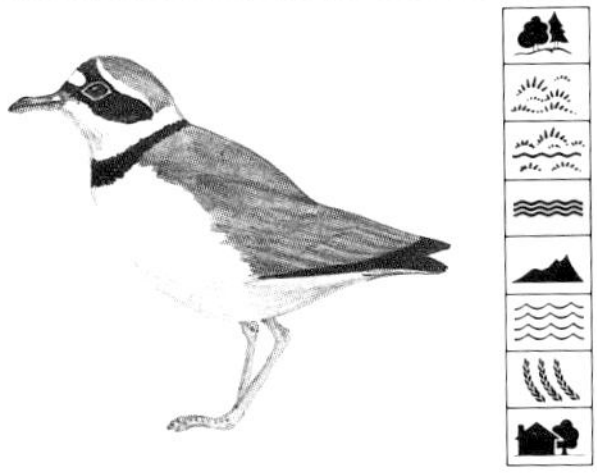

Little Ringed Plover *Length* 6 in (15 cm). *Call* a high, piping 'pee-oo', 'pip-pip' and a repeated song of 'tree-a, tree-a'. *Habitat* fresh water, gravelly river islands, flooded gravel pits; breeding summer visitor.

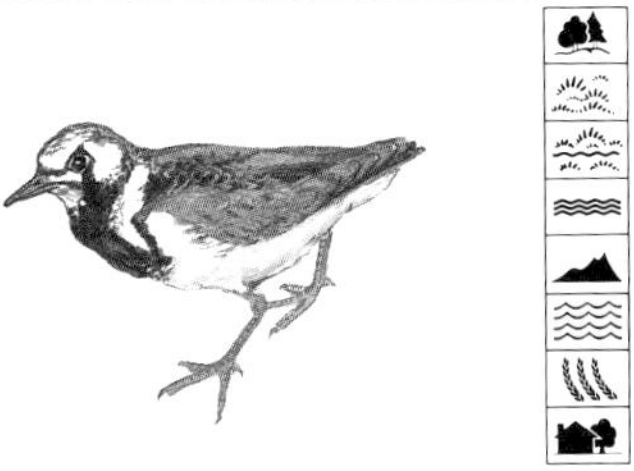

rnstone *Length* 9 in (23 cm). *Call* a rapid 'tuk-a-tuk' d a long trill. *Habitat* a spring/autumn passage grant.

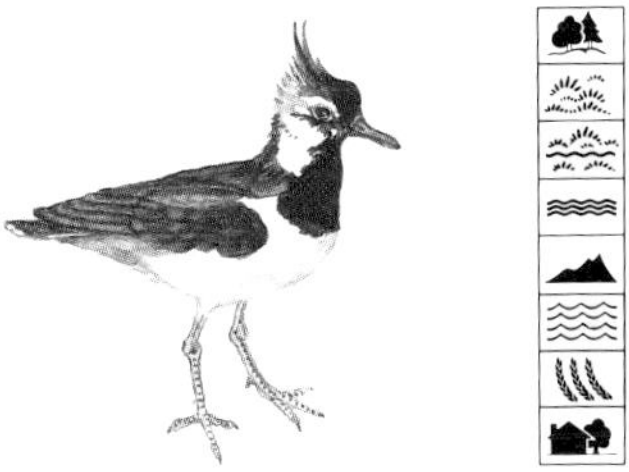

Lapwing *Length* 11¾ in (30 cm). *Call* a nasal 'kee-wi', and a longer 'ker-r-wee', with variants in tumbling display flight: 'pee-wi, pee-wit'. *Habitat* farmland, marshes, moors, mudflats; winter visitor.

nmon Sandpiper *Length* 8 in (20 cm). *Call* high, rapid -weeti, titti-weeti', a piping 'twee-wee-wee' when med. *Habitat* rivers, hill streams, lakes; resident erside nester.

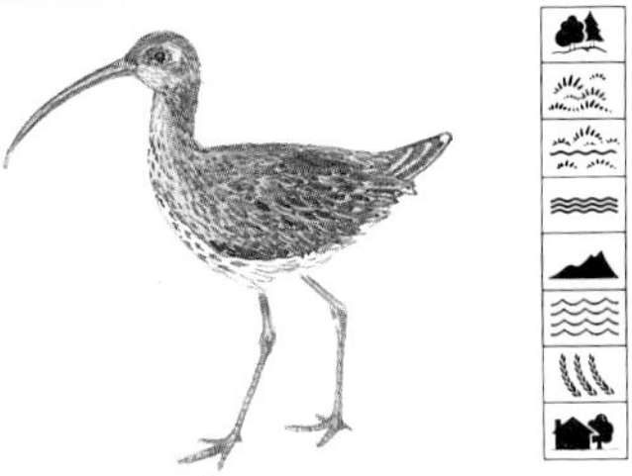

Curlew *Length* 21-22¾ in (53-58 cm). *Call* a pure, ringing 'cour-li', 'crwee', or 'croo-ee'. *Habitat* mudflats, estuaries; a winter visitor.

Stone Curlew *Length* 16 in (41 cm). *Call* mainly in evening, a wailing Curlew-like 'coo-ree' or a shrill 'kee-rrr-eee'. *Habitat* open, dry, stony country, bare, chalky hillsides, heaths; ground-nesting summer visitor in north, resident breeder in south.

Slender-billed Gull *Length* 17 in (43 cm). *Call* a laughing, gull-like 'kau-kau'. *Habitat* coastal waters and estuaries; spring/autumn passage migrant in southern half of country.

Black-headed Gull *Length* 13¾-15 in (35-38 cm). *Call* a harsh, raucous 'kraah'. *Habitat* coastal regions and inland, frequenting lakes, harbours, farms; a winter visitor.

Little Gull *Length* 11 in (28 cm). *Call* a repeated 'ka-ka-ka', with a harsh 'kek-kek-kek'. *Habitat* as for Black-headed Gull; a winter visitor.

Mediterranean Gull *Length* 15½ in (39 cm). *Call* a deep 'kek-ke-ke', 'kee-er' or 'kau-kau-kyau'. *Habitat* as for Black-headed Gull, though less often seen inland; a winter visitor.

Herring Gull *Length* 22-26 in (56-66 cm). *Call* a yelping 'kee-yow' and in spring also, a loud 'gah-gah-gah'. *Habitat* coastal waters, estuaries, fields, often far inland; resident breeder, colonial nesting on cliffs, islands, beaches.

Lesser Black-backed Gull *Length* 21-22 in (53-56 cm). *Call* like a deep, gruff Herring Gull. *Habitat* as for Herring Gull; winter visitor along coasts and inland.

Common Gull *Length* 16 in (41 cm). *Call* a weaker, high pitched version of the Herring Gull's 'kee-yow'. *Habit* coastal waters, estuaries, very often inland; winter visitor throughout, except for Sicily.

Sandwich Tern *Length* 16 in (41 cm). *Call* a loud, harsh 'kirrick' or 'kirr-whit'. *Habitat* almost entirely marine; a passage migrant, spring and autumn.

Common Tern *Length* 13¾ in (35 cm). *Call* high-pitched, strident, usually 'keeerree', 'keeyah', and 'kik-kik-kik'. *Habitat* coastal and inland waters; a spring/autumn passage migrant.

ittle Tern *Length* 9½ in (24 cm). *Call* mainly a high, asping 'kik-kik' and 'pee-e-eer', plus trills. *Habitat* oastal waters, sand, shingle beaches; breeding ummer visitor, nests on beaches, shores of rivers, and akes.

Black Tern *Length* 9½ in (24 cm). *Call* rarely vocal, sometimes a reedy 'kitt' or 'kreek'. *Habitat* inland lakes and marshes; breeding summer visitor in north-east, builds floating nests in shallows, elsewhere, a passage migrant.

/hiskered Tern *Length* 9½ in (24 cm). *Call* rasping arm cries, croaking noises, cheeps. *Habitat* inland esh waters, marshes, brackish coastal lagoons; eeding summer visitor in north-east, colonial nester, sewhere a migrant.

Rock Dove or Feral Pigeon *Length* 13 in (33 cm). *Call* 'oo-roo-coo'. *Habitat* rocky sea cliffs, nearby fields; domestic forms common in cities; breeding resident, nests in rock crevices, on ledges, in caves, on buildings.

ck Dove *Length* 13 in (33 cm). *Call* 'ooo-roo-oo', like od Pigeon, but more monotonous. *Habitat* cliffs, d-dunes, preferring open parkland; resident eder east coast and Sicily, nests in tree holes, rabbit rows, elsewhere a winter visitor.

Wood Pigeon or Ring Dove *Length* 16 in (41 cm). *Call* 'coo-coo-roo, coo-coo', muffled and repeated. *Habitat* almost anywhere with trees; resident breeder, nesting in hedges, trees, and old nests.

Turtle Dove *Length* 10½ in (27 cm). *Call* soft, a repeated, purring 'roor-r-r'. *Habitat* various, open woodland, scattered trees; breeding summer visitor, nesting in scrubby thickets, bushes, orchards.

Great Spotted Cuckoo *Length* 15½ in (39 cm). *Call* harsh, loud cries, including a grating 'keeow-keeow-keeow-keeow' and a crow-like alarm call. *Habitat* scrubby plains, woodland glades and edges; spring/autumn passage migrant.

Barn Owl *Length* 13½ in (34 cm). *Call* long, wild shriek, also, hisses, barks, snores. *Habitat* open, often dry country, with scattered trees; a resident breeder, often nesting in old barns, outhouses, and churches; food mainly rodents.

Eagle Owl *Length* 26-28 in (66-71 cm). *Call* short deep 'ooo-hu', a sharp 'kveck, kveck'. *Habitat* crags, steppes rocky outcrops in forests; resident breeder, nests in rock crevices, hollow trees, old bird-of-prey nests.

Long-eared Owl *Length* 14 in (36 cm). *Call* a long, sighing 'oo-oo-oo', also, yelping and wailing notes and wing clapping. *Habitat* coniferous forests, marshes, heaths, dunes, open areas with scattered trees; resident breeder in old nests.

Scops Owl *Length* 7½ in (19 cm). *Call* a melancholy whistling 'kyew'. *Habitat* open woodland, farmland, open country with scattered trees; resident breeder i south, breeding summer visitor in north, nests in old birds' nests or holes.

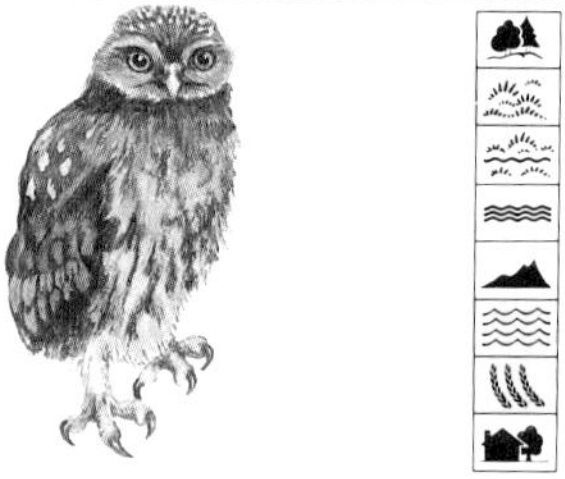

Little Owl *Length* 8¾ in (22 cm). *Call* a barking 'werro' and a shrill 'kiu'. *Habitat* open country with scattered trees, farmland, orchards, dunes; breeding resident, nests in tree holes, burrows, among rocks.

Tawny Owl *Length* 15 in (38 cm). *Call* a shrill 'ke-wick' also, a deep 'hoo-hoo-hoo' followed by a wavering 'oo-oo-oo-oo'. *Habitat* open woodland, open country with scattered trees, large gardens; resident, nests i holes, old nests.

Jightjar *Length* 10½ in (27 cm). *Call* a soft, nasal 'goo-
·k' in flight, a high 'quick-quick-quick' in alarm, a
rolonged churring at night. *Habitat* open woodland,
orest edges and glades, open country; breeding
ummer visitor, eggs on bare ground.

Swift *Length* 6½ in (16.5 cm). *Call* a prolonged shrill screech, chirping at nest. *Habitat* aerial, in areas suitable for nesting; breeding summer visitor, nesting under eaves of buildings, on rocky cliffs, sometimes in tree holes.

llid Swift *Length* 6½ in (16.5 cm). *Call* as for Swift.
bitat as for Swift, with which it often associates;
eeding summer visitor, distinguished from Swift by
tinctly paler-brown and larger, white throat patch.

Alpine Swift *Length* 8¾ in (22 cm). *Call* in flight, a chorus of loud, rising and falling trilling whistles. *Habitat* high mountainous areas, seacliffs; breeding summer visitor, cup-shaped nest in crevices, rock clefts, in colonies.

e-eater *Length* 11 in (28 cm). *Call* in flight, a rather
id 'quilp', also a throaty 'kroop, kroop'. *Habitat* open
hy country, sometimes woodland glades; breeding
nmer visitor, nests in holes in banks, sandy cliffs.

Roller *Length* 12¼ in (31 cm). *Call* a loud, deep, crow-like 'kr-r-r-r-ak' or 'krak-ak'. *Habitat* open country with scattered trees, mature forests; breeding summer visitor, nests in hollow trees, ruins, holes in banks.

fisher *Length* 6½ in (16.5 cm). *Call* a loud, shrill
ee' or 'chikeee'. *Habitat* fresh waters of all kinds in
and areas, estuaries and coasts in winter; resident
der, nests excavated in stream and river banks.

Hoopoe *Length* 11 in (28 cm). *Call* a rapid, clipped, far-carrying 'hoo-hoo-hoo', also several mewing notes and, in alarm, a quiet chattering. *Habitat* open woodlands, grassy plains, farms, orchards; breeding summer visitor, nests in holes in trees.

Green Woodpecker *Length* 12½ in (32 cm). *Call* a loud, ringing 'laugh': 'plue-plue-plue', sometimes loud, yelping cries. *Habitat* broadleaved and mixed forests, parks, gardens; will feed on ground, lawns, anthills; nests in tree holes.

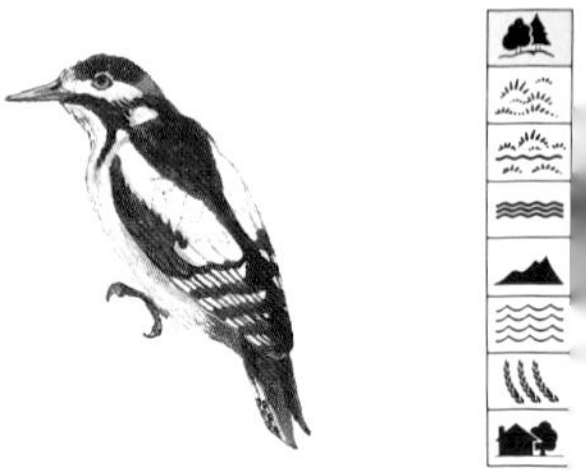

Great Spotted or Pied Woodpecker *Length* 9 in (23 cm). *Call* a loud, sharp, 'tchick' or 'kik'; both sexes drum rapidly on dead branches. *Habitat* woodlands, includin pinewoods; resident breeder, nests in tree holes.

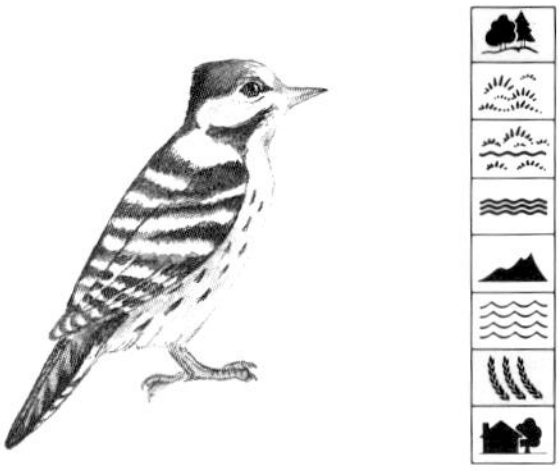

Lesser Spotted or Barred Woodpecker *Length* 5¾ in (14.5 cm). *Call* usually a weak 'pee-pee-pee-pee-pee', like Wryneck, but less ringing. *Habitat* broadleaved woods, pinewoods, orchards; resident breeder, nests in holes bored in trees.

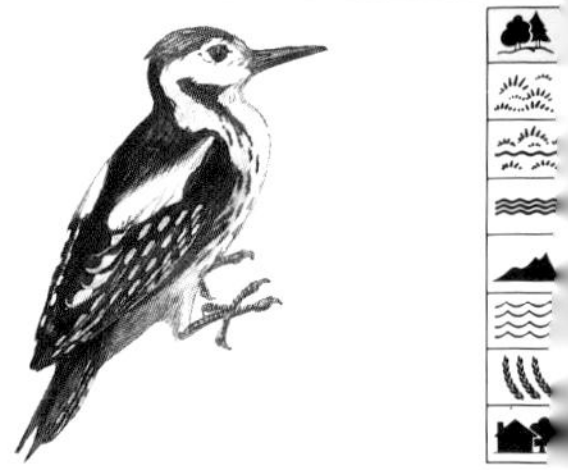

Middle Spotted Woodpecker *Length* 8¾ in (22 cm). *Ca* a repeated 'kik' note and a slow rising or falling 'wait, wait'. *Habitat* usually in high branches of broadleaved and coniferous woodland; resident, nests in high tree hole.

Wryneck *Length* 6½ in (16.5 cm). *Call* a clear, loud, musical 'kew-kew-kew-kew-kew'. *Habitat* deciduous and coniferous forests, open areas with scattered trees, farmland; resident, nests in existing holes in trees, rocks.

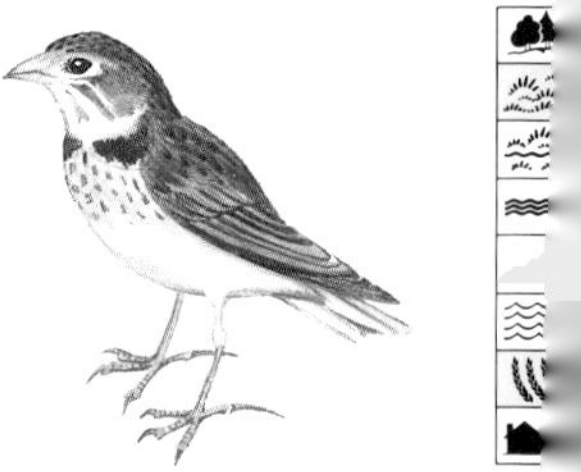

Calandra Lark *Length* 7½ in (19 cm). *Call* a nasal 'klee in high circling flight with final, silent dive. *Habitat* dr stony wastes, steppes, farmland; resident ground nester in southern half.

Short-toed Lark *Length* 5½ in (14 cm). *Call* a short, dry, Sparrow-like chirrup repeated often in high, steeply rising and falling flight. *Habitat* fields, steppes, open sandy and stony areas; breeding summer visitor, nests on ground.

Woodlark *Length* 6 in (15 cm). *Call* a melodious 'toolooeet', interrupted by a liquid trilling 'lu-lu-lu-lu flight or from perch or ground. *Habitat* sandy areas, hillsides, woodland edges; resident ground nester.

Skylark *Length* 7 in (18 cm). *Call* a sustained warbling, usually in flight, in near-vertical ascent or descent or when hovering. *Habitat* open country, heaths, moors, dunes, fields, marshes, farmland; resident ground nester.

Crested Lark *Length* 6¾ in (17 cm). *Call* a rising and falling, liquid 'twee-tee-too', in short, repeated bursts in flight, from perch or on ground. *Habitat* dry, stony, sandy wastes, roadsides; resident ground nester.

wallow *Length* 7½ in (19 cm). *Call* a high 'tswit', which ecomes a rapid twitter in excitement; a high 'tswee' vhen alarmed. *Habitat* open farmland with ponds; reeding summer visitor, open mud and straw nests on afters, ledges.

Crag Martin *Length* 5¾ in (14.5 cm). *Call* rarely vocal; a weak 'chich' or 'tchrri'. *Habitat* rocky inland and coastal cliffs, mountain gorges, though rarely at high altitudes; breeding summer visitor in north, resident in south, open mud nests in rock clefts.

nd Martin *Length* 4¾ in (12 cm). *Call* a reedy 'tchrrip', alarm, a short 'brrit', less musical than Swallow. *bitat* open country with ponds, rivers; breeding mmer visitor, nests communally in tunnels in sand, avel banks.

House Martin *Length* 5 in (12.5 cm). *Call* a clear 'tchirrip', in alarm, a shrill 'tseep', otherwise, a weak, chirruping twitter. *Habitat* open country with ponds; breeding summer visitor, enclosed mud nest with hole on top, on cliffs, under eaves.

er Pipit *Length* 6½ in (16.5 cm). *Call* a thin 'tsip' or ep-eep' in flight. *Habitat* mountain areas; nests in crevices, winters in marshes, mudflats, coasts.

Tawny Pipit *Length* 6½ in (16.5 cm). *Call* variants of 'tzeep', 'tzi-uc', louder than other pipits. *Habitat* dry, open, sandy areas, heaths, dunes, hillsides; breeding summer visitor, nest on ground in scrape sheltered by vegetation.

White Wagtail *Length* 7 in (18 cm). *Call* in flight, a high-pitched 'tschizzick', in alarm, 'tchik'; otherwise, twittering variants of call. *Habitat* open country, often in farmland and near freshwater; resident, nests in rock crevices, buildings.

Grey Wagtail *Length* 7 in (18 cm). *Call* similar to White Wagtail but more metallic; alarm a shrill 'sse-it' or 'siz-eet'. *Habitat* around fast-flowing streams in hill country, winters in lowland cultivated areas; resident, nests in holes.

Great Grey Shrike *Length* 9½ in (24 cm). *Call* a distinctive 'shek-shek', in alarm, a grating 'jaaeg', otherwise, a mixture of harsh and musical notes. *Habitat* woodland edges, heaths, orchards; resident in north, nests in high trees, winter visitor in south.

Lesser Grey Shrike *Length* 8 in (20 cm). *Call* harsh 'she shek' with also a clear 'kviell'. *Habitat* open country w scattered trees and bushes, roadsides; breeding summer visitor, nests in high trees, near to trunk.

Woodchat Shrike *Length* 6¾ in (17 cm). *Call* harsh and variable 'shek-shek' with sparrow-like chatter, otherwise, a musical, warbling song mixed with harsh notes. *Habitat* dry open country; summer visitor, nests in trees.

Red-backed Shrike *Length* 6¾ in (17 cm). *Call* harsh grating 'shach' or 'chee-uk', with a musical, warbling song. *Habitat* thickets, scrubby areas, old quarries; breeding summer visitor, nests in bushes, small trees thorny scrub.

Hedgesparrow or Dunnock *Length* 5¾ in (14.5 cm). *Call* a high, piping 'tseep', with a rapid, jingling song. *Habitat* bushy areas, coppiced woodland, hedges; winter visitor in extreme south, elsewhere resident, nests in bushes, evergreens.

Alpine Accentor *Length* 7 in (18 cm). *Call* a lark-like 'tchir-rip' and a throaty 'churrg', with a sustained warbling song. *Habitat* rocky mountain slopes and crags, wintering in lowlands; resident, nests in vegetation or rock holes.

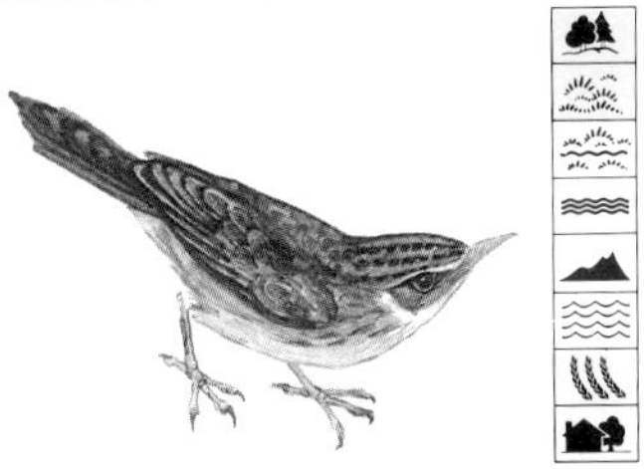

Grasshopper Warbler *Length* 5 in (13 cm). *Call* a short 'twhit' or 'pitt', with distinctive, far-carrying, grasshopper-like churring. *Habitat* undergrowth; ground-nesting summer visitor in northern half, elsewhere a passage migrant.

Reed Warbler *Length* 5 in (12.5 cm). *Call* a rather monotonous 'churr-churr-churr... chirruc-chirruc-chirruc'. *Habitat* reedbeds, waterside vegetation, sometimes cultivated land away from water; summer visitor, nests colonially in reeds.

'reat Reed Warbler *Length* 7½ in (19 cm). *Call* far-arrying, frog-like croaking 'karra-karra-karra'. *Habitat* eedbeds with open water, river banks, claypits; reeding summer visitor, colonial nests suspended from eeds.

Moustached Warbler *Length* 5 in (13 cm). *Call* a soft 't-trrt', a louder 'tchuck' repeated as a churring alarm. *Habitat* swamps and reedbeds; resident breeder, nests in reeds or low vegetation overhanging shallow water.

dge Warbler *Length* 5 in (13 cm). *Call* an explosive :' becoming a stuttering rattle in excitement; song a xture of harsh, chattering and repeated musical es. *Habitat* waterside vegetation, reedbeds; summer itor, nests in dense plant cover.

Cetti's Warbler *Length* 5½ in (14 cm). *Call* 'chee', 'twic', 'huit', and churring note; loud staccato song of 'chewee, chewee, cheweeweeweewee' or 'pit, pit, pitpit'. *Habitat* dense waterside vegetation, where nests are well hidden.

odious Warbler *Length* 5 in (13 cm). *Call* a sharp 'tit, hooeet', and sparrow-like chattering; song a onged, musical babbling. *Habitat* woods, thickets, 'ens, lush waterside vegetation; summer visitor, ing in bushes.

Whitethroat *Length* 5½ in (14 cm). *Call* a repeated 'check', 'tcharr', and a quiet 'wheet, wheet, whit-whit-whit', with urgent, chattering song. *Habitat* open, scrubby country, nettlebeds; summer visitor, nests in vegetation near ground.

Lesser Whitethroat *Length* 5¼ in (13.5 cm). *Call* like Whitethroat, with a song beginning with musical warble, ending with harsh rattle. *Habitat* open country with trees and patches of dense vegetation; summer visitor, nests near ground.

Garden Warbler *Length* 5½ in (14 cm). *Call* 'check, check', a low, harsh 'tchur-r-r', a faint 'whit'; song, a quiet, sustained, musical warble. *Habitat* scrubby areas with brambles, woods; breeding summer visitor in north, elsewhere, a passage migrant.

Blackcap *Length* 5½ in (14 cm). *Call* a sharp 'tac, tac', rapidly repeated in alarm and a harsh churring; song a rich warble. *Habitat* woodland glades with undergrowth, hedges, orchards; resident breeder, nests in brambles, evergreens.

Sardinian Warbler *Length* 5¼ in (13.5 cm). *Call* in alarm a loud, sharp 'cha-cha-cha-cha'; song a mixture of musical notes and snatches of alarm call. *Habitat* dry, open, scrubby areas; resident breeder, nests in undergrowth.

Goldcrest *Length* 3½ in (9 cm). *Call* a high, frequent 'zee-zee-zee'; song a thin, high, double note ending in short twitter. *Habitat* coniferous and mixed woodland, undergrowth; breeding resident, nest suspended under tip of branch.

Spotted Flycatcher *Length* 5½ in (14 cm). *Call* a shrill 'tzee', a rapid 'tzee, tuc-tuc'; song a few thin notes, 'sip-sip-see-sitti-see-see'. *Habitat* woodland edges, parks, gardens; breeding summer visitor, nest agains tree trunk, on building.

Pied Flycatcher *Length* 5 in (13 cm). *Call* a metallic 'whit', 'phweet', 'tic' or 'wheetic', and an explosive 'tschist'. *Habitat* deciduous and coniferous forest, large gardens, orchards; a regular spring/autumn passage migrant.

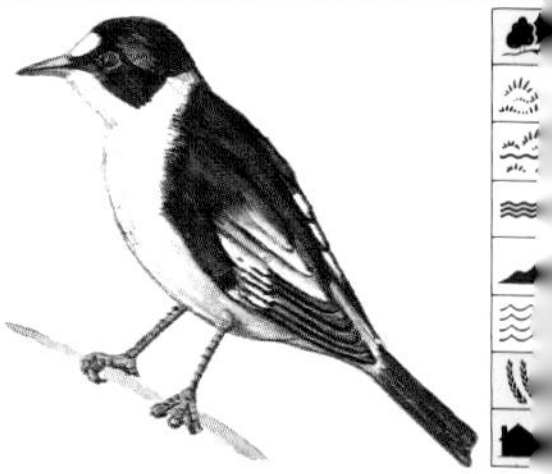

Collared Flycatcher *Length* 5 in (12.5 cm). *Call* a meta 'whit', with short and simple song: 'tsit-tsit-tsit-siu-s *Habitat* forests, orchards, large gardens; regular spring/autumn passage migrant in north, summer vis in south.

Blue Rock Thrush *Length* 8 in (20 cm). *Call* a hard 'tchuck' or a plaintive 'tsec'; loud fluty song especially in morning and at sunset. *Habitat* dry rocky areas, including mountainsides; resident, nests in cliffs, rock crevices, buildings.

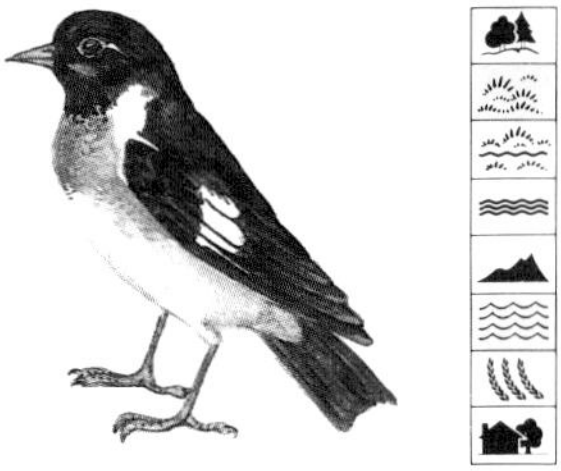

Stonechat *Length* 5 in (12.5 cm). *Call* like two stones hitting together: 'wheet, tsack, tsack'; song an irregular, repeated double note, given from perch or 'dancing' song flight. *Habitat* open bushy country with gorse; resident.

Rock Thrush *Length* 7½ in (19 cm). *Call* 'chack, chack' nd a clear, piping song. *Habitat* open rocky areas from 300-8500 ft (1-2600 m), sometimes lower among trees nd ruins; breeding summer visitor.

Wheatear *Length* 5¾-6 in (14.5-15 cm). *Call* 'chack, chack-weet', 'weet-chack'; song a wheezy yet musical lark-like warbling. *Habitat* open country, tundra, moors, grassy downs; breeding summer visitor, nests in rabbit burrows, holes in walls.

ack-eared Wheatear *Length* 5¾ in (14.5 cm). *Call* a sping note; otherwise, song a wheezy, musical, lark-e warbling preceded by a soft 'plit'. *Habitat* stony pes, dry, open, lightly wooded country; breeding mmer visitor, nests in rock crevices.

Redstart *Length* 5½ in (14 cm). *Call* a liquid 'wheet', a tremulous 'whee-tic-tic', and a clear 'tooick'; song a Robin-like jingle. *Habitat* open country with bushes, old trees, woodland; breeding summer visitor, nests in tree holes, old walls.

in *Length* 5½ in (14 cm). *Call* a rapid, repeated 'tic', ', or 'tsissip' and a thin 'tsee'; song of short, high, bling notes. *Habitat* woodland, coppices, gardens, ges; resident, nests in holes in walls, banks, trees.

Nightingale *Length* 6½ in (16.5 cm). *Call* in alarm, a harsh 'kerr', otherwise, 'tuc', 'tac', or a liquid 'wheet'; song, by DAY and night, bubbling, ending in crescendo. *Habitat* woods, thickets; summer visitor, nests near ground.

Blackbird *Length* 10 in (25 cm). *Call* 'tchook, tchook', becoming a scream in alarm, also 'tchink, tchink, tchink'; song a loud, melodious warble. *Habitat* gardens, bushy areas, gardens, orchards; breeding resident, nests in tree or bush.

Song Thrush *Length* 9 in (23 cm). *Call* mainly a soft 'sip', a loud, rapidly repeated 'tchuck' in alarm; loud musical song of short, repeated phrases. *Habitat* scrub, woodlands, gardens; winter visitor in south, resident in north, mud-lined nests in bushes.

Mistle Thrush *Length* 10½ in (27 cm). *Call* a harsh, grating chatter, a hard 'tuc-tuc-tuc', and a thin 'see-ip'; song loud, Blackbird-like, but less mellow. *Habitat* woodlands, gardens, mountain areas; resident, nests in bare fork in tree.

Long-tailed Tit *Length* 5½ in (14 cm). *Call* a deep 'tupp', repeated spluttering 'tsirrup', and a weak 'tzee-tzee-tzee'. *Habitat* woods, bushy areas; resident, domed nes of interwoven mosses and cobwebs in thorny plants.

Penduline Tit *Length* 4¼ in (11 cm). *Call* a soft, Robin-like 'seeou' and a chatty 'tsi-tsi-tsi'. *Habitat* marshy areas with scrub or willows; resident breeder, egg-shaped nest with funnel-shaped entrance hung from reeds, twigs.

Great Tit *Length* 5½ in (14 cm). *Call* varied; 'tsink, tsink a nasal 'tchair, tchair', a scolding 'chi chi chi'; song ringing variations of 'teechew-teechew-teechew'. *Habitat* mixed woodland, gardens; resident, nests in tree holes.

Marsh Tit *Length* 4½ in (11.5 cm). *Call* 'pitchew', 'pitichewee', a nasal 'tchair', a scolding 'chick-adeedeedee'; song a tuneless rattle. *Habitat* scrub, broadleaved woodland, not specially in marshes; resident, nests in holes.

Nuthatch *Length* 5½ in (14 cm). *Call* very varied, includes a ringing 'chwit, chwit', or 'tsirrup'; song a piping, repeated 'twee', 'pee', or 'chu'. *Habitat* old, deciduous trees in woods, parks, gardens; resident hole nester, entrance plastered with mud.

Wren *Length* 3¾ in (9.5 cm). *Call* a loud, hard 'tit-tit-tit', changing to a trill on alarm; song a vigorous, clear warbling. *Habitat* various, rocky mountains, cliffs, forests, gardens; resident, globular nests in tree holes, banks.

Dipper *Length* 7 in (18 cm). *Call* in flight, a metallic 'clink', otherwise, a short 'zit'; song of grating notes mixed with liquid warble. *Habitat* fast-flowing hill and mountain streams, often 'walks' under water; resident, globular nest always near running water.

Rock Bunting *Length* 6¼ in (16 cm). *Call* a sharp 'tzit'; song a high-pitched, buzzing 'zi-zi-zi-zirr'. *Habitat* rocky mountains and hillsides, wintering on low ground; resident breeder, nests on or near ground.

Golden Oriole *Length* 9½ in (24 cm). *Call* male, a loud, fluting 'weela-weeo', both sexes also a cat-like squawk, in alarm, a harsh 'chr-r-r'. *Habitat* broadleaved woods and forests, large gardens; summer visitor, nests high in trees.

hough *Length* 15½ in (39.5 cm). *Call* a high-pitched, ng 'kyaw' and gull-like cries. *Habitat* mountains, also cky outcrops and cliffs near sea; resident in south, ests in rock crevices, caves, ledges.

Alpine Chough *Length* 15 in (38 cm). *Call* similar to Chough's, but notes more monosyllabic, a distinct, metallic 'chirrish'. *Habitat* high mountains with steep cliffs; resident, nests in rock clefts, ruins.

ven *Length* 25¼ in (64 cm). *Call* a deep, croaking uk, pruk' and a high, metallic 'tok', other clucking and aking noises. *Habitat* open hill country, sea cliffs, untain crags, and woods; resident, nests on rock ges, trees.

Hooded Crow *Length* 18½ in (47 cm). *Call* a harsh, croaking 'kraa, kraa, kraa', a muffled, metallic 'konk', and a repeated 'keerk'. *Habitat* open country with some trees, seashores; resident, nests in trees, sometimes on cliffs.

Pool Frog *Size* 2¾-3½ in (7-9 cm). *Call* a harmonious 'bre-ke-ke-ke-kek'. *Habitat* shallow ponds, particularly in breeding season, but may be found basking in sunlight near edge.

Common Tree Frog *Length* 1½-2 in (4-5 cm). *Call* a harsh, noisy 'krak-krak-krak' repeated very rapidly; males sing at night when breeding. *Habitat* in branches of shrubs and small trees; return to ground to breed in ponds; largely nocturnal.

Agile Frog *Length* 3¼-3½ in (8-9 cm). *Call* a soft, rapid 'quar-quar-quar'. *Habitat* wet vegetation near to water; spends most of year on land.

Green Toad *Length* 2¾-4 in (7-10 cm). *Call* long, high-pitched churring beginning at dusk; males sing in chorus. *Habitat* sandy areas, where it hides under stones during day. In south, common near streetlamps hunting insects.

Common Toad *Length* 5-6 in (13-15 cm). *Call* a short harsh 'qwark-qwark-qwark' heard around dusk and at night. *Habitat* under stones and logs in fields, woodland, and gardens; emerge at night to feed. Only found in ponds, in large numbers, in breeding season.

Yellow-bellied Toad *Length* 1¼-1½ in (3-4 cm). *Call* a melodious 'poop-poop-poop' heard mainly in the evening. *Habitat* in shallow water, streams, ditches, ponds, and temporary pools; active by day.

Slow Worm *Length* 17½-20 in (45-50 cm). *Colour* variable; juveniles brighter with golden scales; males with scattered blue spots. A legless lizard. *Habitat* under logs and stones in damp grassland, woods, and embankments.

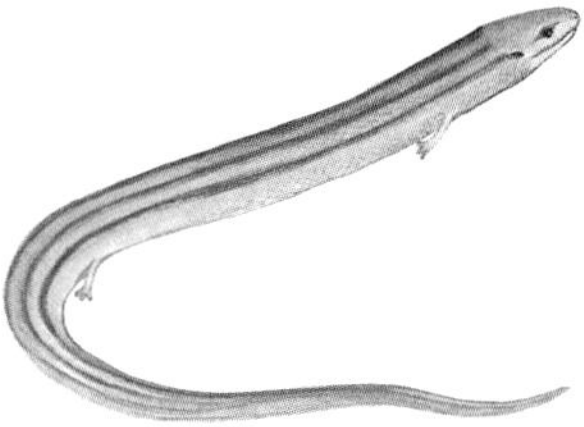

Three-toed Skink *Length* 13¾-15¾ in (35-40 cm). *Colo* green to golden with variation in number of stripes. *Habitat* among dense, wet vegetation near water, usually low-lying fields. Active during day if warm.

Common Wall Lizard *Length* 7-8¾ in (18-22 cm) including tail. *Colour* very variable; males conspicuous spotted pattern with orange belly; southern forms black with green spots. *Habitat* dry, sunny walls, rockfaces; often in or near houses.

Italian Wall Lizard *Length* 2¾-3½ in (7-9 cm). *Colour* pale to dark green with occasional black; variable pattern of spots or stripes. *Habitat* from open coastal areas to cultivated fields, gardens, and embankments; occurs on ground and on walls.

Green Lizard *Length* 11¾-15¾ in (30-40 cm) with tail. *Colour* variable in females from green to brown; juvenile nales without blue chin. *Habitat* wooded or scrubby areas in south; heathland in north.

Fire Salamander *Length* 7-11 in (18-28 cm) with tail. *Colour* and paterrn variable; main colour yellow or black with spots or stripes in contrasting colour. *Habitat* damp, mountainous regions near water; nocturnal.

uropean Pond Terrapin *Length* 7-10 in (18-25 cm). uveniles much smaller, with bright colouring. *Habitat* overgrown ponds and ditches with slow-moving ater.

Smooth Snake *Length* 23½-27½ in (60-70 cm). *Colour* variable from grey to red; distinguish from vipers by smoother, less-prominent head scales. *Habitat* dry, open, stony areas in south, woodland or scrub in north.

Viper *Length* 23½-29½ in (60-75 cm). *Bite* CAN BE AL. *Colour* some forms completely black, especially orth. *Habitat* mainly dry stony areas, cultivated fields vineyards; occasionally in cooler mountain ons.

Aesculapian Snake *Length* 53-79 in (135-200 cm). *Colour* variable; juveniles with dark spots. *Habitat* mainly sunny, sheltered places in woodland and shrubby areas; good climbers, so found in trees and old walls.

Ephippiger or 'Tizi' *Length* 11½-13 in (29-33 mm). *Song* usually males only, a short, double chirp. *Habitat* low bushes on dry mountains and hillsides, active in daylight, preying on other insects and small invertebrates. Summer-autumn.

Field Cricket *Length* 8-8¾ in (20-22 mm). *Song* loud, shrill bursts of chirping by males, often audible at 100 m. *Habitat* dry fields, warm, well-drained hillsides in summer, where it feeds on plants and small insects.

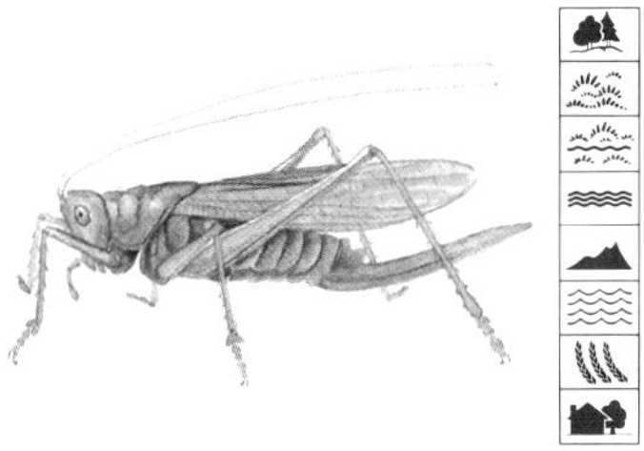

Great Green Bush Cricket *Length* 15¾-19¾ in (40-50 mm). *Song* males only, a prolonged, harsh chirping, like sound of bicycle freewheeling. *Habitat* shrubby areas with long grasses, feeding on small insects and plant material, in summer.

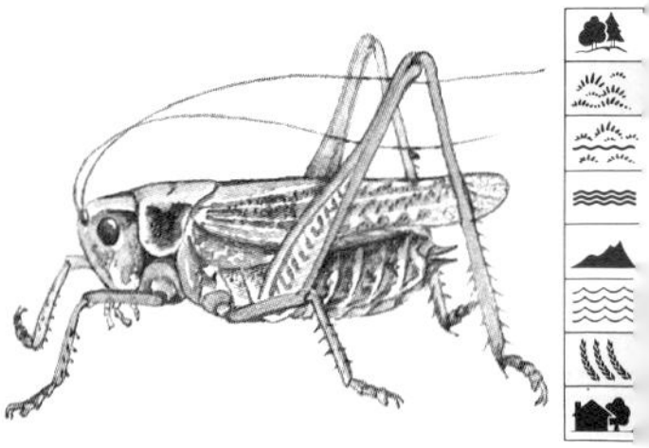

Large Brown Bush Cricket *Length* 13¾-21½ in (35-55 mm). *Song* males only, a loud, very shrill, bird-like chirp. *Habitat* in bushes and small trees in dry, parched areas, in summer.

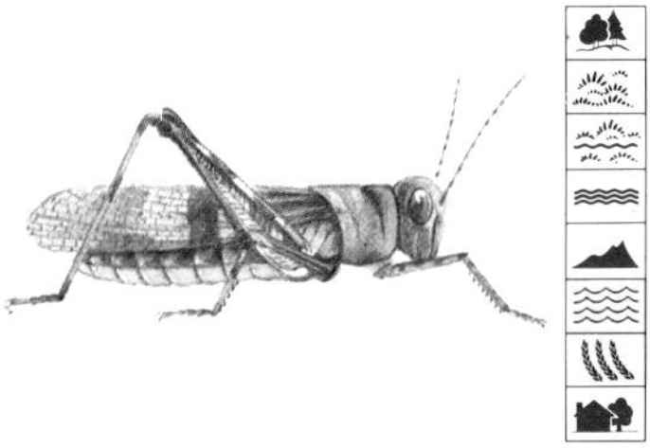

German Grasshopper *Length* 7-11 in (17-28 mm). *Song* males only, a regular, rasping chirp. *Habitat* dry hillsides, *garrigue* vegetation, feeding on low plants and plant debris; readily takes to flight, exposing red hindwings, in summer.

Common Field Grasshopper *Length* 6-9 in (15-23 mm). *Song* short, brisk chirp, males only. *Habitat* open, dry, stony areas, dry agricultural land, woodland clearings sand-dunes, in summer.

Praying Mantis *Length* 15¾-27½ in (40-70 mm). *Habitat* bushes and low vegetation almost everywhere in the south, sitting still for long periods in attitude of 'prayer', waiting to grasp insect prey with powerful, raptorial front legs.

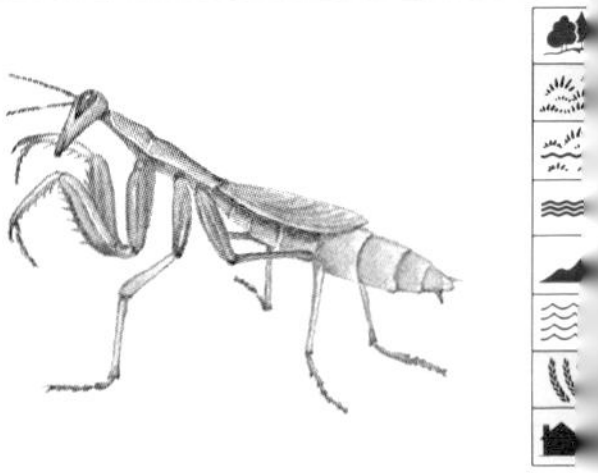

Lesser Praying Mantis *Length* 14-15¾ in (36-40 mm). *Habitat* small bushes and trees in dry, stony areas fro August onwards; not so common as Praying Mantis.

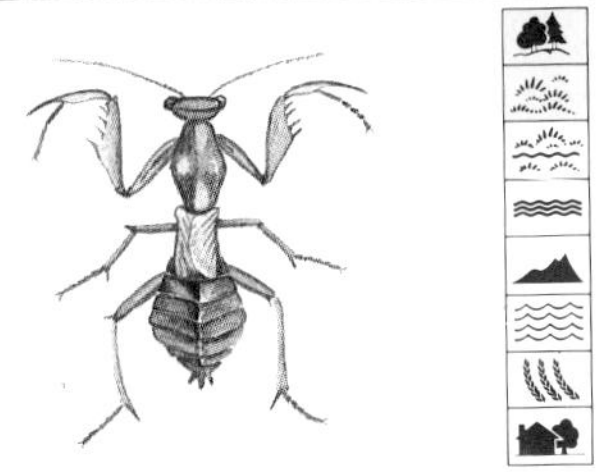

Small Mantis *Length* 8-10 in (20-25 mm). *Habitat* in groves of Evergreen Oak, in autumn, sometimes on the ground, where well camouflaged.

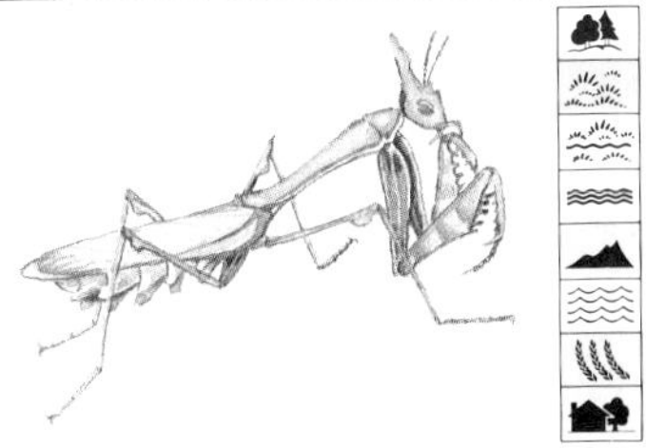

Pennate Mantis *Length* 2-2¼ in (50-60 mm). *Habitat* parched vegetation in dry, stony areas, perching in characteristic posture, body supported by hind two pairs of legs, forebody and head held vertically; well camouflaged against dry vegetation.

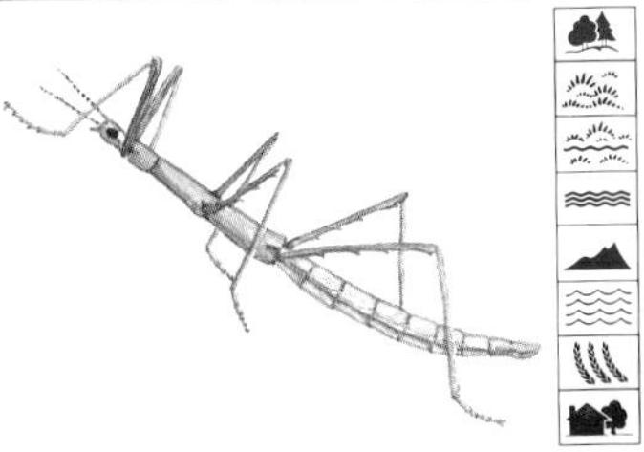

Stick Insect *Length* 17¾-29½ in (45-75 mm). *Habitat* in coarse vegetation, where it spends long periods motionless, with forelegs extended in front, enhancing resemblance to twig; males rare, eggs developing unfertilized; July onwards, feeding on leaves.

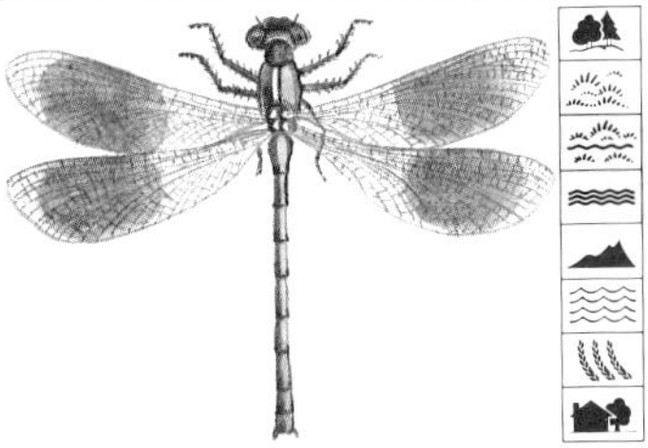

Splendid Damselfly *Length* male abdomen 1¼-1½ in (33-39 mm), hindwing 1⅒-1¼ in (27-32 mm); female abdomen 1¼-1⅗ in (33-40 mm) hindwing 1⅕-1⅖ in (31-36 mm). *Habitat* slow-flowing rivers, ponds, still waters. *Season* May-end September.

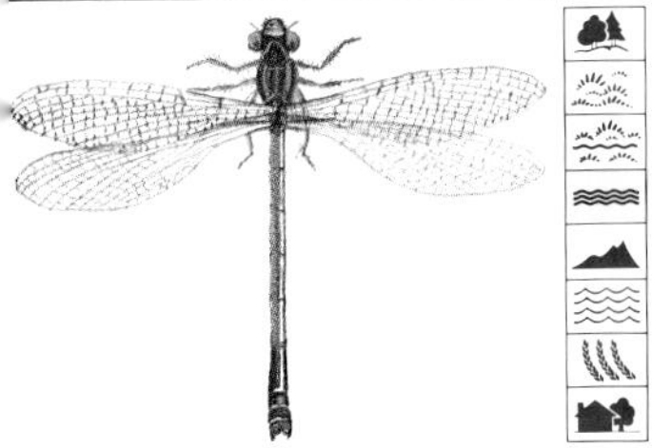

ed Damselfly *Length* male abdomen 1-1⅒ in (25-9 mm), hindwing ¾-9/10 in (19-22 mm); female abdomen -1⅒ in (26-28 mm), hindwing ⅘-9/10 in (21-24 mm). *abitat* around small, clear streams, ponds, lakes, etc. o to 4000 ft (1200 m). *Season* April-September.

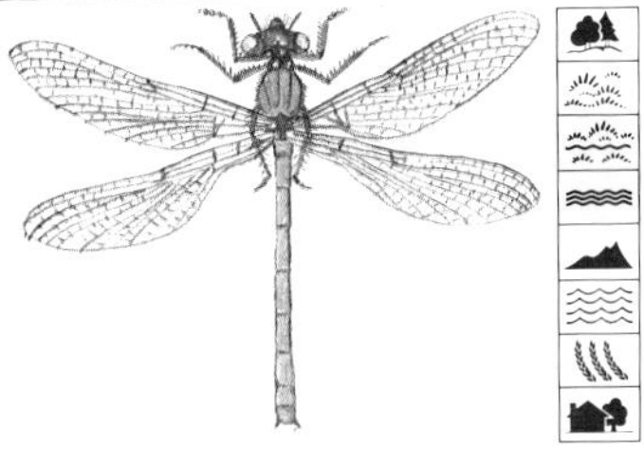

Green Lestes Damselfly *Length* male abdomen 1-1⅗ in (33-40 mm), hindwing 9/10-1 in (23-25 mm); female abdomen 1⅕-1⅖ in (30-35 mm), hindwing 1-1⅒ in (25-28 mm). *Habitat* usually around stagnant waters. *Season* June-beginning of November.

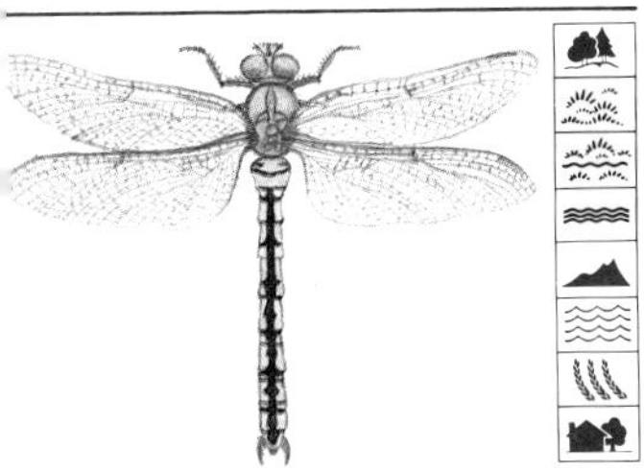

nperor Dragonfly *Length* male abdomen 2⅒-2⅖ in 3-61 mm), hindwing 1¾-2 in (45-50 mm); female domen 1 9/10-2¼ in (49-57 mm), hindwing 1⅘-2 in (46-mm). *Habitat* around ponds, lakes, stagnant ditches, t very often far from water. *Season* May-September.

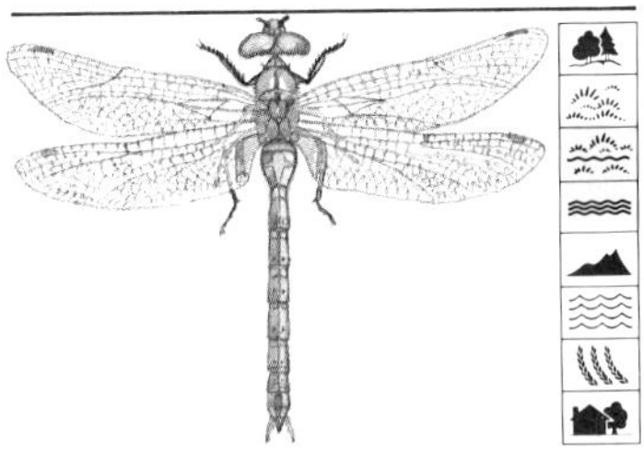

Norfolk Hawker Dragonfly *Length* male abdomen 1⅘-2 in (47-50 mm), hindwing 1½-1¾ in (39-42 mm); female abdomen 2-2⅒ in (50-54 mm), hindwing 1⅗-1¾ in (41-45 mm). *Habitat* usually around stagnant waters, not often far from water. *Season* May-August.

Common Darter Dragonfly. *Length* male abdomen 1-$1\frac{1}{5}$in (25-30mm), hindwing 1-$1\frac{1}{5}$in (25-30mm); female abdomen 1-$1\frac{1}{10}$in (25-29mm), hindwing 1-$1\frac{1}{10}$in (26-30mm). *Habitat* around stagnant water, peat bogs, streams to 6000ft (1800m). *Season* May-October.

Ruddy Darter Dragonfly *Length* male abdomen $\frac{4}{5}$-1in (20-25mm), hindwing $\frac{9}{10}$-$1\frac{1}{10}$in (23-28mm); female abdomen $\frac{9}{10}$-1in (22-25mm), hindwing 1-$1\frac{1}{10}$in (25-29mm). *Habitat* near stagnant, acid waters, ponds, peat bogs. *Season* June-early October.

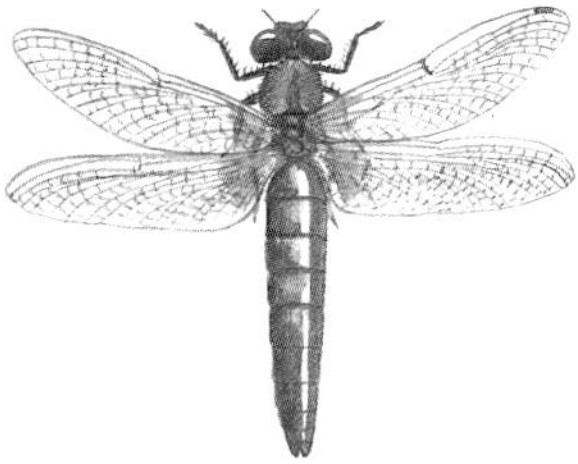

Red Darter Dragonfly *Length* male abdomen $\frac{9}{10}$-$1\frac{1}{10}$in (23-29mm), hindwing $1\frac{1}{10}$-$1\frac{1}{4}$in (27-32mm); female abdomen $\frac{9}{10}$-$1\frac{1}{10}$in (22-28mm), hindwing $1\frac{1}{10}$-$1\frac{1}{4}$in (27-32mm). *Habitat* around stagnant ponds, lakes, lagoons, etc. *Season* April-November.

Ringed Darter Dragonfly *Length* male abdomen $\frac{9}{10}$in (22-24mm), hindwing 1-$1\frac{1}{5}$in (26-30mm); female abdomen $\frac{9}{10}$in (22-24mm), hindwing $1\frac{1}{10}$-$1\frac{1}{4}$in (28-32mm). *Habitat* near stagnant or running water, on rocks. *Season* April-November, in south only.

Black-tailed Skimmer Dragonfly *Length* male abdomen $1\frac{1}{5}$-$1\frac{2}{5}$in (30-35mm), hindwing $1\frac{2}{5}$-$1\frac{3}{5}$in (35-40mm); female abdomen $1\frac{1}{10}$-$1\frac{2}{5}$in (29-34mm), hindwing $1\frac{2}{5}$-$1\frac{3}{5}$in (35-41mm). *Habitat* near ponds, lakes, peat bogs. *Season* April-end of September.

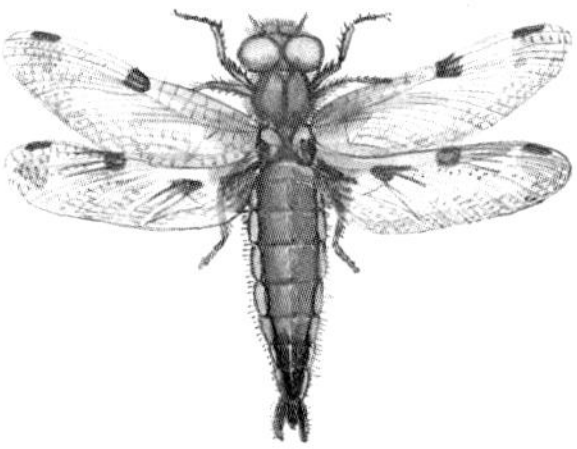

Four-spotted Chaser Dragonfly *Length* male abdomen $1\frac{1}{10}$-$1\frac{1}{4}$in (27-32mm), hindwing $1\frac{1}{4}$-$1\frac{2}{5}$in (32-36mm); female abdomen $1\frac{1}{10}$-$1\frac{1}{5}$in (28-31mm), hindwing $1\frac{1}{2}$-$1\frac{1}{2}$in (33-39mm). *Habitat* near weedy, stagnant waters up to 6575ft (2000m) and more. *Season* April-September.

Ant Lion *Length* abdomen $1\frac{1}{2}$in (37mm), wingspan $1\frac{4}{5}$in (47mm). *Habitat* dry, stony hillsides, adult with characteristic 'lazy' rising and falling flight; name derived from larvae which excavate pits in sand and feed on insects, mainly ants, which fall in.

Ribbon Wing *Length* including ribbon-like hindwings $1\frac{3}{4}$in (43-45mm). *Habitat* warm, dry, open country, flying at dusk with characteristic, bobbing action; larvae in caves, outbuildings, feeding on other insects

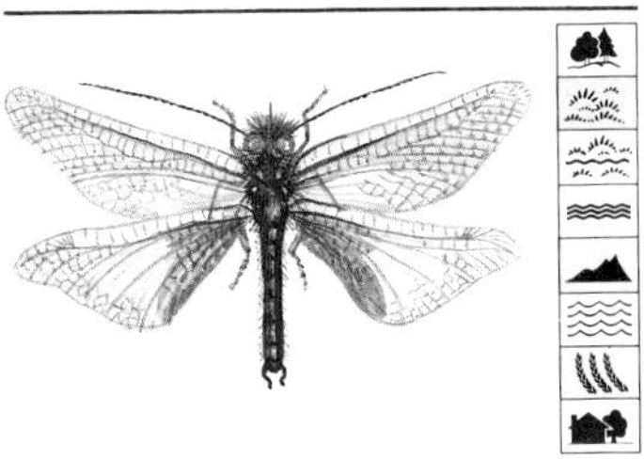

Ascalaphid *Wingspan* 2⅒ in (53-55 mm). *Habitat* fields, waysides, alpine grasslands, in the summer; adults hunt insect prey on the wing in a rapid, darting flight; larvae seek prey in leaf litter and under stones and have sharply toothed jaws.

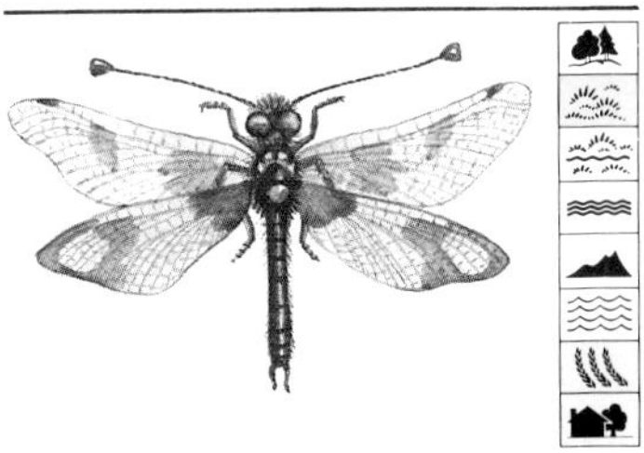

Spotted Ascalaphid *Wingspan* 1⅘-1⁹⁄₁₀ in (46-48 mm). *Habitat* dry, open country in summer months, adults hunting insect prey on the wing with rapid, fluttering flight; larve hunt prey on the ground.

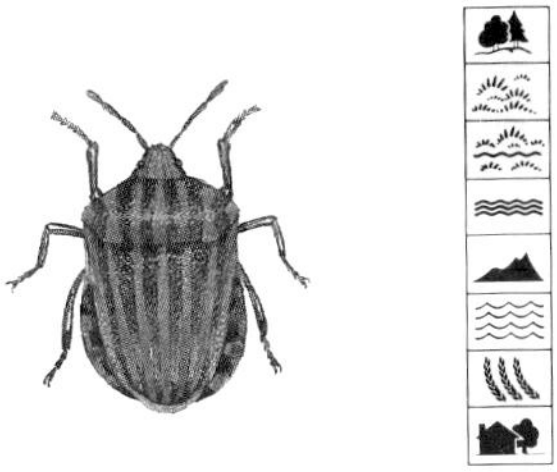

larlequin Shieldbug *Length* ⅓-⅖ in (9-11 mm). *Habitat* ound mainly on umbellifers, sucking sap, among oadside vegetation, marginal areas and waste rounds; common in summer months.

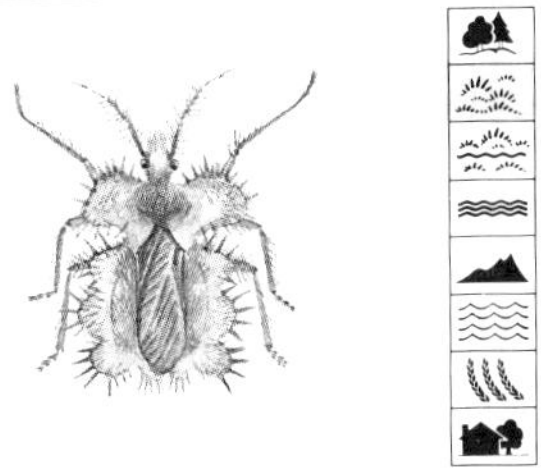

Spiny Squashbug *Length* ⅓-⅗ in (9-10 mm). *Habitat* dry, stony, open country, usually found on papery flowers of Silvery Paronychia or dry flowerheads of Lavender, against which it is well camouflaged; common in summer.

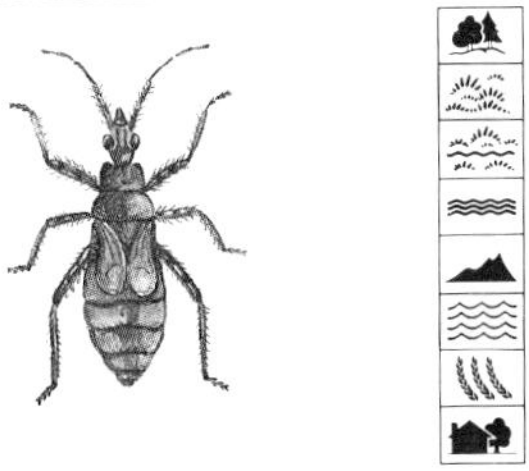

ath Assassin Bug *Length* ⅓-⅖ in (9-11 mm). *Habitat* y, sandy areas such as heaths and sand-dunes, ually seen walking over sand in search of insect prey which it feeds with its piercing and sucking uthparts; common July to October.

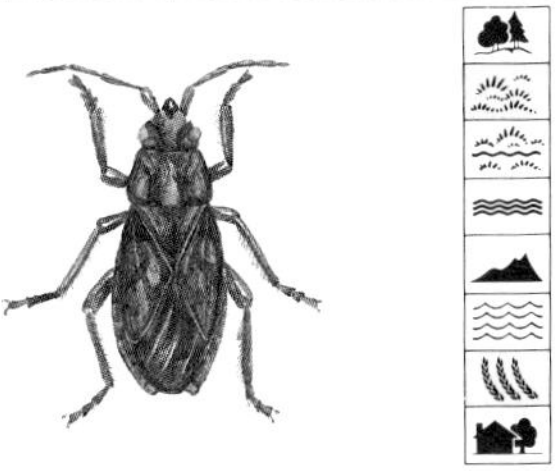

Ground Bug *Length* ⅖ in (10-11 mm). *Habitat* open country, roadside vegetation, on a variety of plants and also around the margins of cultivated land; common throughout summer.

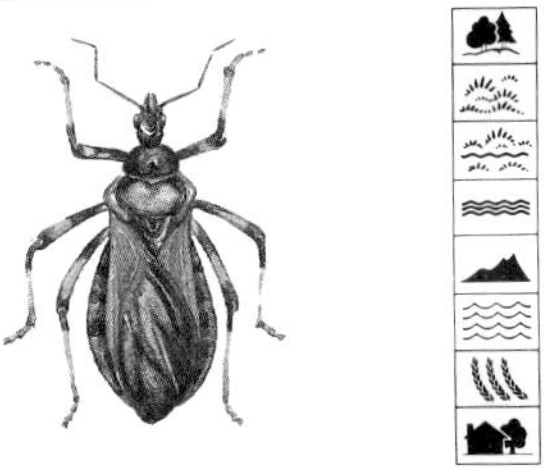

sassin Bug *Length* ⅖ in (10-11 mm). *Habitat* etation including flowers, in marginal areas of ods, fields, cultivated plots, where it preys on other ects; often walking about with prey impaled on king mouthparts, in summer.

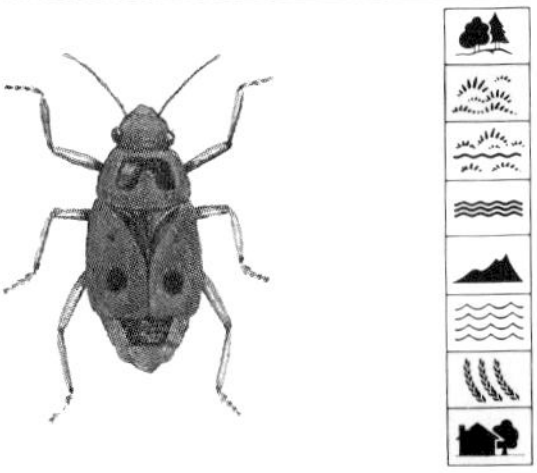

Firebug *Length* ⅓-⅖ in (8-10.5 mm). *Habitat* on Mallows and Lime trees, feeding on seeds though sometimes carnivorous and will prey on small insects; also, mating pairs often seen running on bare ground; April-May.

Swallowtail *Description* male forewing 1¼-1½in (32-38mm); sexes similar. *Flight* 2 broods, April/May, July/August. *Habitat* flowery meadows and banks, sea-level to 6600ft (2000m). *Larvae* on Wild Carrot, Fennel, and other umbellifers.

Corsican Swallowtail *Description* male forewing 1⅖-1½in (36-38mm); sexes similar, very like Swallowtail, but tails shorter. *Flight* May-July. *Habitat* mountains 2000-4275ft (600-1300m), Corsica and Sardinia only. *Larvae* on umbellifers.

Southern Swallowtail *Description* male forewing 1¼in (31-33mm); female often larger, otherwise similar. *Flight* April-July. *Habitat* mountainous areas up to 4275ft (1300m), attracted to thistles in south. *Larvae* on umbellifers.

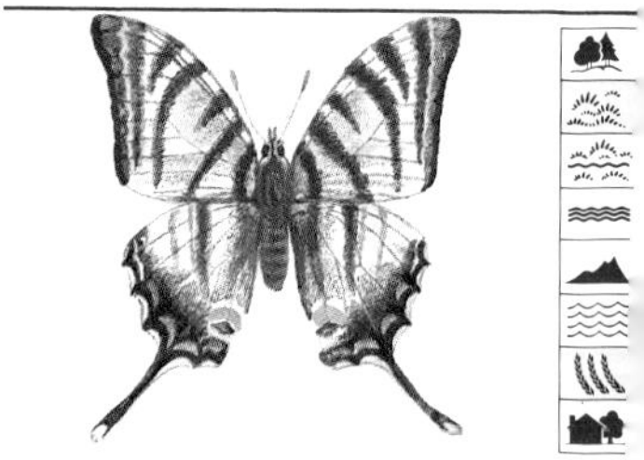

Scarce Swallowtail *Description* male forewing 1¼-1⅗in (32-40mm), female larger; wing patterns liable to vary. *Flight* March-September. *Habitat* lowlands to 6600ft (2000m) or higher, often flying around orchards. *Larvae* on sloe, cultivated fruit trees.

Southern Festoon *Description* male forewing $\frac{9}{10}$-1in (23-26mm); sexes similar. *Flight* single brooded, end April/May. *Habitat* rough, stony areas, from lowlands to 3300ft in (1000m). *Larvae* on Birthwort plants.

Apollo *Description* 1⅓-1⅔in (35-42mm); sexes similar except females may have red spots larger. *Flight* July-August. *Habitat* mountain regions at subalpine levels, from 2730-6600ft (830-2000m). *Larvae* on Stonecrop.

Clouded Apollo *Description* male forewing 1-1⅕in (26-31mm); sexes similar, though some females with dark suffusions on wings. *Flight* single brooded, May-July. *Habitat* damp meadows in hills and mountains up to 5425ft (1650m). *Larvae* on corydalis.

Large White (Cabbage White) *Description* male forewing 1$\frac{1}{10}$-1¼in (28-33mm); female hindwing yel tinged. *Flight* April/May, and July/August. *Habitat* gardens, flowery waysides, and fields up to 6600ft (2000m). *Larvae* on Cabbage and related plants.

Southern Small White *Description* male forewing 4/5-9/10 in (20-23 mm), female sometimes larger, black areas larger. *Flight* 3-4 broods, March-summer. *Habitat* rocky areas up to 5250 ft (1600 m). *Larvae* on members of cabbage family.

Peak White *Description* male forewing 4/5-1 in (21-26 mm); female with stronger dark markings. *Flight* late June-August. *Habitat* alpine, grassy slopes from 6900 ft (2100 m upwards). *Larvae* on Smooth Mignonette and alpine cabbage family.

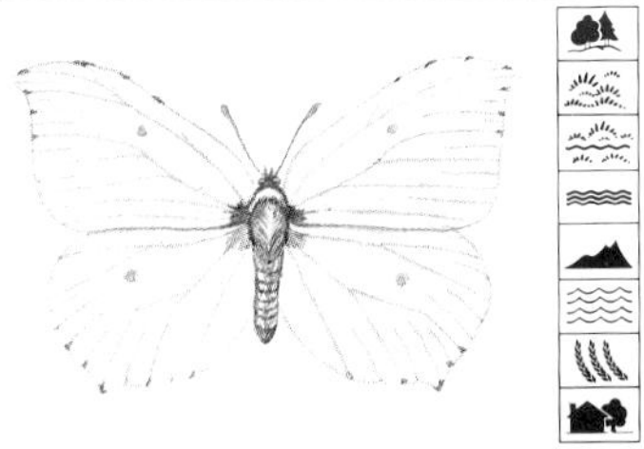

rimstone *Description* male forewing 1-1⅕ in (26-
)mm); female wing markings similar, wings greenish
hite. *Flight* June, hibernated individuals appearing
llowing spring. *Habitat* open areas to 6600 ft (2000 m).
arvae on Buckthorn.

Nettle-tree Butterfly *Description* male forewing 3/4-9/10 in (17-22 mm); females similar; colour pattern very constant. *Flight* June-August/September, March/April. *Habitat* lowlands up to 1650 ft (500 m), usually near Nettle-trees. *Larvae* on Nettle-tree.

vo-tailed Pasha *Description* male forewing 1½-1⅗ in
3-41 mm); female similar, larger. *Flight* two broods,
ay/June and August/September. *Habitat* from sea-
vel to 1650 ft (500 m). *Larvae* on Strawberry Tree.

Lesser Purple Emperor *Description* male forewing 1¼-1⅓ in (32-35 mm); female larger, without purple flush. *Flight* two broods, May/June and August/September. *Habitat* open woodland in valley bottoms. *Larvae* on poplars and willows.

berwell Beauty *Description* male forewing 1¼-
n (30-34 mm); female similar. *Flight* June/July and
n in spring after hibernation. *Habitat* open, usually
or mountainous country. *Larvae* willows, birch,
r deciduous forest trees.

Peacock *Description* male forewing 1⅒ in (27-29 mm); female similar, slightly larger. *Flight* July onwards, again in spring after hibernation. *Habitat* flowery areas to 6600 ft (2000 m). *Larvae* usually on nettles.

Red Admiral *Description* male forewing $1\frac{1}{10}$-$1\frac{1}{5}$in (28-31mm); female similar. *Flight* May-October, in south, hibernated individuals appear in spring. *Habitat* flowery areas to 6600ft (2000m). *Larvae* on nettles, sometimes on thistles.

Painted Lady *Description* male forewing $1\frac{1}{10}$in (27-29mm); female similar. *Flight* from April onwards. *Habitat* flowery meadows and banks from lowlands to 6600ft (2000m). *Larvae* on thistles and nettles.

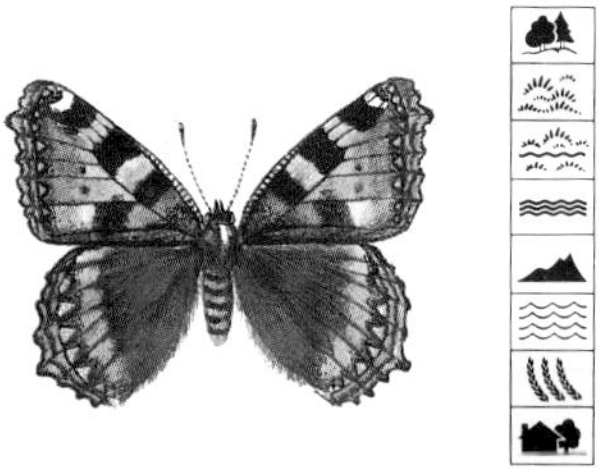

Small Tortoiseshell *Description* male forewing $\frac{9}{10}$-1in (22-25mm); female similar, slightly larger. *Flight* May onwards in several broods, hibernated individuals in March. *Habitat* flowery places to 7500ft (2300m). *Larvae* on nettles.

Comma *Description* male forewing $\frac{9}{10}$in (22-24mm); sexes similar. *Flight* two broods, June/August; hibernated individuals active March/April. *Habitat* flowery gardens, to 6000ft (1800m). *Larvae* on nettles, hops, willows, other trees.

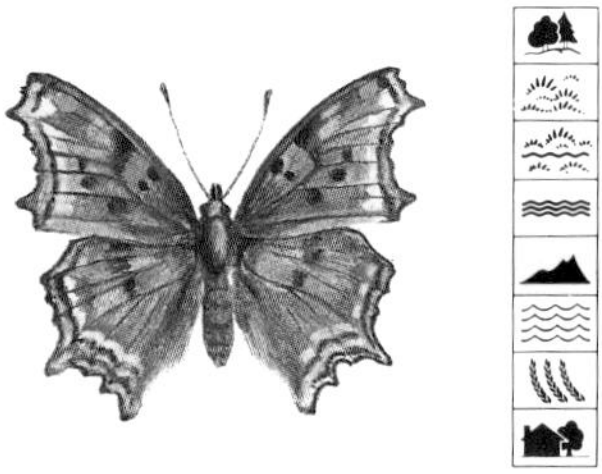

Southern Comma *Description* male forewing $\frac{9}{10}$in (22-23mm), sexes similar. *Flight* double brooded, May/June and August/September, then again in spring, after hibernation. *Habitat* hot, dry, rocky valleys to 4000ft (1200m). *Larvae* on Pellitory, nettles.

Dark Green Fritillary *Description* male forewing $\frac{9}{10}$-$1\frac{1}{10}$in (24-29mm); female similar, with ground colour slightly paler. *Flight* June-July. *Habitat* heaths, dune hollows, flowery meadows to treeline. *Larvae* on viole and Redshank.

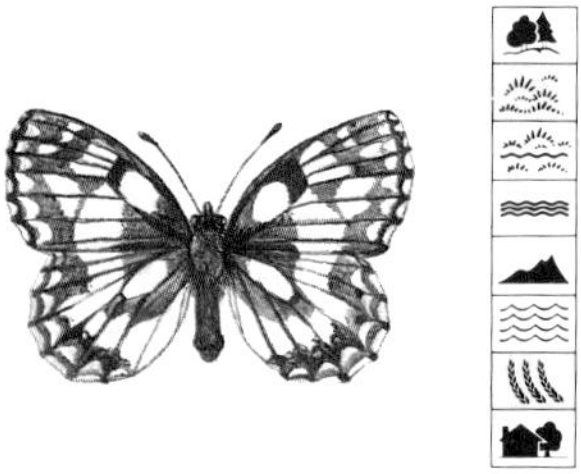

Marbled White *Description* male forewing $\frac{9}{10}$-1in (23-26mm); female larger, hindwings beneath with pale yellow ground colour and yellow-brown marks. *Flight* June-July. *Habitat* grassy areas to 5250ft (1600m). *Larvae* on grasses.

Italian Marbled White *Description* male forewing 1 i (25-26mm); female often larger, otherwise similar. *F* May/June. *Habitat* hillsides and mountains, in small, localized colonies, up to 5000ft (1500m). *Larvae* on grasses.

Woodland Grayling *Description* male forewing 1¼-1½ in (33-38 mm); female larger, bands paler, more sharply defined. *Flight* July-August. *Habitat* among bushes and trees up to 3300 ft (1000 m). *Larvae* on grasses, especially Fog Grass.

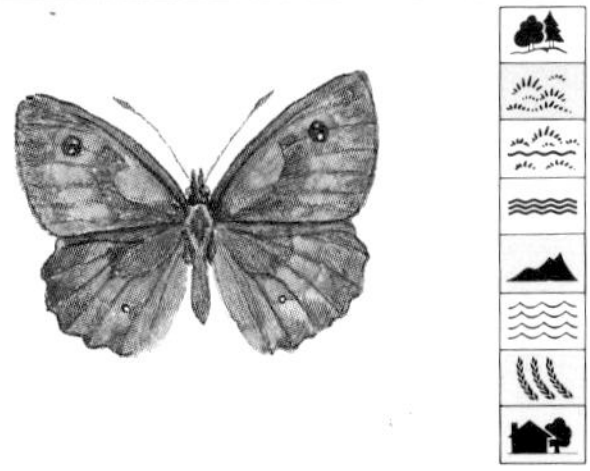

Gatekeeper *Description* male forewing ⅔-¾ in (17-19 mm); female larger, upperside ground colour brighter. *Flight* July-August. *Habitat* around brambles in lowlands and up to 3300 ft (1000 m). *Larvae* on meadow grasses and millets.

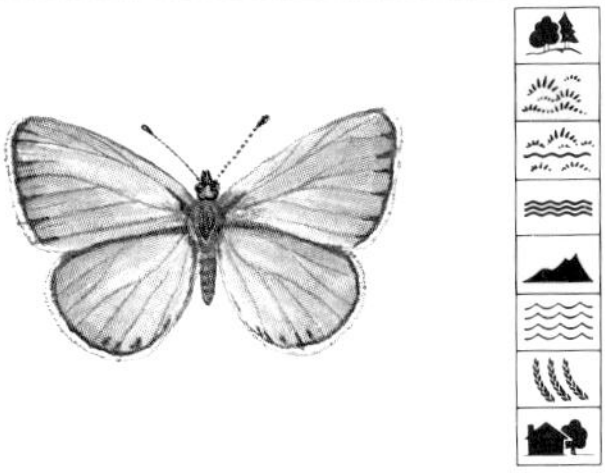

:scher's Blue *Description* male forewing ⅔-¾ in (17-9 mm); female uppersides brown, orange markings on ides. *Flight* late June-July. *Habitat* usually mountains p to 6600 ft (2000 m), sometimes in lowlands. *Larvae* on etches.

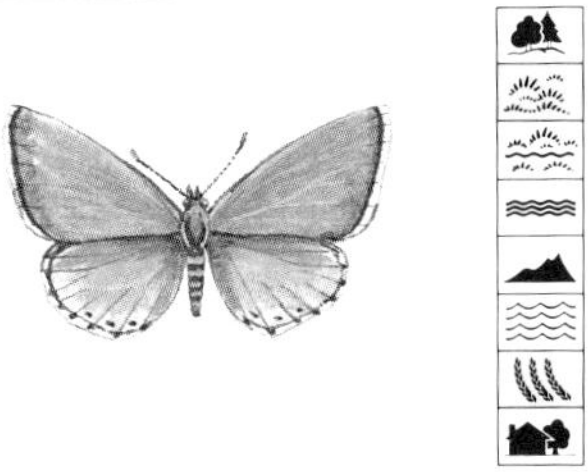

Common Blue *Description* male forewing ⅗-¾ in (14-18 mm); female wings brown with blue flushes at bases. *Flight* two to three broods, from April onwards. *Habitat* open spaces, flowery meadows and waysides to 6600 ft (2000 m). *Larvae* on clovers, vetches.

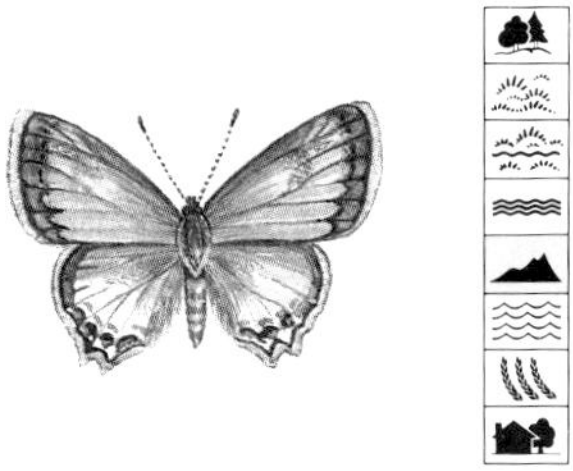

eleager's Blue *Description* male forewing ¾ in (18-mm); female a deeper blue, hindwings more deeply alloped. *Flight* June, single brood. *Habitat* warm, wery hillsides up to 4750 ft (1450 m). *Larvae* on tches, Thyme.

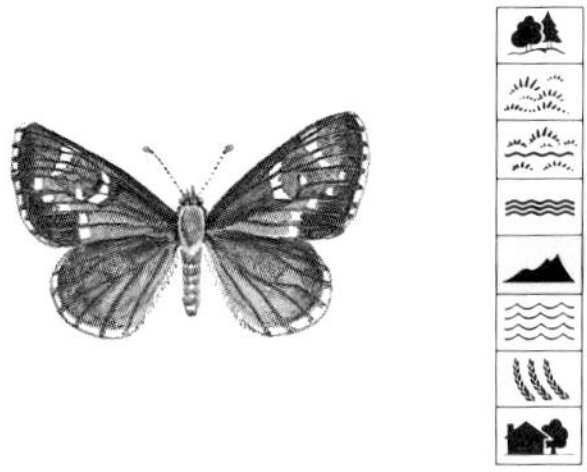

Carline Skipper *Description* male forewing ½ in (13-14 mm); female with yellowish flush to uppersides. *Flight* July-August. *Habitat* mountain pastures, often in large gatherings on damp paths. *Larvae* on *Potentilla*.

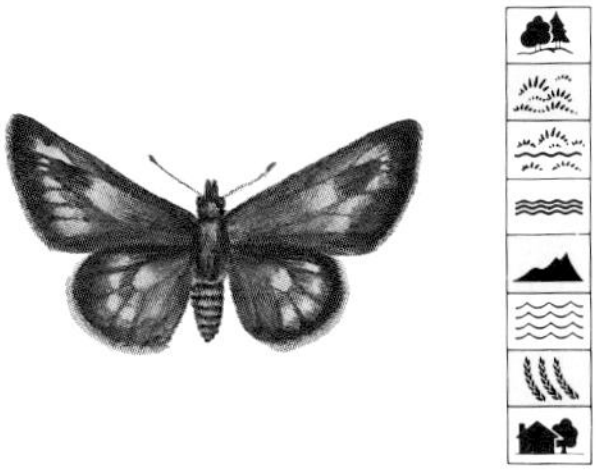

ge Skipper *Description* male forewing ⅗-⅔ in (14-ım); female wings with series of pale spots. *Flight* e-August. *Habitat* fields and grassy banks up to)ft (1800 m). *Larvae* on grasses and rushes.

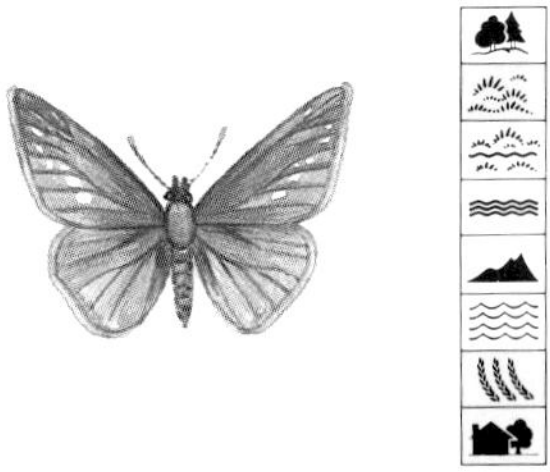

Pigmy Skipper *Description* male forewing ⅗ in (14 mm); female similar but paler, with pale spots. *Flight* throughout summer. April-October. *Habitat* often seen resting on rocks in full sunlight or hot paths in lowlands. *Larvae* on grasses.

Hornet Clearwing *Wingspan* 1⅖ in (36 mm). *Flight* May/June. *Habitat* lowlands, river banks, and waysides with poplars. *Larvae* feed in roots and lower trunks of poplars, taking three years to develop, before pupating under bark or in soil.

Six-spot Burnet *Wingspan* 1¼-1⅖ in (33-36 mm). *Flight* July/August. *Habitat* hillsides, cliffs, grassland, in chalky areas, also on sand-dunes. *Larvae* on clover, trefoils, and vetches, completing growth and pupating in spring.

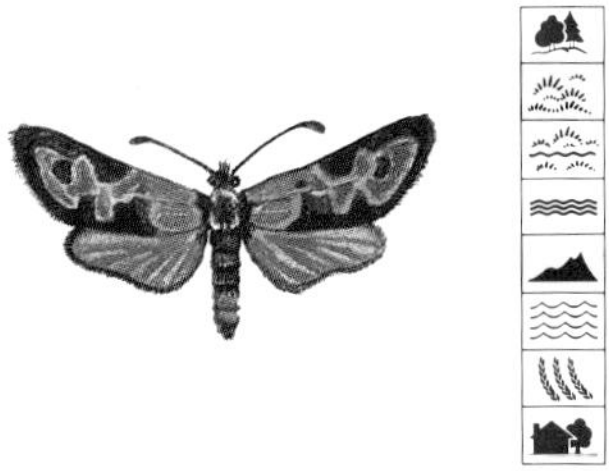

Faust Burnet *Wingspan* 9/10-1 1/10 in (22-28 mm). *Flight* late spring-summer. *Habitat* scrubby thickets on chalk and limestone hills. *Larvae* on Crown Vetch and Scorpion Senna.

Buff-tip *Wingspan* 1¾-2¼ in (42-55 mm). *Flight* May-July. *Habitat* deciduous woodland, urban parks. *Larvae* on willows, hazels, oaks, limes, living gregariously when young, often stripping branches of leaves.

Puss Moth *Wingspan* 1¾-2¾ in (45-70 mm). *Flight* April-July. *Habitat* damp, waterside vegetation, woodland edges and in valleys, mountains up to 8225 ft (2500 m). *Larvae* on willows and poplars.

Garden Tiger *Wingspan* 1¾-2¼ in (45-65 mm). *Flight* June-August. *Habitat* lowlands, including agricultural land, mountains up to 6600 ft (2000 m), but mostly on mountain-slope areas at about 2000 ft (600 m). *Larvae* wide variety of plants, covered in irritant hairs.

Cinnabar Moth *Wingspan* 1¼-1¾ in (32-42 mm). *Flight* May-July. *Habitat* meadows, warm and cool steppes, up to 5250 ft (1600 m). *Larvae* gregarious, conspicuous black and yellow-ringed, feeding on ragworts and groundsels, HIGHLY POISONOUS.

Heart and Dart Moth *Wingspan* 1¼-1⅗ in (30-40 mm). *Flight* June-September. *Habitat* almost everywhere except high mountains. *Larvae* on wide range of foodplants, including Goosefoot, Plantain, Chickweed, lettuce, turnips.

Red Underwing *Wingspan* $2\frac{1}{2}$-3 in (65-75 mm). *Flight* July-October. *Habitat* urban parks, moist deciduous woodlands in the north, often near water. *Larvae* on various kinds of poplars and willows.

Emperor Moth *Wingspan* $1\frac{3}{5}$-$2\frac{1}{3}$ in (40-60 mm); females without feathery antennae, ground colour of wings grey rather than orange-brown. *Flight* April/May. *Habitat* lowlands, mountains to 6600 ft (2000 m). *Larvae* on Blackthorn, willows, Bilberry.

eath's Head Hawkmoth *Wingspan* $3\frac{1}{10}$-$4\frac{3}{4}$ in (80-20 mm). *Flight* May/June, immigrant from Africa and outh-west Asia. *Habitat* cultivated areas in lowlands. *arvae* on potato family: potatoes, Woody Nightshade, horn-apple.

Eyed Hawkmoth *Wingspan* $2\frac{3}{4}$-$3\frac{1}{10}$ in (70-80 mm). *Flight* May-July. *Habitat* lowlands, mountains up to 6600 ft (2000 m), urban parks; nocturnal. *Larvae* on poplars and willows, sometimes fruit trees.

mmingbird Hawkmoth *Wingspan* $1\frac{3}{5}$-2 in (40-50 mm). *ght* June-October. *Habitat* day-flying, at flowers in an flowerbeds, flowery meadows, margins of fields, ting flowers with rapid, darting and hovering flight. *vae* on bedstraws.

Poplar Hawkmoth *Wingspan* $2\frac{1}{2}$-$3\frac{1}{2}$ in (65-90 mm). *Flight* May-August. *Habitat* scrub, riverside trees, damp deciduous forest in the north. *Larvae* on poplars and willows, sometimes on low shrubs.

rge Hawkmoth *Wingspan* $2\frac{1}{4}$-3 in (55-75 mm). *Flight* -August. *Habitat* waste areas, marginal land, dry, bby waysides. *Larvae* on various kinds of spurge.

Mediterranean Hawkmoth *Wingspan* $3\frac{1}{3}$-4 in (85-100 mm). *Flight* May-September. *Habitat* dry hillsides, scrubby waysides, margins of open woodlands. *Larvae* on various kinds of spurge.

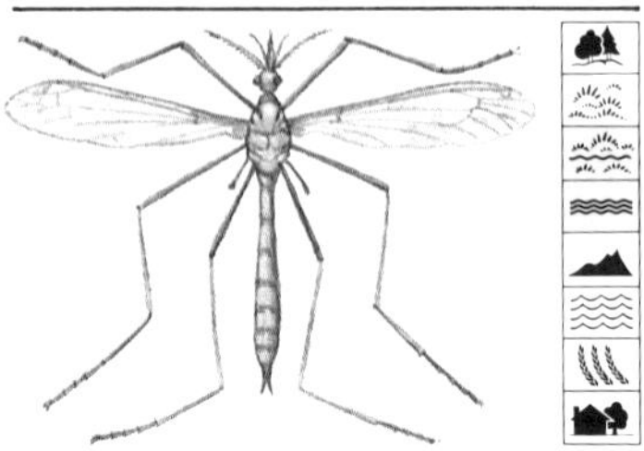

Great Cranefly *Wingspan* 2½in (65mm). *Season* spring and summer. *Habitat* damp, marshy areas, stream- and lakesides, ditches. *Larvae* semiaquatic, in saturated margins of ponds, streams, or, sometimes living under water.

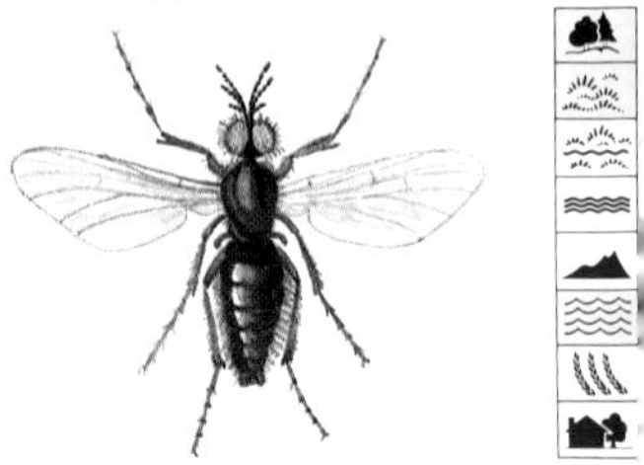

St Mark's Fly *Wingspan* ⅘-9⁄10in (20-22mm). *Season* spring. *Habitat* varied, grasslands, downs, dunes, woodland; shiny black adults sluggish in flight, often seen in swarms, rising and descending. *Larvae* feed in leaf litter, pupate in the ground.

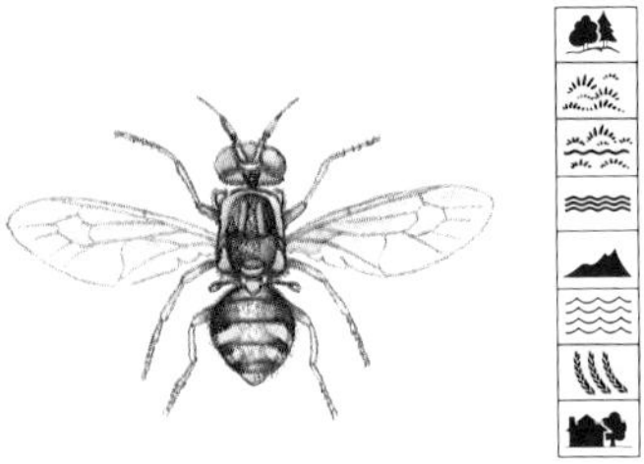

Soldier Fly *Wingspan* ⅖-½in (10-12mm). *Season* summer. *Habitat* marshy areas, including damp meadows, ditches, waterside vegetation, often seen on umbellifer flowers. *Larvae* in ponds, ditches, preying on small water animals, including insects.

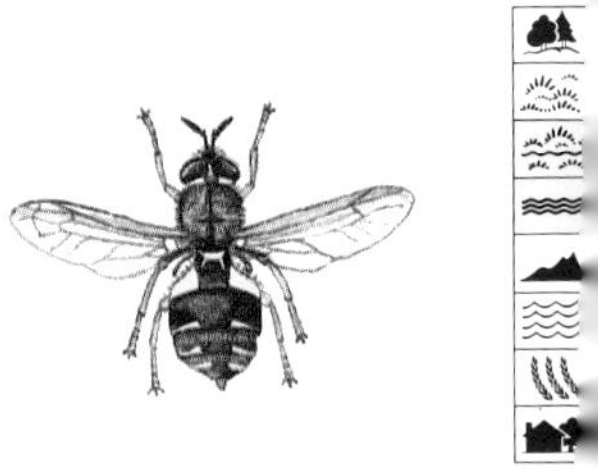

Soldier Fly *Wingspan* 1-1⅒in (26-28mm). *Season* summer. *Habitat* waterside vegetation, often seen at flowers of Water Hemlock; heavy flight, with wasp-lik hum. *Larvae* aquatic, feeding on small water creature and other insects.

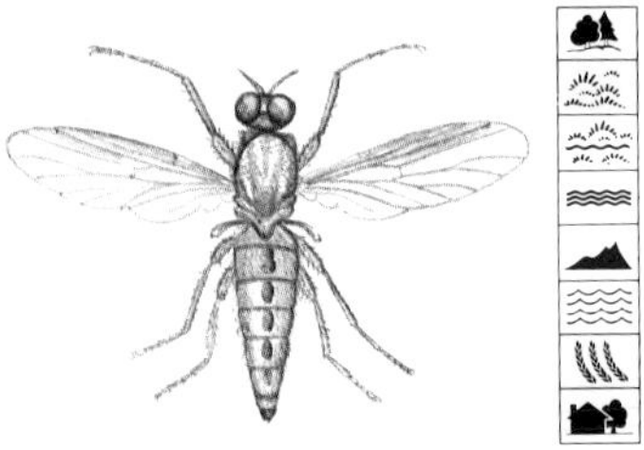

Snipe Fly *Wingspan* 1-1⅒in (26-28mm). *Season* summer-early autumn. *Habitat* hedgerows, meadows, woodland edges, often seen resting head down on treetrunks. *Larvae* carnivorous, living in leaf litter, under bark of fallen trees.

Horsefly *Wingspan* 1⅒-1⅕in (27-30mm). *Season* M September. *Habitat* fields, open woodlands, females sucking blood of livestock; males nectar-feeders, at flowers. *Larvae* carnivorous, preying on worms, inse larvae in soil, dead wood.

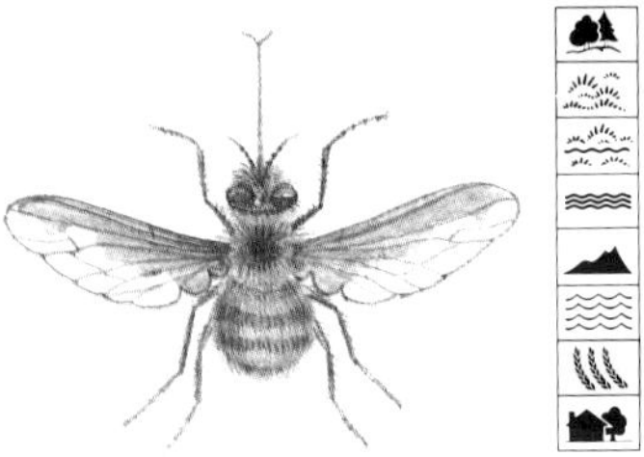

Bee-fly *Wingspan* 1-1⅒in (26-28mm). *Season* spring, early summer. *Habitat* fields, waysides, woodland glades with patches of bare earth; often seen at flowers or hovering near mining bee nests. *Larvae* parasites of solitary mining bee larvae.

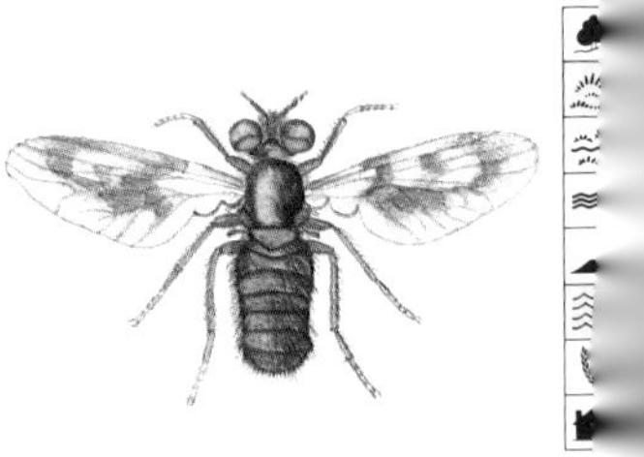

Bee-fly *Wingspan* ⅘-9⁄10in (20-22mm). *Season* Jun August. *Habitat* dry, sandy areas, heaths, sand-dur often seen resting on bare sand. *Larvae* parasites o caterpillars.

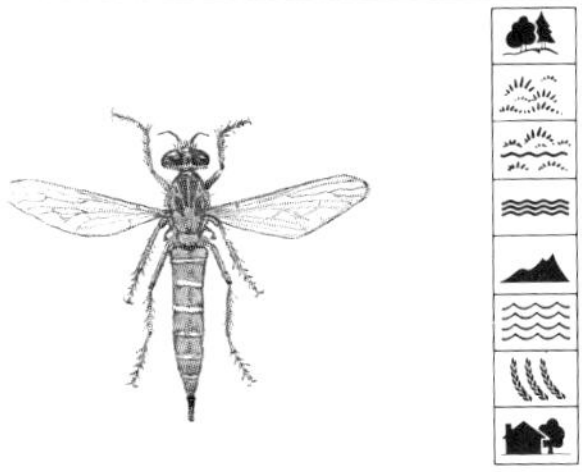

Robberfly *Wingspan* 9/10 in (22 mm). *Season* spring and summer. *Habitat* dry sandy areas in coastal regions, especially sand-dunes, where the flies prey on other insects. *Larvae* feed on decaying vegetable matter in soil, sand.

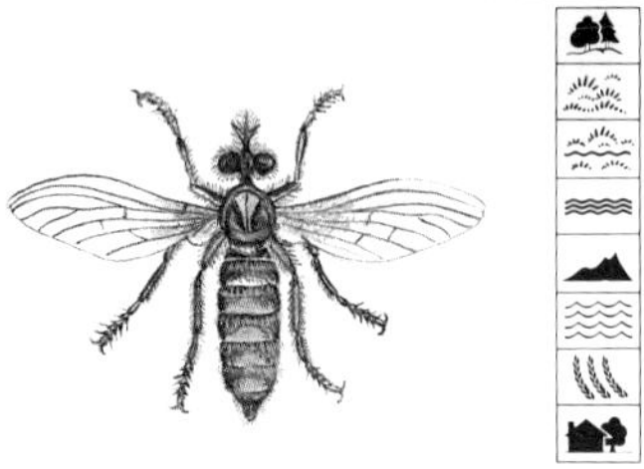

Robberfly *Wingspan* 4/5-9/10 in (21-23 mm). *Season* late spring-summer. *Habitat* open woodlands, sunny clearings, meadows, leaping on insect prey from vantage points such as treestumps, rocks. *Larvae* live in soil, feeding on humus and other decaying matter.

low Flower Fly *Wingspan* 1 1/10-1 1/5 in (28-30 mm). *eason* spring-summer. *Habitat* hot, dry, stony, and andy places where often seen sipping nectar from owers while hovering. *Larvae* possibly parasites of eetle larvae.

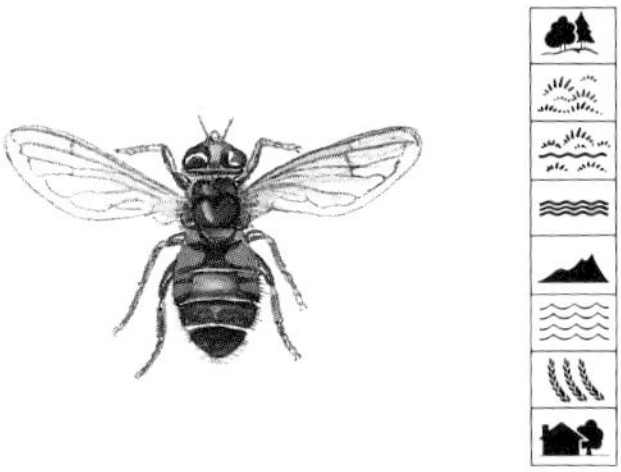

Dronefly *Wingspan* 1-1 1/10 in (26-29 mm). *Season* early spring to autumn. *Habitat* flowers in waysides, woodlands, hedgebanks, gardens, farmyards, closely resembling Honeybee. *Larvae* in stagnant water, called 'rat-tailed maggots'.

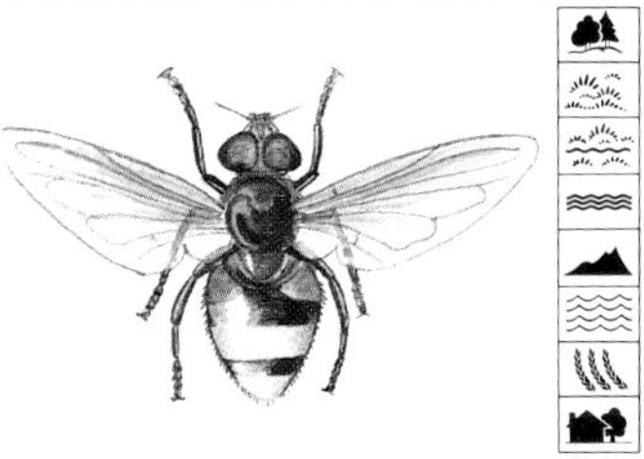

verfly *Wingspan* 1 1/10-1 1/4 in (28-33 mm). *Season* ne-September. *Habitat* flower-rich meadows, lsides, and woodlands. *Larvae* live as scavengers in rnet nests.

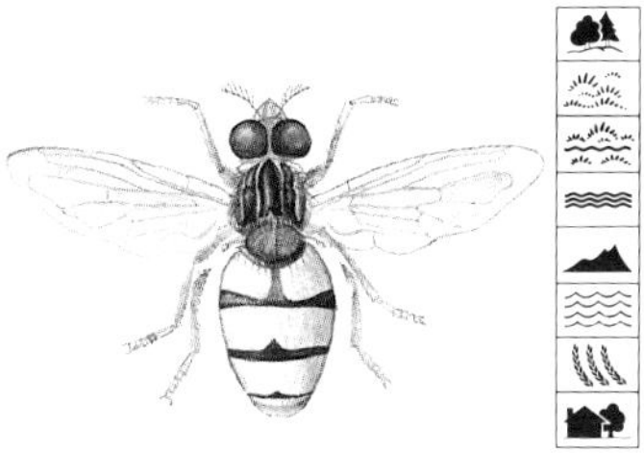

Hoverfly *Wingspan* 1 1/2-1 3/5 in (39-41 mm). *Season* April-September. *Habitat* flower-rich areas, often near damp or marshy ground; at flowers of umbels, mint. *Larvae* feeding on damp, rotting plant material and other decaying organic matter.

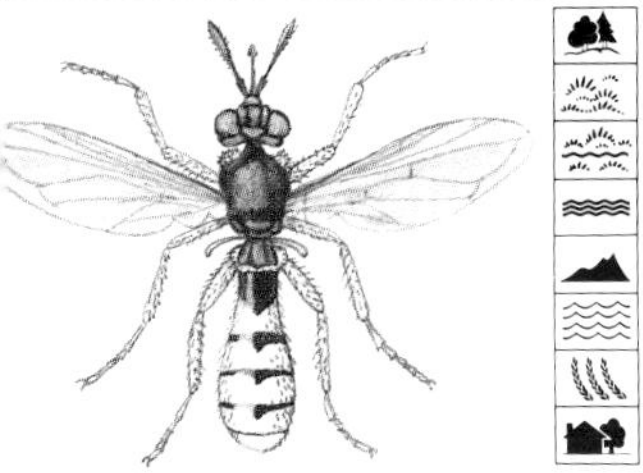

ck-headed Fly *Wingspan* 3/5-2/3 in (16-18 mm). *Season* e-August. *Habitat* woodland glades, flowery adows, hedgerows; often at umbels, bramble, and er Mint flowers. *Larvae* internal parasites of social ps and bumblebees.

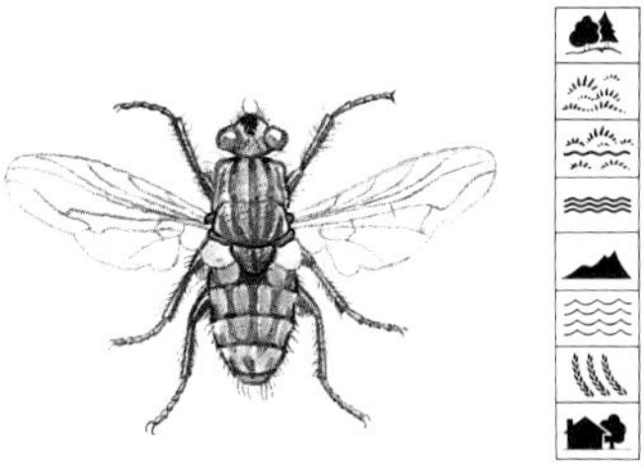

Fleshfly *Wingspan* 9/10-1 in (23-25 mm). *Season* March-November. *Habitat* varied, almost everywhere, including towns; at umbels and other flowers, attracted to rotting meat. *Larvae* female lays small larvae on meat, dead animals.

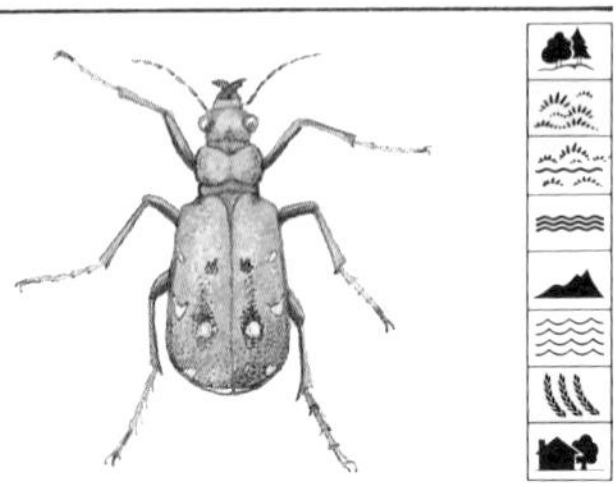

Field Tiger Beetle *Length* 2/5-3/5 in (10.5-14.5 mm). *Season* April-September. *Habitat* dry, sandy areas, dry fields with bare earth; runs rapidly, flies readily, preys on insects. *Larvae* live in short burrows, darting out to catch insect prey.

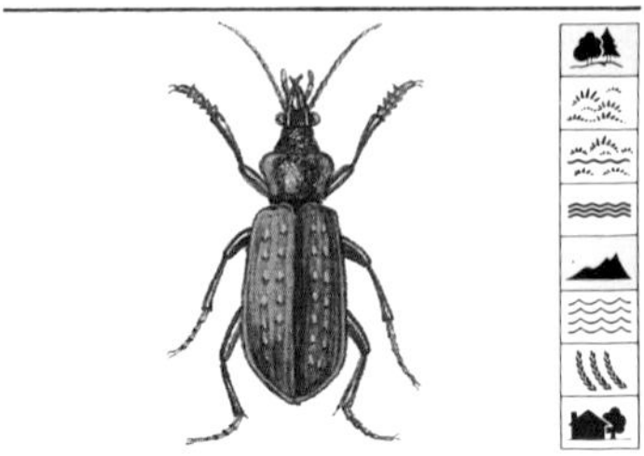

Golden-dimpled Ground Beetle *Length* 4/5-1 1/5 in (20-30 mm). *Season* spring-autumn. *Habitat* dry woodland, hillsides, under stones; feeds on other insects, especially caterpillars, at night. *Larvae* carnivorous, under stones.

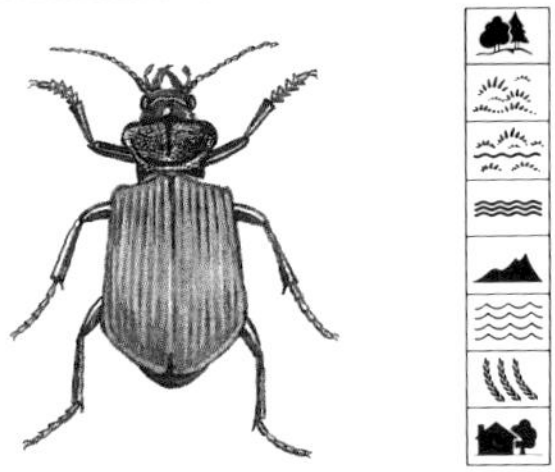

Green Caterpillar-hunting Ground Beetle *Wingspan* 2/3-1 1/10 in (17.5-28 mm). *Season* spring-summer. *Habitat* woodland, under bark of dead trees, logs, and stones, feeding on caterpillars at night in tree canopy. *Larvae* nocturnal, carnivorous.

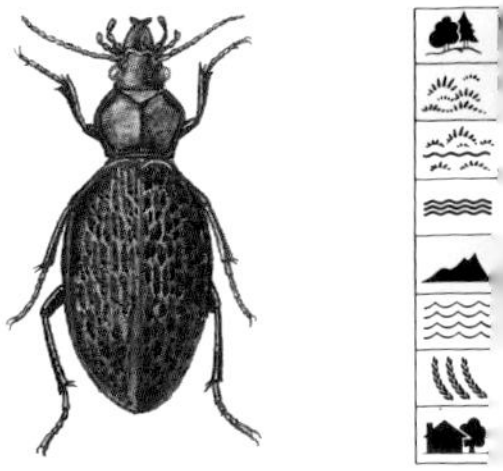

Coriaceous Ground Beetle *Length* 1 1/5-1 3/5 in (30-40 mm *Season* spring-autumn, hibernating through winter; adults may live 2-3 years. *Habitat* varied, ranging from lowlands to mountains, under stones during day. *Larva* prey on other insects.

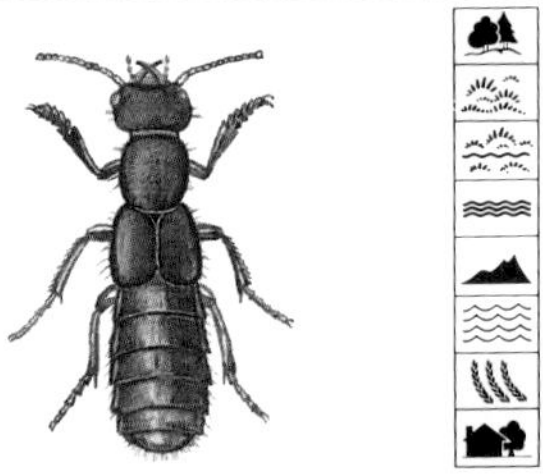

Devil's Coach Horse *Length* 9/10-1 1/4 in (22-32 mm). *Season* most times of the year. *Habitat* open country, gardens, woods, under stones and logs in day; by night, preys greedily on other insects. *Larvae* similar habits to adults.

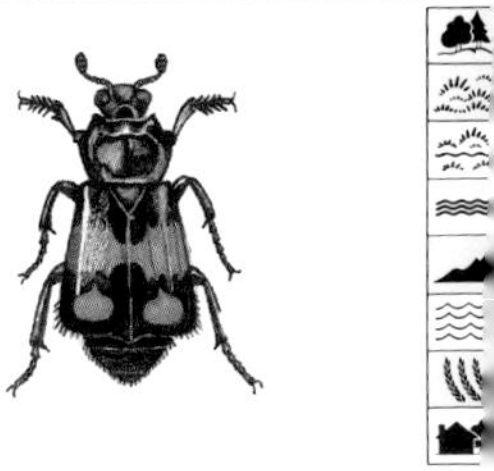

Sexton Beetle *Length* 1/2-9/10 in (12-22 mm). *Season* spring-autumn. *Habitat* almost everywhere, on carrio which they bury as future food for offspring; active fliers at night. *Larvae* in carrion buried by parent.

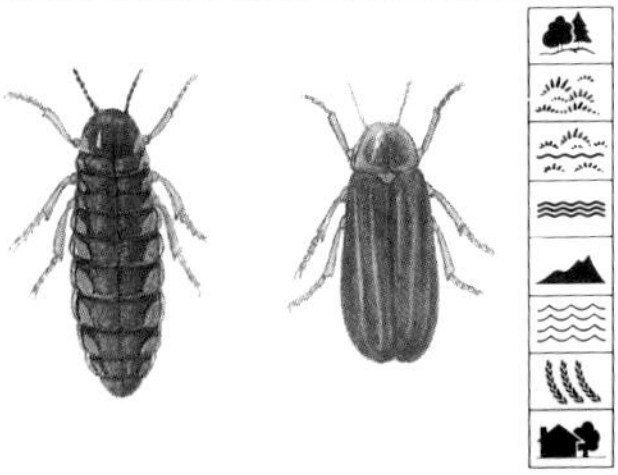

Glowworm *Length* male 2/5-1/2 in (10-12 mm), female 3/5-4/5 in (15-20 mm). *Season* June-September. *Habitat* chalky areas; prey on snails; female resembles larva, is flightless, and produces green light on warm evenings to attract males. *Larvae* eat snails.

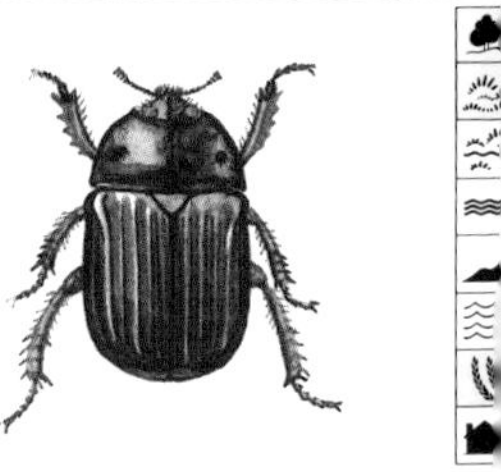

Dor Beetle *Length* 3/5-1 in (16-25 mm). *Season* spring-autumn. *Habitat* grasslands in lowland areas, open woodland; feed on dung, excavating nest tunnels immediately under dung pat, laying eggs in dung ca into brood chamber. *Larvae* on dung in brood cells.

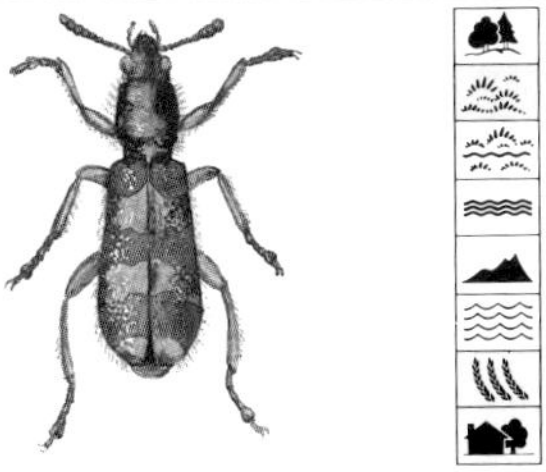

Bee-eating Beetle *Length* ⅓-⅗in (9-16mm). *Season* summer. *Habitat* warm, open country, on umbelliferous flowers. *Larvae* live in nests of Honeybees and solitary mining bees and eat larvae.

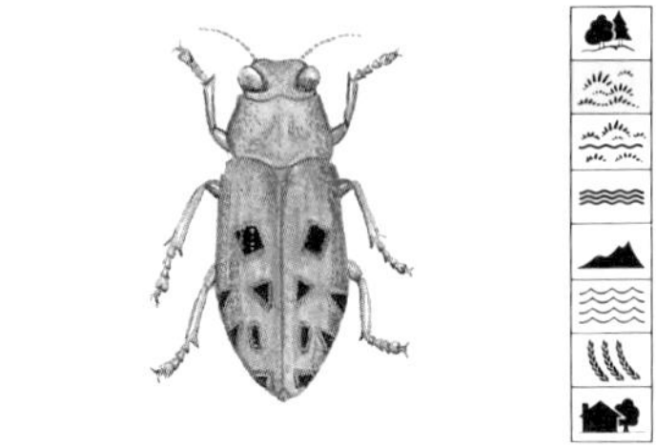

Jewel Beetle *Length* ¼-½in (6-12mm). *Season* June-August. *Habitat* open grassland, flying around Juniper trees. *Larvae* feed on Juniper, under the bark.

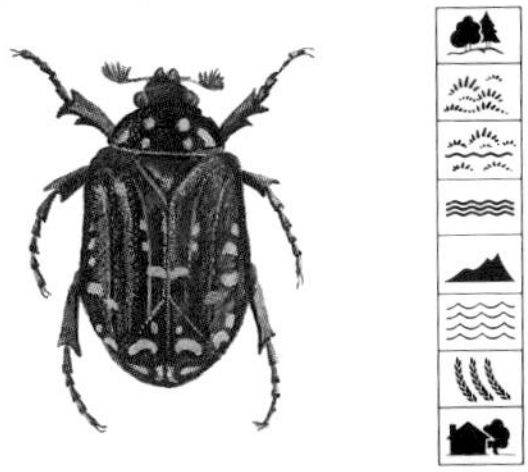

'lower Chafer *Length* ⅓-½in (8-12mm). *Season* May/ 'une. *Habitat* flowery meadows, waysides, marginal ınd, woodland clearings in dry areas, usually sitting on .owers; flies readily. *Larvae* feed on the roots of plants.

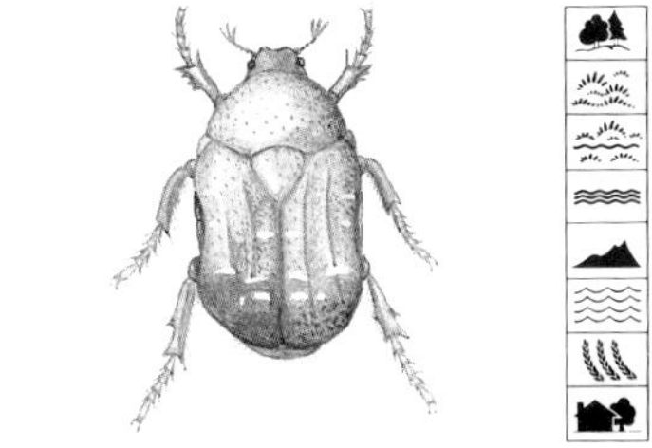

Rose Chafer *Length* ⅗-⅘in (14-20mm). *Season* April-September. *Habitat* open country with flowery areas, waysides, usually sitting on flowers; takes to flight readily. *Larvae* feed on rotting wood and humus.

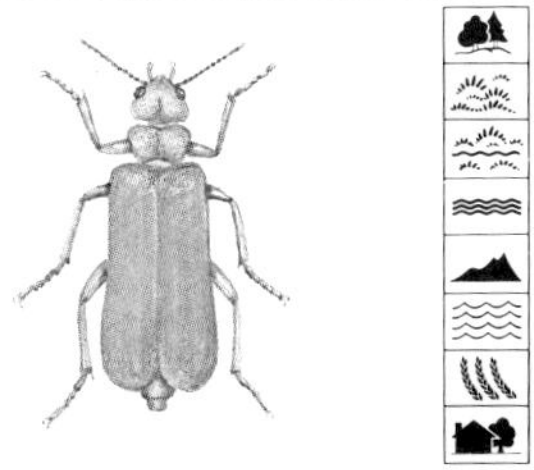

anish Fly *Length* ⅓-⅘in (9-21mm). *Season* spring-mmer. *Habitat* flowery meadows; beetles once sold an aphrodisiac, contain the toxin cantharadin; ISTERING IF HANDLED. *Larvae* parasites of ısshopper eggs.

Variegated Ladybird *Length* ⅙-⅕in (3-5.5mm). *Season* spring-autumn. *Habitat* almost everywhere, but especially in coastal regions, where they may swarm in large numbers near the water's edge. *Larvae* feed on aphids, as do the adults.

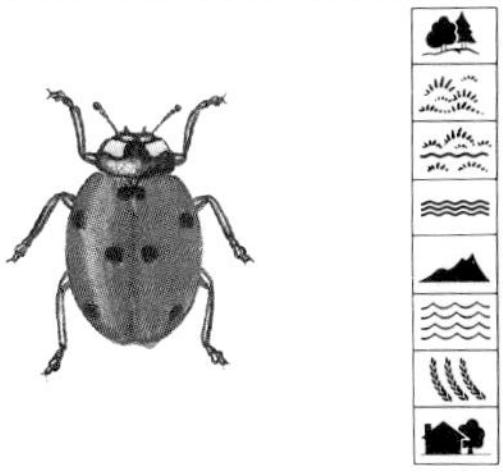

en-spot Ladybird *Length* ⅕-⅓in (5.2-8mm). *Season* y spring-late autumn. *Habitat* almost everywhere, especially in rich vegetation, cultivated areas, dlands, feeding on aphids. *Larvae* on plants, 'ing on aphids.

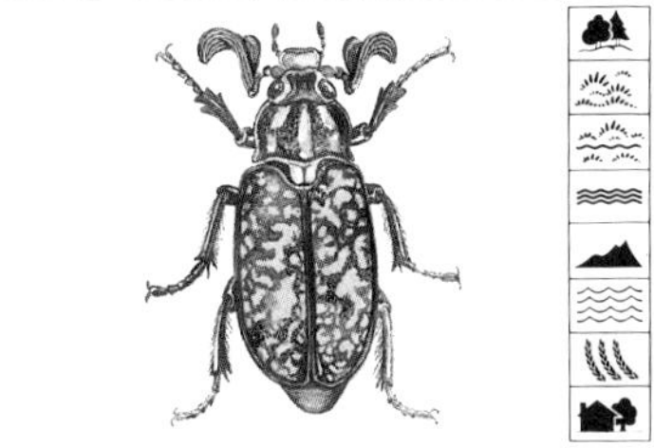

Large Chafer *Length* 1-1⅖in (25-36mm). *Season* late spring-early summer. *Habitat* lowland areas, including cultivated land; adults fly in evening. *Larvae* carnivorous, preying on the larvae of other beetles, development taking 3-4 years.

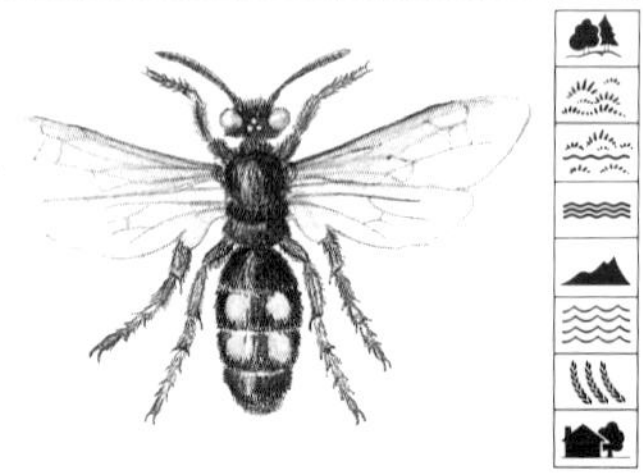

Large Scolia *Wingspan* 1⅓-2⅓ in (35-60 mm). *Season* early summer-autumn. *Habitat* dry, open, stony country, both sexes often on flowers, especially umbels. *Larvae* external parasites of chafer beetle larvae.

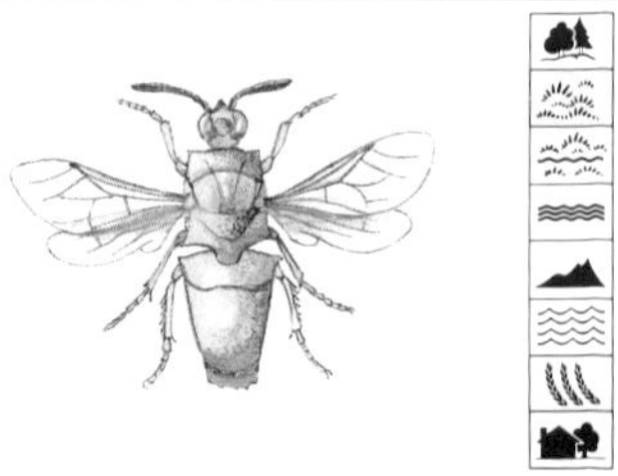

Great Ruby-tailed Wasp *Wingspan* ¾-⅘ in (17-20 mm). *Season* late spring-summer. *Habitat* warm, dry, and usually stony fields and hillsides, often at flowers. *Larvae* parasitize the larvae of wasps and bees which build exposed mud nests.

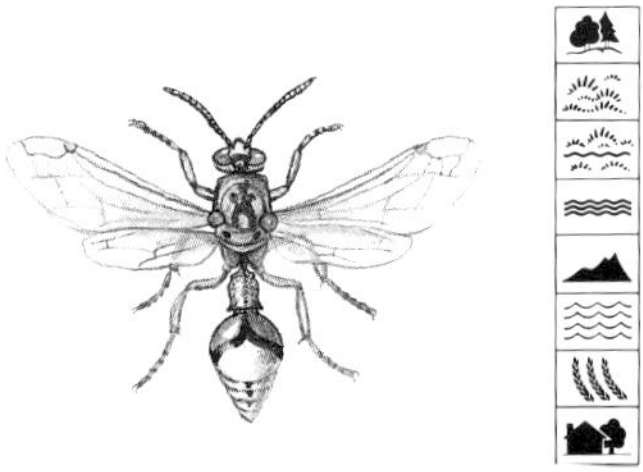

Large Potter Wasp *Wingspan* 1⅒-1⅗ in (28-40 mm). *Season* late spring-summer. *Habitat* warm, dry, stony fields and hillsides; solitary females build exposed nest out of mud. *Larvae* feed on paralyzed caterpillar collected by female wasp.

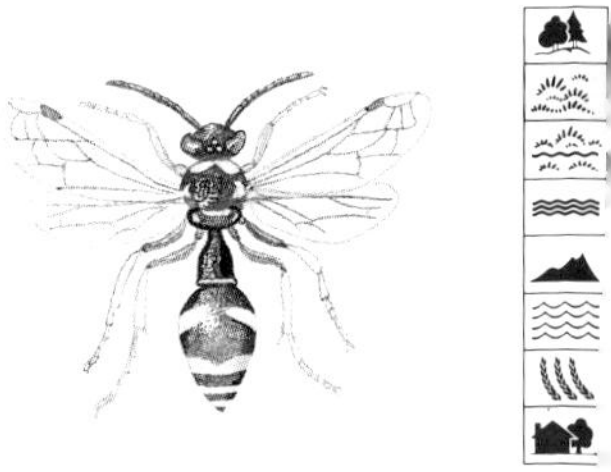

Heath Potter Wasp *Wingspan* ⅗-⅘ in (16-20 mm). *Season* summer. *Habitat* dry, open, areas and heaths with heather; solitary females build mud nest suspended from heather twig. *Larvae* feed on caterpillar provided by female wasp.

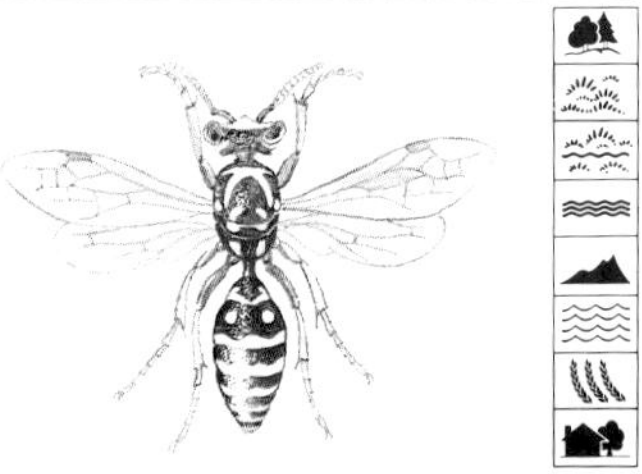

French Polistes *Wingspan* 9/10-1 in (23-26 mm). *Season* spring-summer. *Habitat* open country; founding female (queen) builds paper nest from branch, female offspring act as non-reproductive workers. *Larvae* eat chewed insect prey provided by workers.

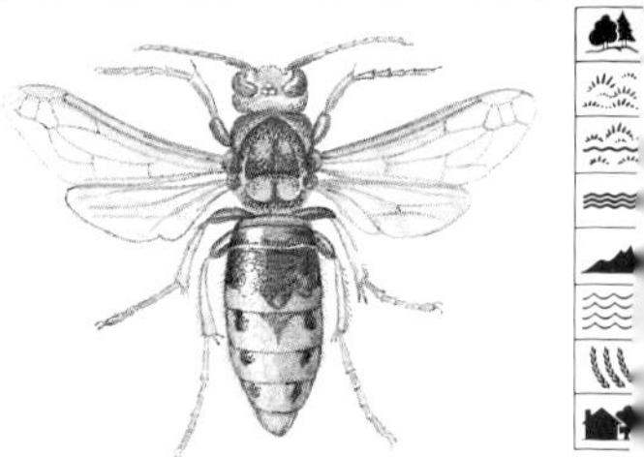

Western Hornet *Wingspan* 1⅓-2 in (35-50 mm). *Seasor* spring-autumn. *Habitat* open woodland, parkland with mature trees; colonies build paper nests in hollow trees. *Larvae* feed on chewed insect prey caught by workers.

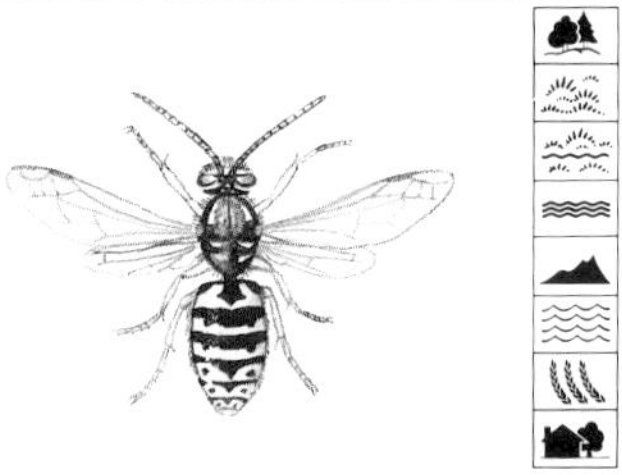

Common Social Wasp *Wingspan* 1⅕-1¾ in (30-45 mm). *Season* spring-autumn. *Habitat* almost everywhere, especially in north of country; colonies nest in holes in ground. *Larvae* feed on chewed insect prey provided by workers.

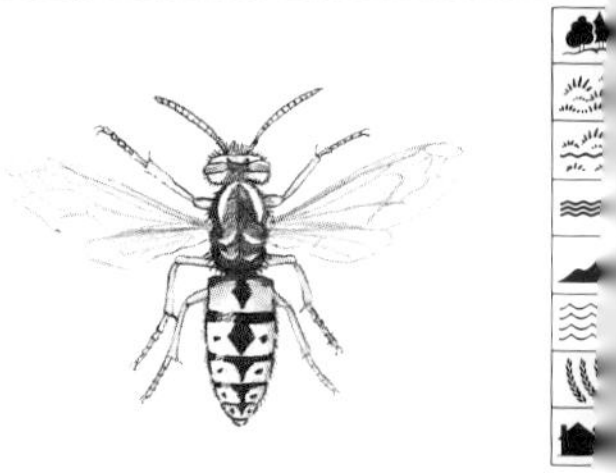

German Wasp *Wingspan* 1⅒-1⅔ in (28-43 mm). *Sea* spring-autumn. *Habitat* almost everywhere in open country, woodland edges, hedgerows; nest usually underground. *Larvae* eat chewed insect prey caught workers.

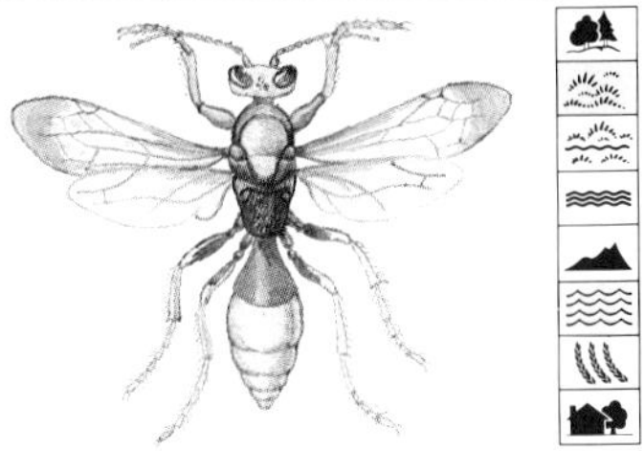

Yellow Spider-hunting Wasp *Wingspan* $1\frac{2}{3}$-$1\frac{9}{10}$in (43-48mm). *Season* summer. *Habitat* hot, dry, sandy areas, dunes, hillsides; females store paralyzed spiders in nest in ground. *Larvae* each feeds on a single spider collected by mother wasp.

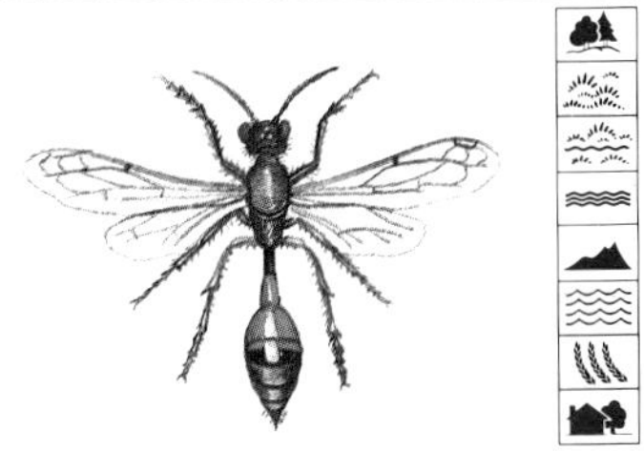

Solitary Digger Wasp *Wingspan* 22-25mm. *Season* late spring-summer. *Habitat* dry, sandy wastes; open, dry jrasslands; females provision each nest with several aterpillars. *Larvae* live in nest in ground, eat prey captured by female.

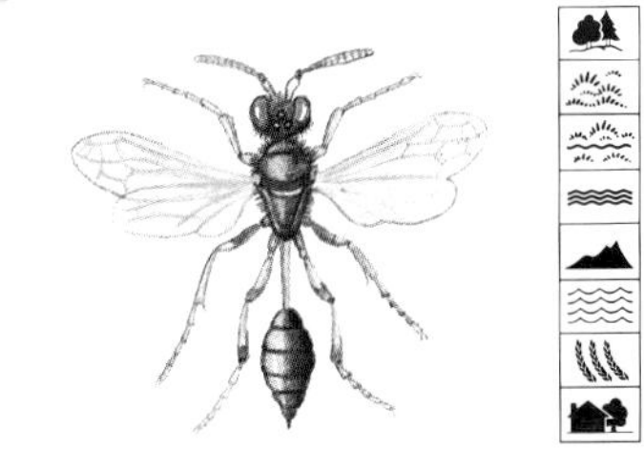

ud-dauber Wasp *Wingspan* 1-$1\frac{1}{5}$in (25-30mm). *eason* spring-summer. *Habitat* dry, rocky areas; male builds exposed mud nest of several cells, ovisions each cell with several spiders and lays egg in *Larvae* eat spiders.

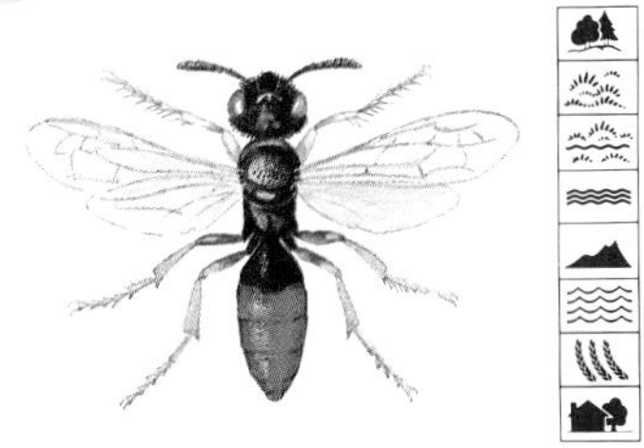

e Wolf *Wingspan* $\frac{4}{5}$-$1\frac{1}{10}$in (20-30mm). *Season* mmer. *Habitat* dry sandy or stony areas with posures of clay soil; female provisions underground st with captured bees, including Honeybees. *Larvae* ed on bees.

Red Spider-hunting Wasp *Wingspan* $\frac{2}{3}$-$\frac{9}{10}$in (18-22mm). *Season* late spring-summer. *Habitat* dry, sandy areas on chalk or sand, especially dunes near sea; heaths; female paralyzes spider with sting. *Larva* feeds on spider caught by female.

Bush Cricket-hunting Wasp *Wingspan* $1\frac{1}{3}$-$1\frac{3}{5}$in (35-40mm). *Season* spring-summer. *Habitat* dry, stony wastes and hillsides; females provision nest with paralyzed bush crickets. *Larvae* in nest in ground, one per nest, eat bush crickets.

Sand Wasp *Wingspan* 1-$1\frac{1}{5}$in (25-30mm). *Season* summer. *Habitat* dry, sandy areas; females collect flies, sting and paralyze them, provide them as food for larvae in nest dug in sand; very rapid, darting flight. *Larvae* eat flies.

Great Digger Bee *Wingspan* 1-$1\frac{1}{5}$in (25-30mm). *Season* spring-summer. *Habitat* open country, marginal land; nests dug in ground by single females, which collect pollen and nectar from wide range of flowers. *Larvae* eat pollen.

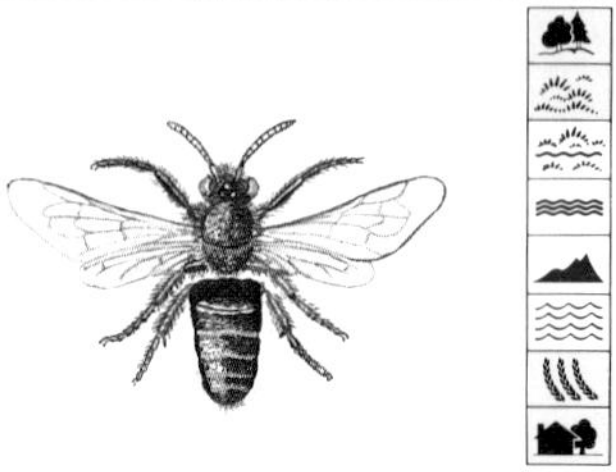

Rose Leaf-cutter Bee *Wingspan* $\frac{3}{5}$-$\frac{3}{4}$ in (16-19 mm). *Season* late spring-summer. *Habitat* woodland edges, open hedgerows, gardens, nests in beetle borings in dead wood, hollow plant stems, lined with cut leaf pieces; *Larvae* feed on pollen/nectar.

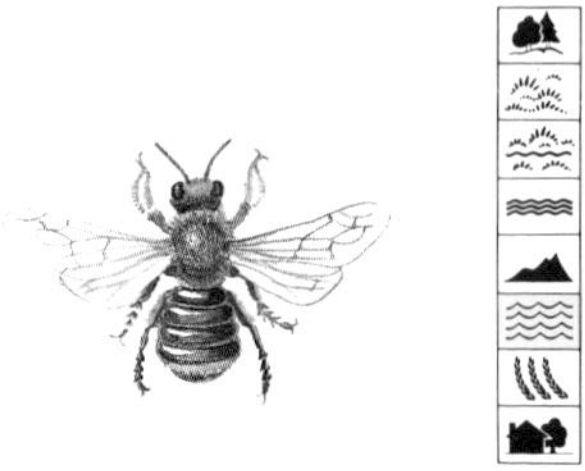

Coastal Leaf-cutter Bee *Wingspan* $\frac{9}{10}$-1$\frac{1}{10}$ in (22-28 mm) *Season* July-August. *Habitat* sandy areas near the coast; females excavate nest in ground, line cells with cut leaf pieces. *Larvae* eat pollen/nectar mixture collected by female.

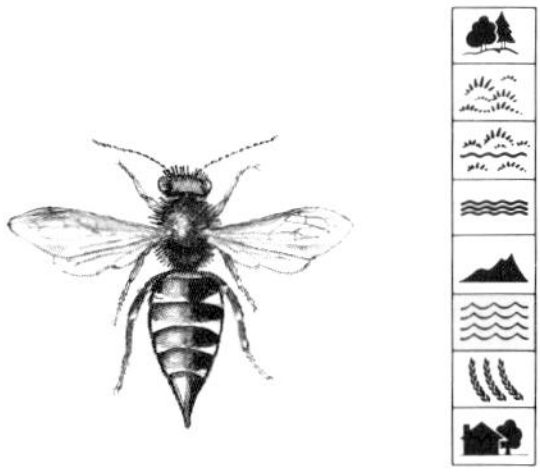

Cuckoo Bee *Wingspan* $\frac{3}{5}$-$\frac{4}{5}$ in (15-21 mm). *Season* July-August. *Habitat* sandy areas near coast; female uses spiny tip of abdomen to make holes in nest cells of leaf-cutter bees, then lays egg. *Larvae* eat food stores of leaf-cutter bee host.

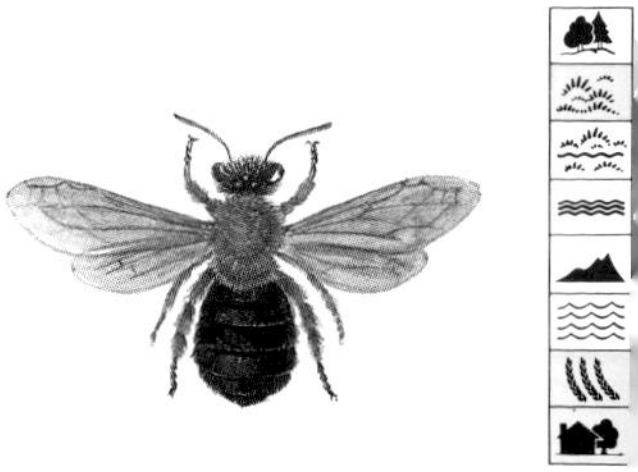

Shrub Mason Bee *Wingspan* $\frac{9}{10}$-1$\frac{1}{10}$ in (23-28 mm). *Season* spring. *Habitat* open, stony countryside; females build exposed mud nests on branches, shrubs or rocks, collect pollen from vetches, bugloss flowers. *Larvae* eat pollen/nectar.

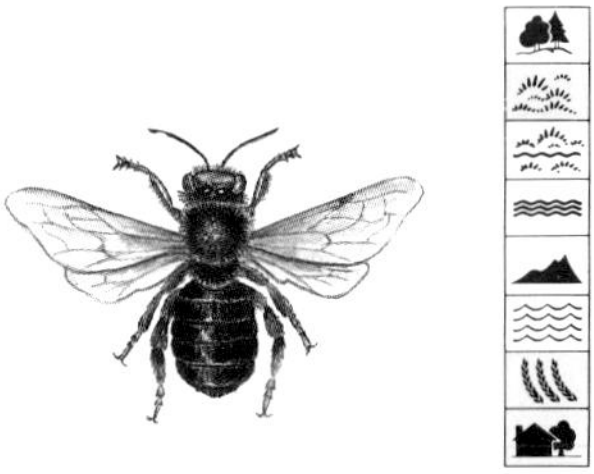

Wall Mason Bee *Wingspan* $\frac{9}{10}$-1$\frac{1}{10}$ in (22-27 mm) *Season* spring-summer. *Habitat* dry, open, stony, and rocky areas; females build exposed mud nests on rocks, stones, walls, ancient monuments. *Larvae* eat pollen/nectar mixture.

Variegated Carder Bee *Wingspan* $\frac{3}{5}$-$\frac{4}{5}$ in (16-20 mm). *Season* summer. *Habitat* dry, scrubby hillsides, sandy wastes; females nest in beetle borings in dead wood o hollow plant stems, lining them with plant hairs. *Larvae* eat pollen/nectar mixture.

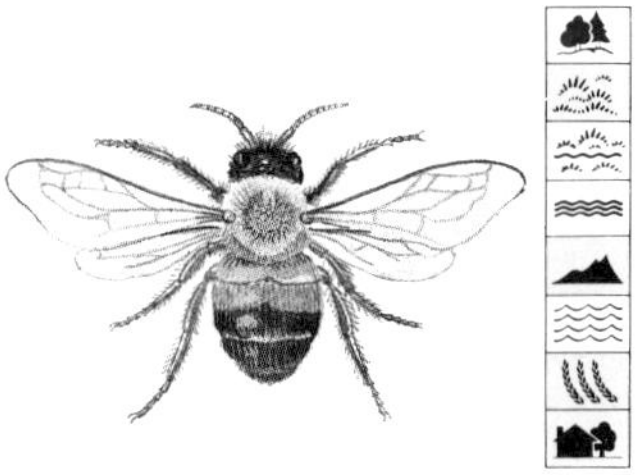

Spanish Anthophora *Wingspan* 1$\frac{1}{5}$-1$\frac{1}{3}$ in (30-34 mm). *Season* spring. *Habitat* open country and hillsides with flowery areas; females nest in ground, forage at deep-tubed flowers. *Larvae* eat nectar/pollen mixture.

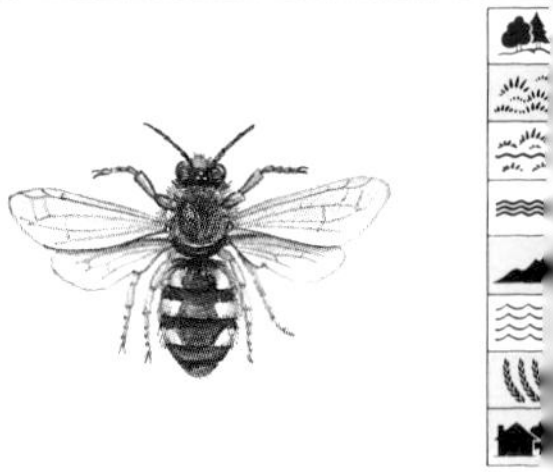

Cuckoo Bee *Wingspan* $\frac{9}{10}$-1$\frac{1}{10}$ in (24-27 mm). *Seasor* spring. *Habitat* rocky areas with cliffs; females enter nests of anthophora bees and lay eggs there. *Larvae* food store after killing host egg or young larva.

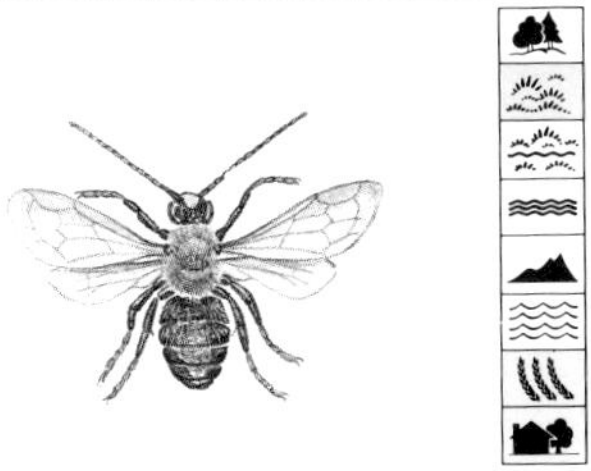

Long-horned Bee *Wingspan* 9⁄10-1 (22-25 mm); females lack long antennae, have white hairs at side of abdomen. *Habitat* flowery meadows. *Larvae* eat pollen/nectar mixture stored by females.

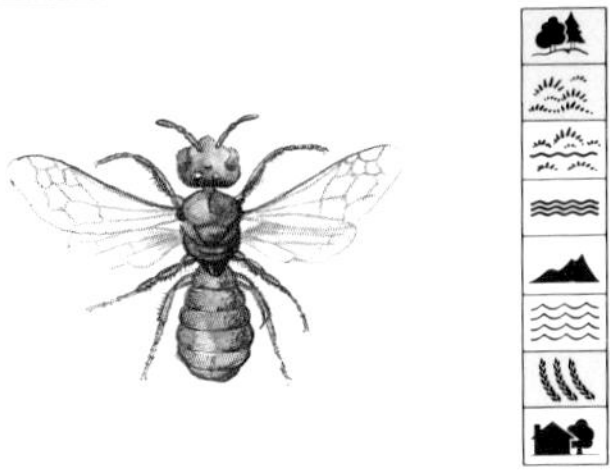

Dwarf Carpenter Bee *Wingspan* 2⁄5-1⁄2 in (10-12 mm). *Season* summer. *Habitat* dry, shrubby areas, marginal land, edges of woods and cultivated areas; females nest in hollow plant stems. *Larvae* eat pollen/nectar mixture.

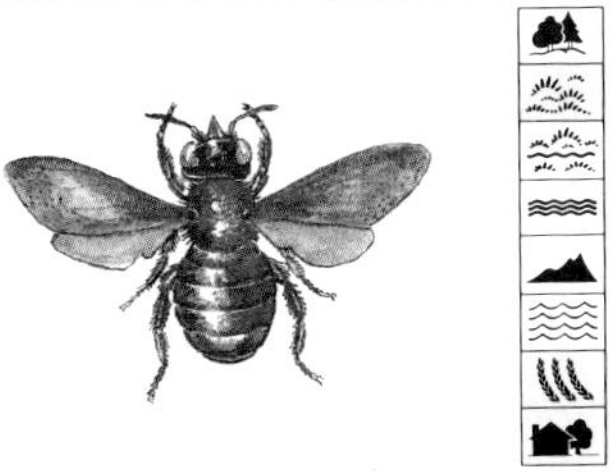

Violet Carpenter Bee *Wingspan* 1¾-2 in (45-50 mm). *Season* spring-summer. *Habitat* open country, scrubby areas; females bore in solid wood or use hollow stems; nest partitioned with wood fragments. *Larvae* eat pollen/nectar mixture.

Black Carpenter Bee *Wingspan* 1⅗-1¾ in (40-45 mm). *Season* summer. *Habitat* scrubby areas, marginal land; females nest in hollow plant stems, especially those of large umbellifers. *Larvae* eat pollen/nectar mixture.

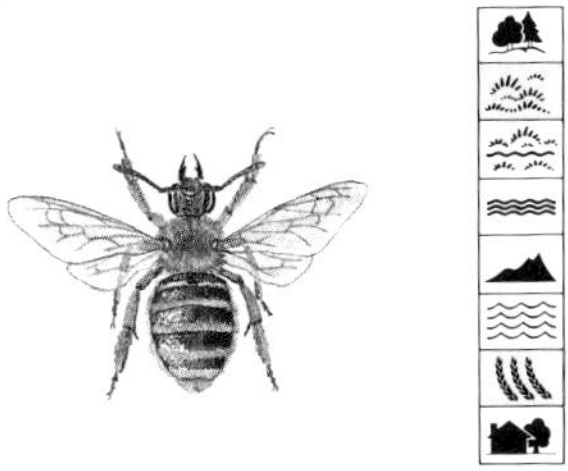

ivier's Carpenter Bee. *Wingspan* 1 1⁄10-1⅓ in (28-
mm). *Season* late spring-summer. *Habitat* lowland
eas with clay banks and cliffs; females make nest
urrows in the ground. *Larvae* eat pollen/nectar
ixture.

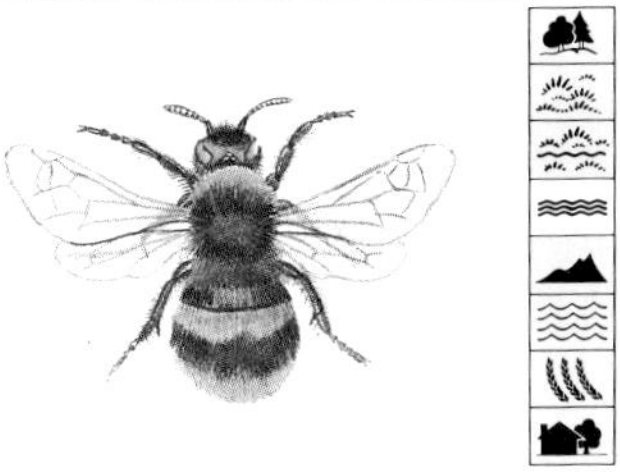

Buff-tailed Bumblebee *Wingspan* 1 1⁄10-1⅔ in (28-42 mm); queens larger than workers. *Season* spring-early autumn. *Habitat* most kinds of countryside to 6000 ft (1800 m); queen founds nest in old rodent nest. *Larvae* reared in wax cells.

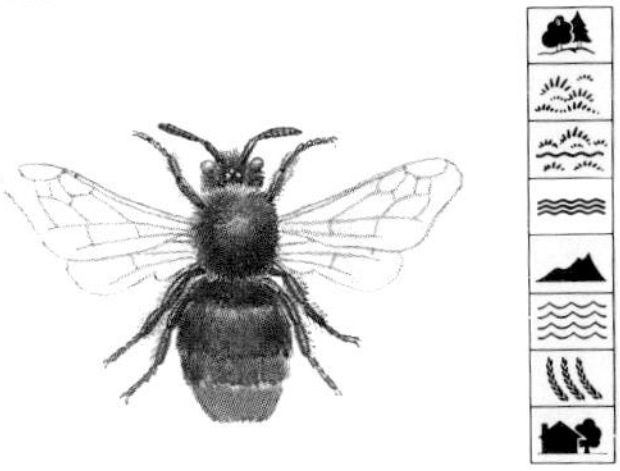

d-tailed Bumblebee *Wingspan* 9⁄10-1⅗ in (22-40 mm)
ason spring-summer. *Habitat* scrubby areas,
dgerows, waste ground, gardens; nests in old rodent
rows, under rocks and garden refuse. *Larvae* reared
vax cells.

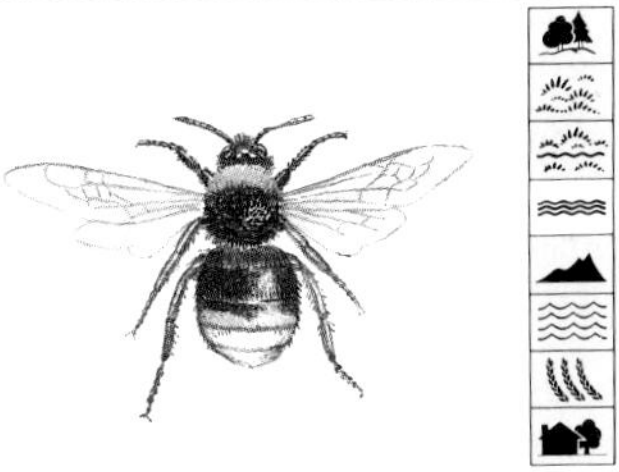

Vestal Cuckoo Bee *Wingspan* 1⅓-1½ in (35.5-39 mm). *Season* early summer-autumn. *Habitat* most kinds of countryside, including mountains up to 6000 ft (1800 m); females lay eggs in nests of Buff-tailed Bumblebee. *Larvae* reared by workers of host.

Purse-web Spider *Length* male $\frac{1}{4}$-$\frac{1}{3}$in (7-9mm), female $\frac{2}{5}$-$\frac{3}{5}$in (10-15mm). *Habitat* dry, sandy areas; silk-lined nest tube excavated under lowplants, often in mounds of Yellow Meadow Ant. *Season* older females all year, otherwise, mainly autumn.

European Trap-door Spider *Length* male $\frac{2}{5}$in (11mm), female $\frac{3}{5}$-$\frac{4}{5}$in (15-20mm). *Habitat* dry, sandy areas, unbranched, silk-lined tunnel $4\frac{3}{4}$-5in (12-13cm) deep, lid camouflaged with moss and other vegetation. *Season* all year.

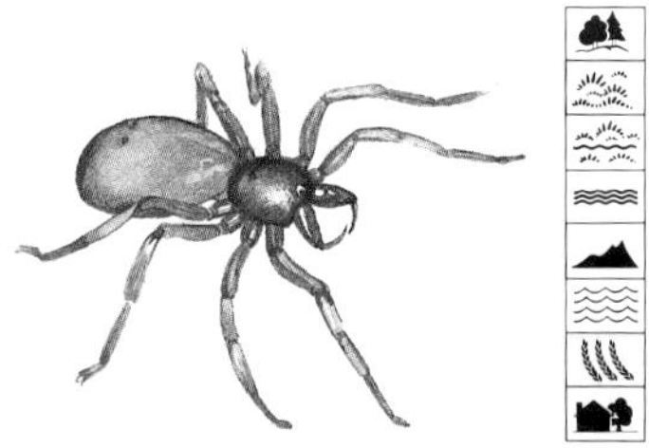

Woodlouse-hunting Spider *Length* male about $\frac{2}{5}$in (10mm), female about $\frac{1}{2}$in (12mm). *Habitat* under stones and logs in warm, dry places, where it preys on woodlice. *Season* all year.

Trap-line Spider *Length* $\frac{1}{4}$-$\frac{2}{5}$in (7-10mm). *Habitat* under bark, stones, holes in old walls, where it lives in silk tube with about 12 threads radiating from entrance, which act as trap-lines, alerting spider to prey. *Season* spring.

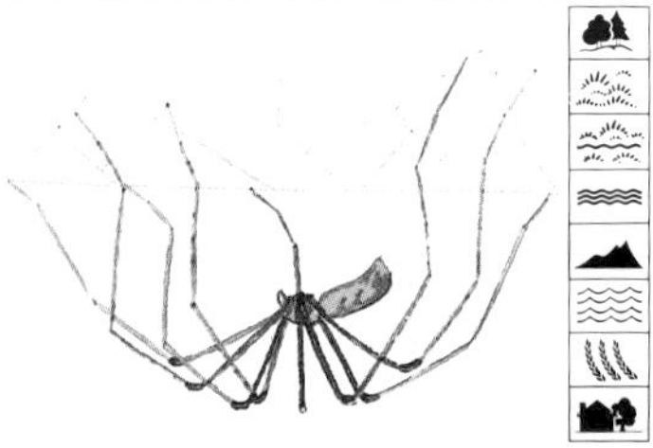

Daddy-longlegs Spider *Length* $\frac{1}{3}$-$\frac{2}{5}$in (8-10mm). *Habitat* buildings, in the ceiling corners of rooms; dry caves, spiders hanging upside-down in webs, gyrating rapidly if disturbed. *Season* females most of year, otherwise, mainly spring.

Southern Pinewood Spider *Length* male $\frac{1}{10}$in (3mm), female $\frac{1}{10}$in (3.5mm). *Habitat* among stones in pinewoods; feeds on ants, biting at bases of antennae and waiting for venom to take effect; prey often dragged to retreat. *Season* spring.

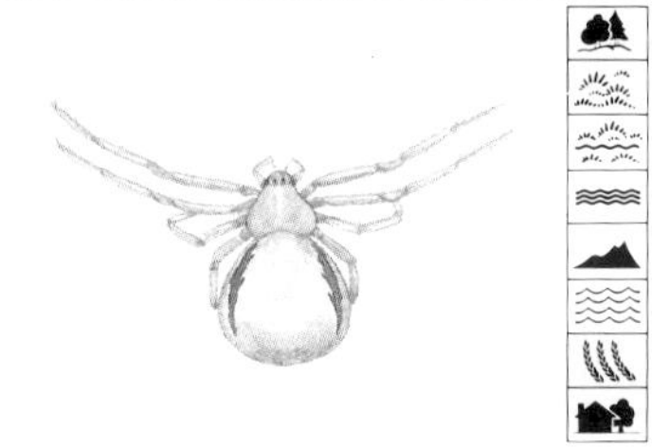

Common Crab Spider *Length* male $\frac{1}{6}$in (4mm), female $\frac{2}{5}$in (10mm); male body dark brown, female's variable, changes with floral background colour. *Habitat* usually white or yellow flowers. *Season* early and midsummer.

Bark Crab Spider *Length* male $\frac{1}{5}$in (5mm), female $\frac{1}{4}$i (6mm). *Habitat* bark and leaves of lichen-covered tree well camouflaged, where they lie in wait for insect pre *Season* early summer.

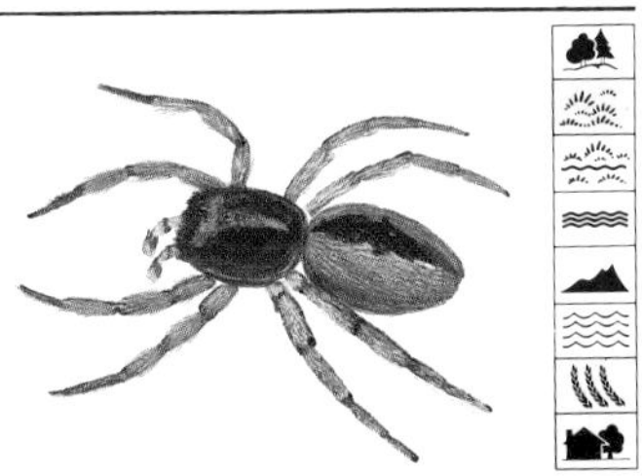

Orange Jumping Spider *Length* ¼-½in (7-12mm); female with central black stripe flanked by light brown, unlike bright orange of male. *Habitat* sometimes low bushes, otherwise mainly among rocks and stones. *Season* summer.

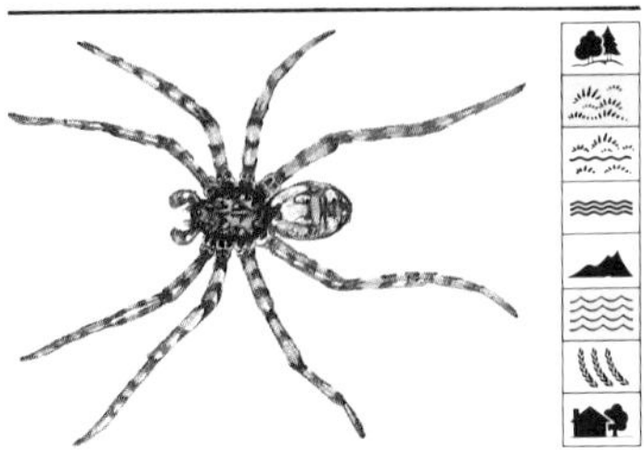

Dune Wolf Spider *Length* male ⅓in (8.5mm), female ⅓in (8mm). *Habitat* sandy places, both inland and coastal; excavates burrow, though both sexes often seen running over sand surface. *Season* autumn, spring, early summer.

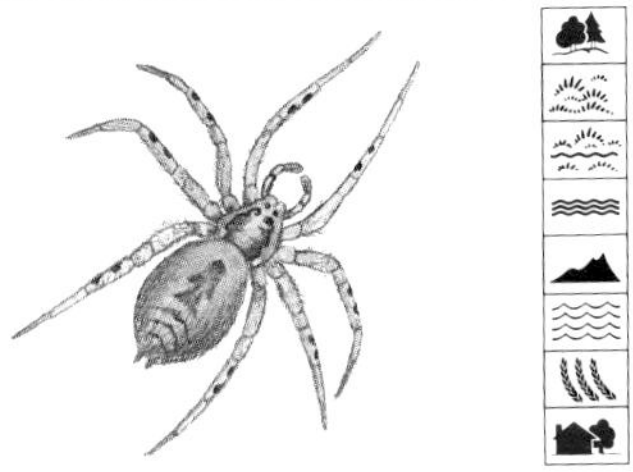

European True Tarantula *Length* ⅖-⅔in (10-18mm). *labitat* dry, stony hillsides with Thyme; spiders live in urrows from which they leap out and capture insects, specially grasshoppers. *Season* spring-summer.

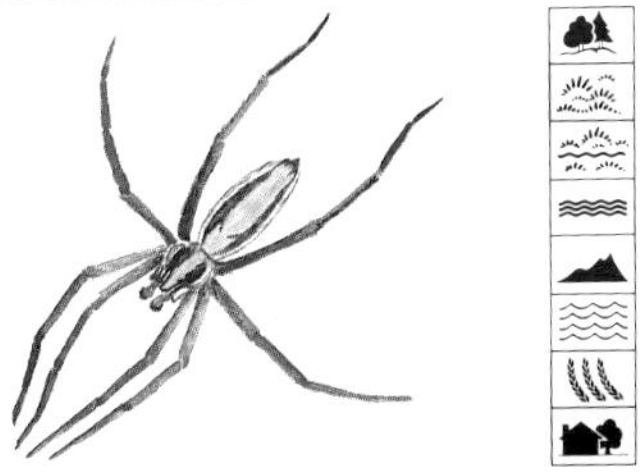

Slim Wolf Spider *Length* male ⅖-½in (10-12mm), female ½-⅗in (12-15mm). *Habitat* woods, heaths, lush hedgerows and gardens, female often seen carrying white egg sac. *Season* early summer

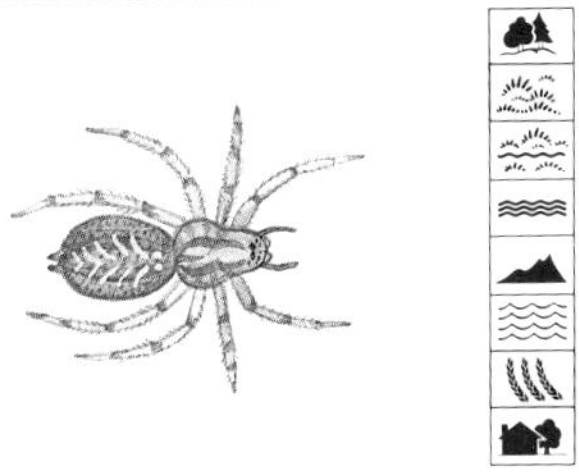

heet-web Spider *Length* male ⅓in (9mm), female up ½in (12mm) *Habitat* low vegetation and bushes, in rge sheet web with tubular retreat at each end; egg ac made higher than sheet, guarded by female until her eath. *Season* midsummer.

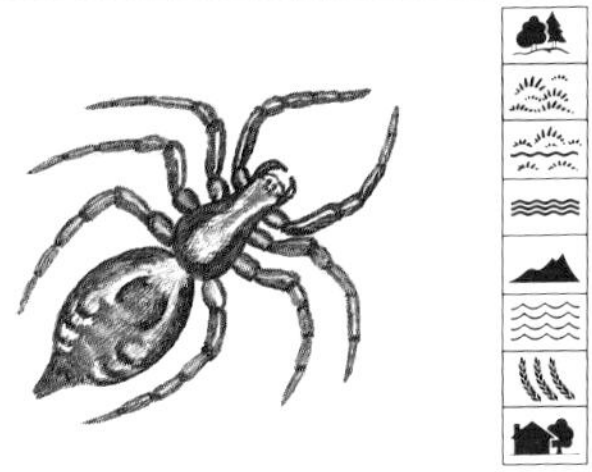

Hammock-web Spider *Length* male ¼in (6-7mm), female ¼-⅓in (6-8mm). *Habitat* dry, stony country, drystone walls, where small, hammock-like web is suspended between stones. *Season* males early summer, females throughout the year.

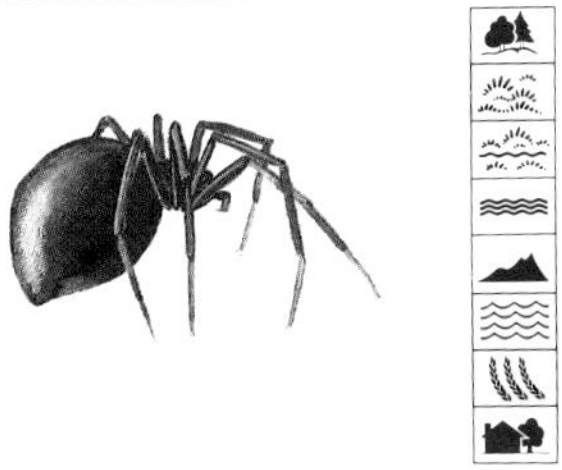

ropean Black Widow Spider. *Length* male ⅒-⅕in 5mm), female ⅓-⅕in (8-12mm). *Bite* female's VERY SONOUS causing intense pain. *Habitat* low getation in dry areas, small web strung close to und. *Season* spring-summer.

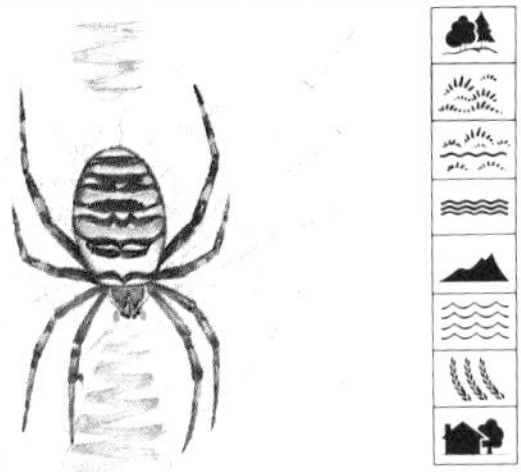

Golden Orb Web Spider *Length* male ⅙in (4mm), female ⅗in (15mm); male with elongate abdomen, with two vague brown stripes. *Habitat* grassy areas, low vegetation, large web up to 12in (30cm) across. *Season* spring-early autumn.

Grove Snail *Shell* height ½-9/10 in (12-22 mm), width ⅔-1 in (18-25 mm). *Habitat* very varied, ranging from sand-dunes and grasslands to scrub, hedgerows, and woodlands, up to 4000 ft (1200 m) in the Alps and 6000 ft (1800 m) in the Pyrénées.

Roman Snail *Shell* height 1⅕-2 in (30-50 mm), width 1¼-2 in (32-50 mm). *Habitat* tall herbage, hedges, and woodland in chalk and limestone areas; often a pest in vineyards, although 'cultivated' as food in some areas.

Garden Snail *Shell* height 1-1⅓ in (25-35 mm), width 1-1⅗ in (25-40 mm). *Habitat* varied, banks, ivy-covered walls, cliffs, quarries, hedges, evergreen shrubs in gardens, dunes, woods, individuals returning to fixed home after feeding trips.

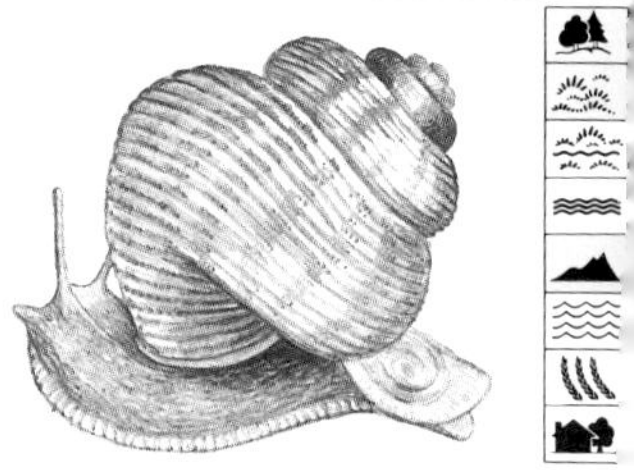

Round-mouthed Snail *Shell* height ½-⅗ in (13-16 mm), width ⅓-½ in (9-12 mm). *Habitat* chalky areas with dry, friable soil in which it burrows; hedgebanks, open woodland, screes.

Bulin Snail *Shell* height ½-1 in (12-25 mm), width ⅓-½ in (8-12 mm). *Habitat* mainly on lime-rich soils, where it can be seen on dry, exposed places; open grasslands, screes, vineyards; up to 5000 ft (1500 m).

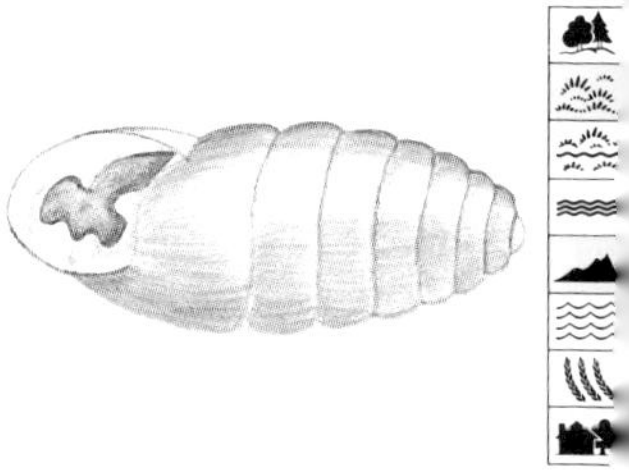

Four-toothed Snail *Shell* height ¼-½ in (7-12 mm), wid about ⅕ in (5 mm). *Habitat* usually in very dry and exposed places, among scree falls and limestone and dolomite rocks, less commonly in grassland; up to 6600 ft (2000 m) and above.

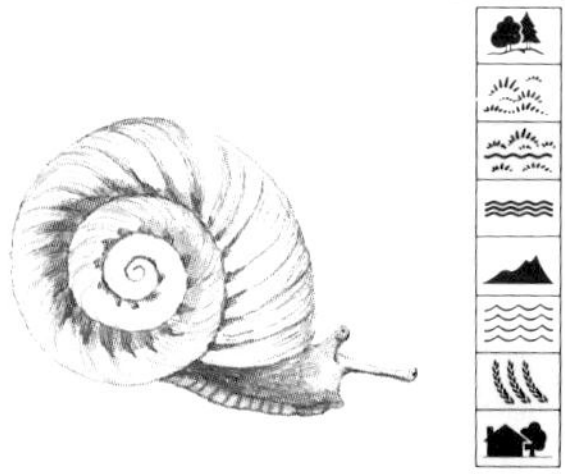

Mediterranean Garden Snail *Shell* height ⅙ in (4-5 mm), width ¼--⅓ in (7-9 mm). *Habitat* prefers damp sites, mostly in cultivated areas; gardens, meadows, under litter and stones.

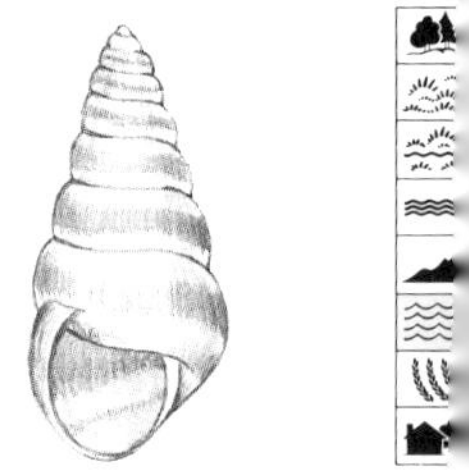

Dune Pointed Snail *Shell* height ⅓-½ in (8-12 mm), width ⅕-⅓ in (5-8 mm). *Habitat* dry exposed areas in coastal regions, such as dunes and low cliffs.

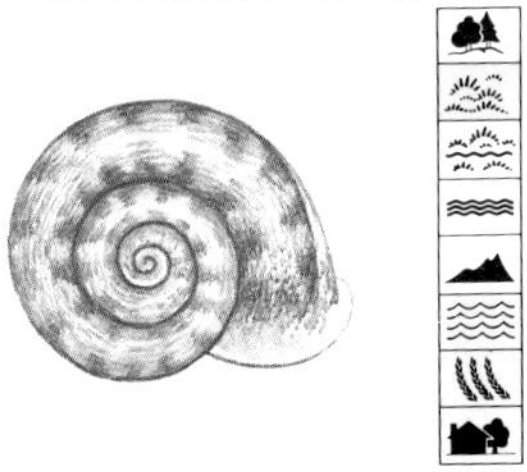

Common Mediterranean Snail *Shell* height 3/5-1 1/10 in (14-27 mm), width 9/10-1 1/5 in (22-30 mm). *Habitat* dry, grassy places, fields, waysides, gardens, Olive groves, vineyards, and hedgerows.

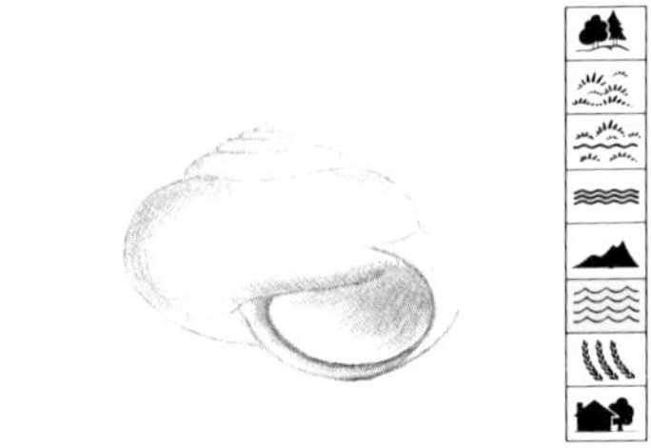

White Snail *Shell* height 1/3-4/5 in (9-20 mm), width 1/2-1 in (12-25 mm). *Habitat* usually near the sea, in dry, exposed places, often on dunes, where it sits out on plant stems in dry weather.

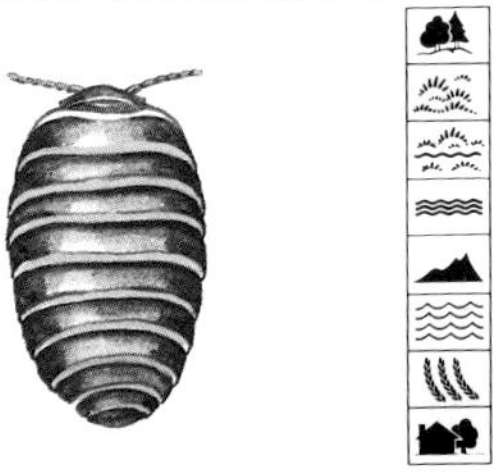

Pill Millipede *Length* 2/3-4/5 in (17-20 mm). *Habitat* among vegetation in a variety of situations, including dry areas such as sand-dunes and heaths; when disturbed, rolls up into a ball for protection.

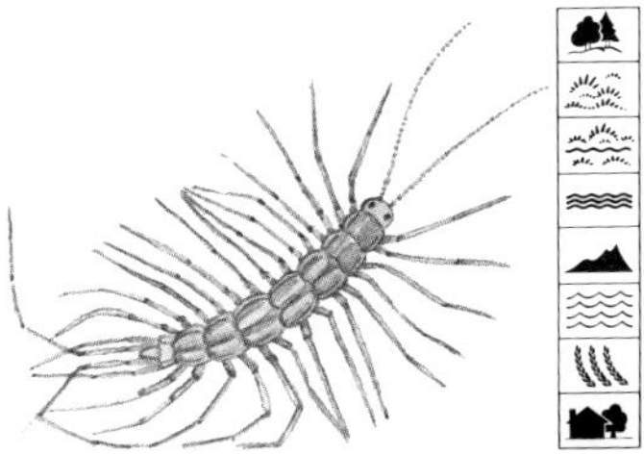

House Centipede *Length* up to 1 1/5 in (30 mm). *Habitat* usually near buildings, where it preys on insects and other small animals; extremely fast runner, especially at night, when disturbed by light.

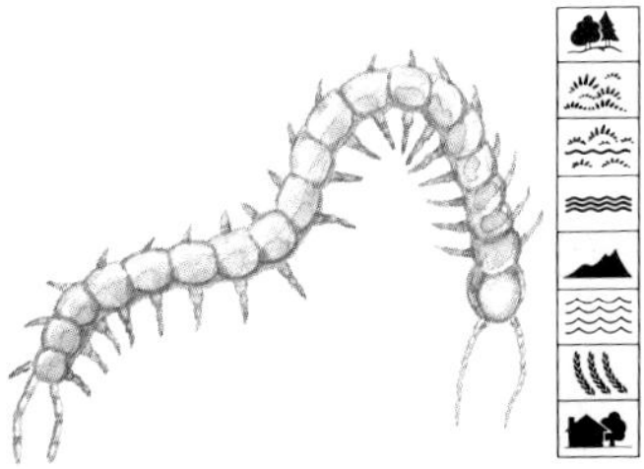

Mediterranean Centipede *Length* up to 1 in (25 mm). *Habitat* in rock crevices, between boulders, often in buildings, where it preys on insects and other small animals, even small lizards.

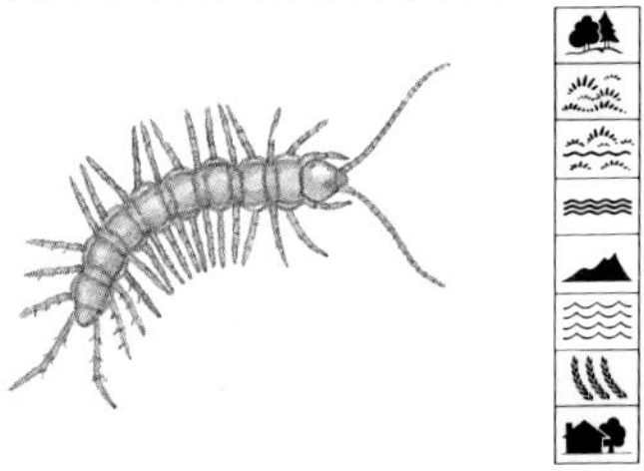

Stone-dwelling Centipede *Length* 2/3-1 1/5 (18-30 mm). *Habitat* varied, open woodland, under bark of dead trees, under logs, open country under stones, gardens, houses; feeds on insects, slugs, and earthworms, BITES IF HANDLED.

boscqui's Centipede *Length* 1/4-1/3 in (5.5-9.5 mm). *Habitat* woodland, gardens, cultivated land, mainly in the north; curls up when disturbed; feeds on small insects and worms.

Mediterranean Scorpion *Length* up to 1 1/3 in (35 mm). *Habitat* under stones in dry areas, coming out at dusk and throughout night to feed on insects and other small animals, which it kills with venomous sting. PAINFUL STING IF HANDLED.

Sponge Crab *Length* up to 3¼ in (8 cm). *Shell* very broad. *Habitat* lower shore, among stones, and in sea down to 100 ft (30 m). Often carries a small sponge on its back, using fourth and fifth pairs of legs.

Swimming Crab *Length* up to 1½ in (4 cm). *Shell* pink to red-brown, hairy. Fifth pair of legs end in swimming paddle. *Habitat* in open water or sometimes near water's edge among weeds.

Common Shore Crab *Length* up to 2¼ in (6 cm). *Shell* variable, green to mottled black; juveniles sandy coloured. *Habitat* middle to lower shore and water's edge; also saltmarsh.

Hairy Crab *Length* up to ½ in (1.5 cm). *Shell* and legs ver hairy. *Habitat* lower shore and water's edge under stones.

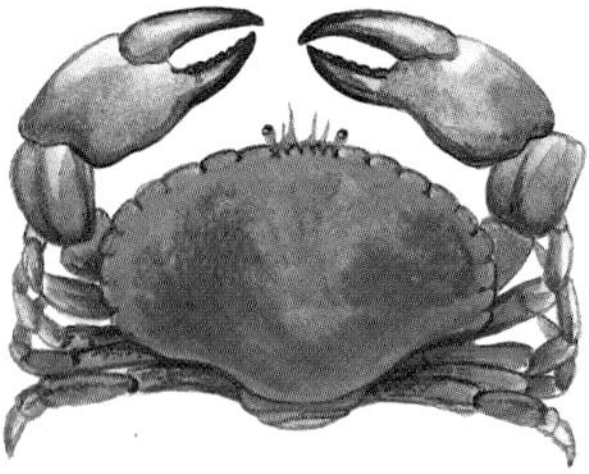

Edible Crab *Length* up to 6¼ in (16 cm). *Shell* very broad, almost oblong, smooth. *Habitat* lower shore under stones, in rock crevices, and on sea bottom to depth of 330 ft (100 m).

Marbled Crab *Length* up to 2 in (5 cm). *Shell* almost square, varying from green to violet or brown with stripes. *Habitat* upper and lower shore in rock crevice very fast runner.

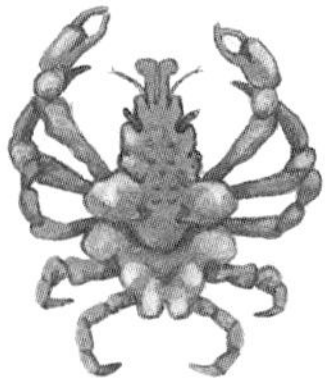

Red Spider Crab *Length* up to 1½ in (4 cm). *Shell* pear shaped, with knobbly, encrusted surface. Legs quite short with spines and protuberances at joints. *Habitat* on sandy bottoms from depths of 100 to 265 ft (30 to 80 m).

Spiny Spider Crab *Length* up to 10 in (25 cm). *Shell* pe shaped, encrusted with knobs and spines. Legs very hairy. *Habitat* on sandy bottoms to depth of 165 ft (50 r

Broad-clawed Porcelain Crab *Length* up to ½ in (1.5 cm). *Shell* round and hairy. Walking legs and pincers with hairy edges. *Habitat* among small stones on lower shore and shallow water.

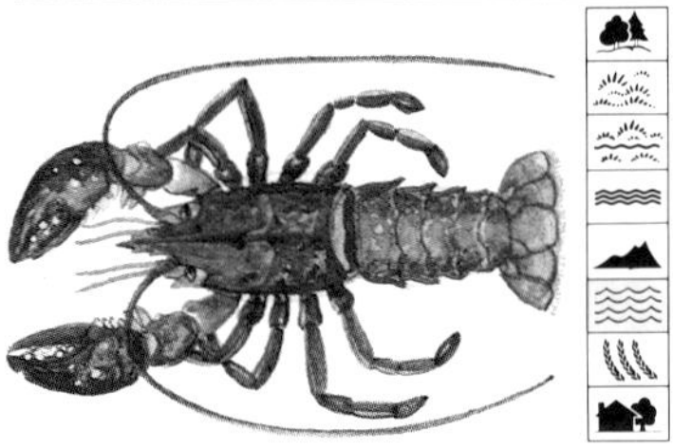

Common Lobster *Length* up to 17½ in (45 cm). *Colour* blue with orange areas, but turns red when boiled. *Habitat* underwater caves and rock crevices; collected commercially in lobster pots made of wicker.

Dublin Bay Prawn or Scampi *Length* up to 8 in (20 cm), emale smaller. *Habitat* soft, sandy bottom at depths of 30-260 ft (40-80 m); collected commercially and eaten hroughout Europe. Not a true prawn but a lobster.

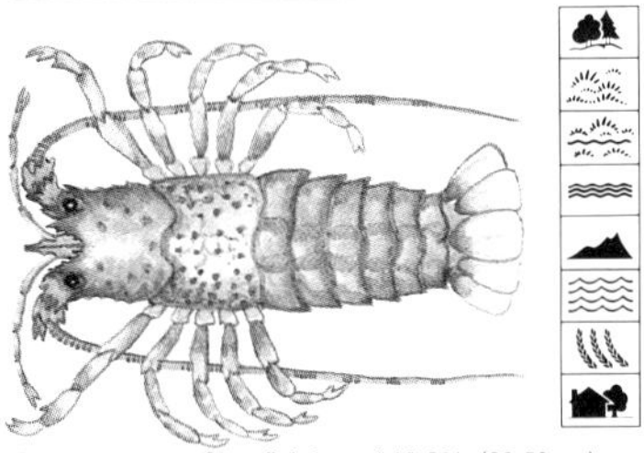

Spiny Lobster or Crawfish *Length* 12-20 in (30-50 cm). Unlike Common Lobster has no pincers, but very spiny body which causes deep wounds if stepped on. *Habitat* underwater caves and rock crevices to depth of 230 ft (70 m).

ommon Shrimp *Length* up to 2 in (5 cm). *Colour* emitransparent, grey-brown with red markings; turns nk when boiled. *Habitat* lower shore and shallow ater; also found in estuaries where water is saline.

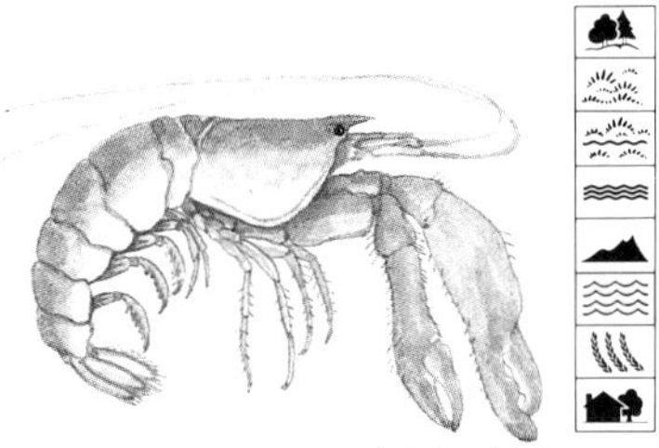

Snapping Prawn *Length* up to 2¼ in (6 cm). *Colour* pink or red, darker on back. *Habitat* among stones and weeds on muddy bottom at depths of 6-130 ft (2-40 m); presence detected by loud clicking noises made by snapping the pincers shut.

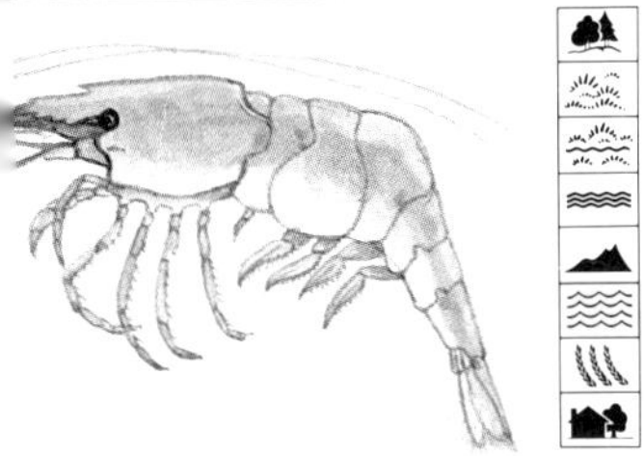

ameleon Prawn *Length* up to 1 in (2.5 cm). *Colour* nitransparent blue at night, either green, brown, or during the day. *Habitat* among weeds on lower re, and on stony bottom to depth of 165 ft (50 m).

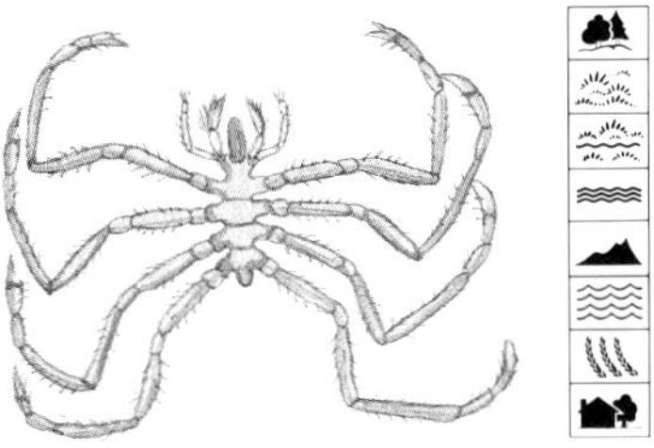

Sea Spider *Length* body up to ⅘ in (2 cm); legs up to 2 in (2.5 cm). Extra short pair of legs used by male to carry egg batch below body. *Habitat* middle and lower shore, feeding on sea anemones. Not a true spider.

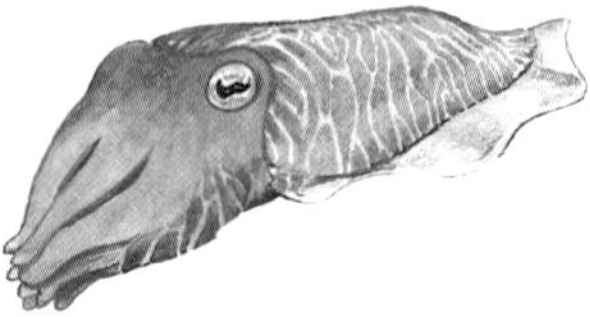

Common Cuttlefish *Length* up to 12 in (30 cm); body flattened and streamlined; internal oval shell or 'cuttlebone'; 10 tentacles bearing suckers around mouth. *Colour* varies with background and mood. *Habitat* open water, often near shore.

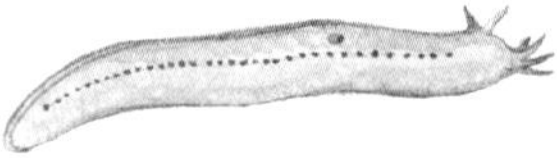

Hagfish *Length* up to 16 in (40 cm); appearance eel-like, with slimy, scaleless body and single fin around tail; no eyes; sensory tentacles near mouth. *Habitat* on sea bottom down to 2650ft (800 m); feeds on dead and dying fish, rasping with tongue.

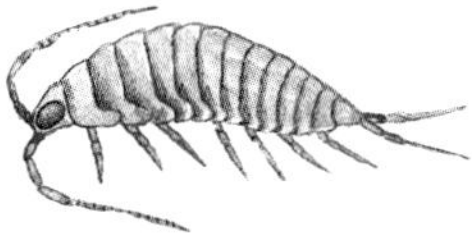

Italian Sea Slater *Length* up to $\frac{1}{2}$ in (1.5 cm); head prominent, with large eyes and very long antennae. *Habitat* on rocks, wooden pilings, and jetties near water's edge; emerges from hiding to feed on material washed up on beach; rapid mover.

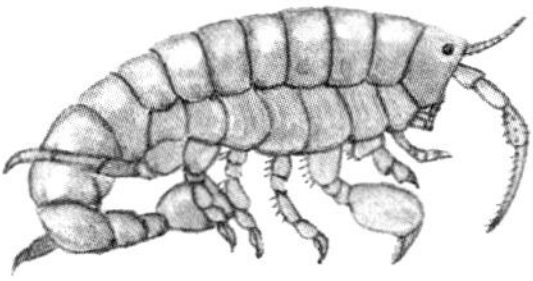

Sand Hopper *Length* up to $\frac{4}{5}$ in (2 cm); tail end curved under body; one pair of legs modified to form tiny claw. *Habitat* on shore under driftwood and dead plants; restricted to damp sand; if disturbed will spring short distance off the ground.

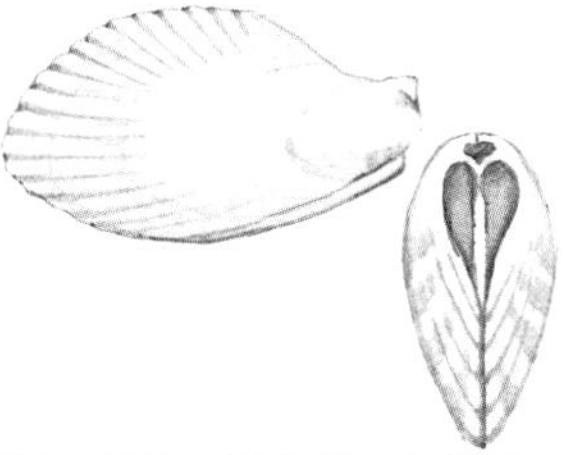

Gaping File Shell *Shell* length up to $1\frac{1}{5}$ in (3 cm); oblong, asymmetrical, gap between shell halves; thick orange tentacles protrude between shell halves around edge. *Habitat* lower shore and to depth of 330 ft (100 m) among rocks and weeds.

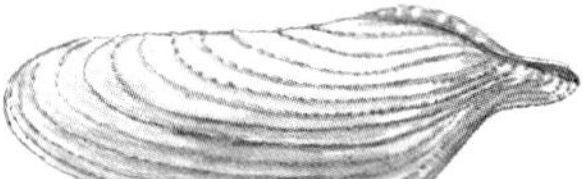

Common Piddock *Shell* length up to 6 in (15 cm); shell halves equal, thin, edges do not meet at sides, surface ridged, with small spines. *Habitat* bores into soft rock using internal 'teeth' and rough shell surface; lower shore, shallow water.

Thin Tellin *Shell* length up to $1\frac{1}{5}$ in (3 cm); shell halves almost equal, oval, surface with concentric rings, thin and fragile. *Colour* alternating dark and light bands of pink, red, yellow, or grey. *Habitat* in sand, lower shore to shallow water.

Mediterranean Jewel Box *Shell* length about $1\frac{1}{2}$ in (4 cm), depth $1\frac{1}{2}$ in (4 cm); shell halves unequal, lowe dish-like, attached to surface, upper flatter, functioni as lid; inner surface grooved, purple to brown. *Habit.* on rocks in shallow water.

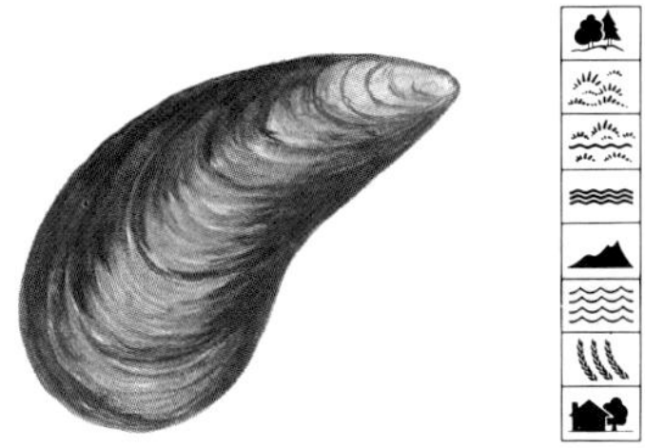

Common Mussel *Shell* length up to 4 in (10 cm); shell halves equal, asymmetrical. *Colour* dark blue, black, or brown. *Habitat* attached to rocks and stones by narrow threads on lower shore and shallow water; cultured commercially.

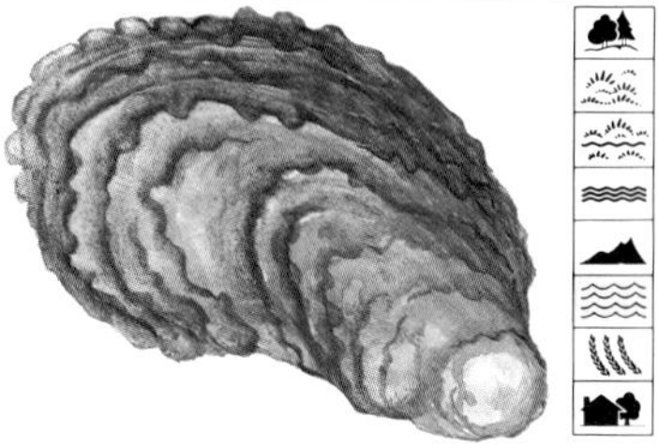

European Oyster *Shell* length up to 4 in (10 cm), very broad, almost circular; surface sculpted into irregular ridges; inner surface smooth pearly white. *Habitat* attached to rocks, in water to depth of 165 ft (50 m); fished commercially.

:ommon Saddle Oyster *Shell* length up to 2¼ in (6 cm); hell halves unequal, upper domed and heavily culpted, lower much flatter and c-shaped with hole ırough which it attaches to rock. *Habitat* lower shore) deep water.

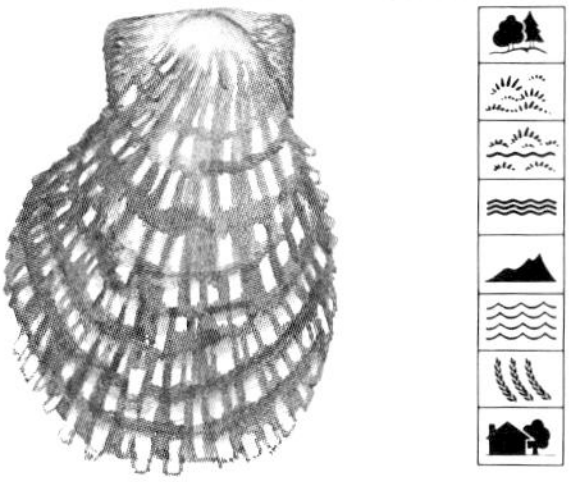

Thorny Oyster *Shell* length up to 4 in (10 cm); shell halves unequal, upper flatter with many sharp spines, lower more convex with broad spines. *Colour* brown to purple. *Habitat* attached to rocks on seabed.

een Scallop *Shell* length up to 3½ in (9 cm); shell lves unequal, upper more curved than lower. *Colour* y variable, white, yellow, red, brown, often with ıts or stripes. *Habitat* on sand and gravel down to ıth of 660 ft (200 m).

Great Scallop *Shell* length up to 6 in (15 cm); shell halves unequal, lower concave, upper flat with deep ridges forming fan. *Colour* red to brown. *Habitat* on sand and gravel; swim for short distances by forcing water out through valve.

ımon Otter Shell *Shell* length up to 4¾ in (12 cm); ıd, oblong, shell halves equal, surface with centric grooves. *Colour* horny outer layer often s to show paler shell surface. *Habitat* burrows in or gravel, to depth of 330 ft (100 m).

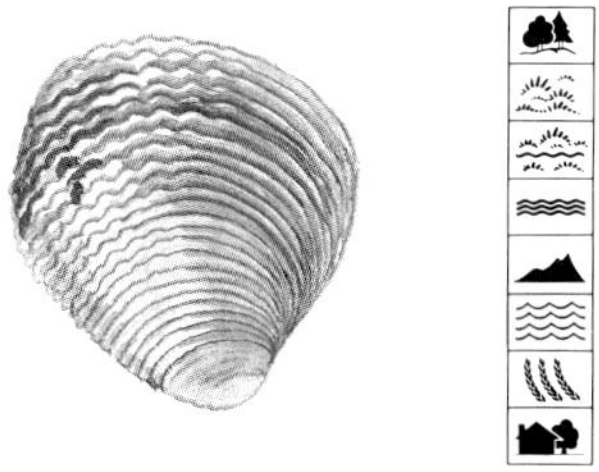

Warty Venus *Shell* length up to 2¼ in (6 cm); shell halves equal, surface concentric rings rough textured. *Colour* white, cream, or grey with brown markings. *Habitat* just below sediment surface to water depth of 330 ft (100 m).

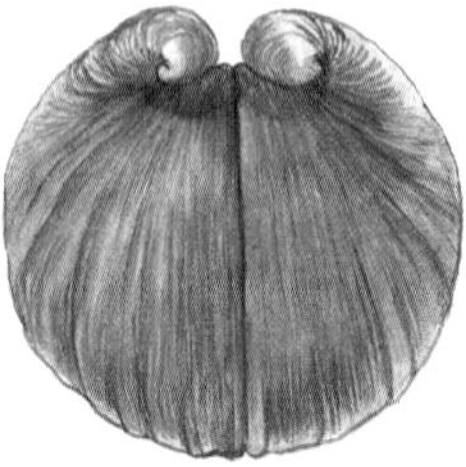
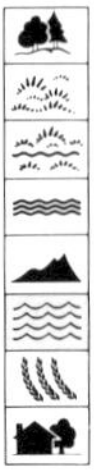

Heart Shell *Shell* length up to 4 in (10 cm); shell halves equal, outline circular with coil near hinge, heart shaped when seen from side. *Habitat* soft sand and mud in deeper water.

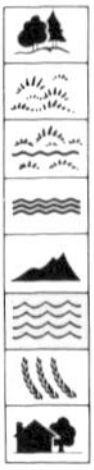

Dog Cockle *Shell* length up to 3¼ in (8 cm); shell halves equal, broad, almost circular, inner margin toothed. *Colour* variable, cream with brown-red patches, or red zig-zag pattern. *Habitat* burrowing in soft bottom to water depth of 265 ft (80 m).

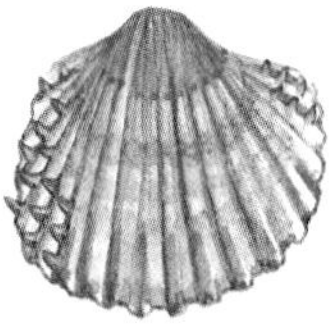
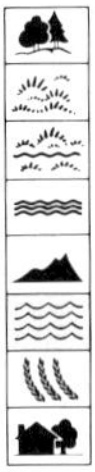

Prickly Cockle *Shell* length up to 2¾ in (7 cm); shell halves equal, outer surface ribbed, with short, blunt spines near margin. *Colour* cream to fawn. *Habitat* burrows in mud or sand from water depth of about 33 ft (10 m).

Common Edible Cockle *Shell* length up to 2 in (5 cm); shell-halves equal, outer surface and inner margin finely grooved. *Colour* pale brown to yellow. *Habitat* burrows in sand, lower shore to shallow water; eaten by birds and humans.

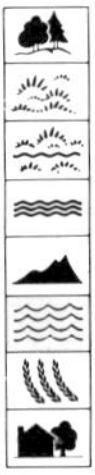

Violet Sea Snail *Shell* height up to ½ in (1.5 cm), broad, flat whorls with wide shell entrance. *Habitat* floating on sea surface, using air bubbles trapped in web of mucus to give buoyancy; preys on other surface floaters.

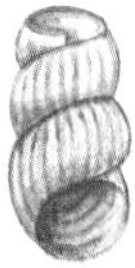
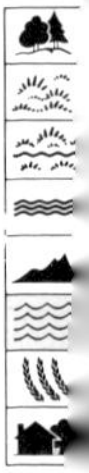

Looping Snail *Shell* height about ⅕ in (0.5 cm), with whorls of spire at the apex absent in adults, present in juveniles. *Habitat* on lower shore among weeds and stones.

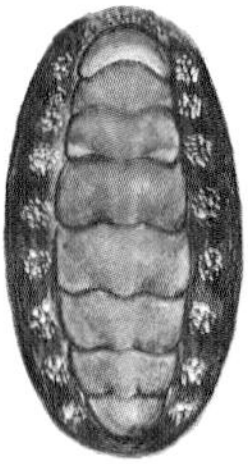
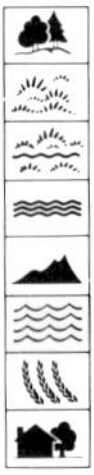

Chiton or Coat-of-mail Shell *Shell* length up to 2 in (5 cm), flattened, with 8 central overlapping plates and a middle ridge; tufts of spines around edges. *Colour* grey to yellow. *Habitat* rock surfaces, among weeds, in shallow water.

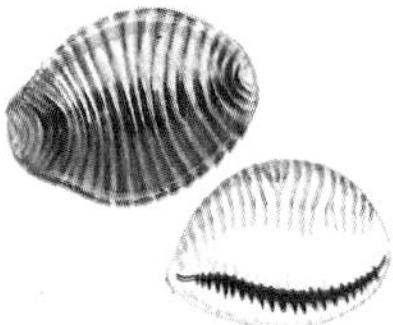
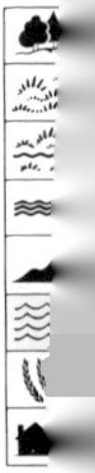

European Cowrie *Shell* height ½ in (1.25 cm); surfac sculpted into narrow, transverse ridges; shell openi lengthwise slit. *Habitat* lower shore to shallow wate rock surfaces and among sea-squirts.

Small Limpet *Shell* length up to $1\frac{1}{2}$ in (4 cm) roughly ridged surface. *Colour* variable, grey to pale brown. *Habitat* rock surfaces on the shore.

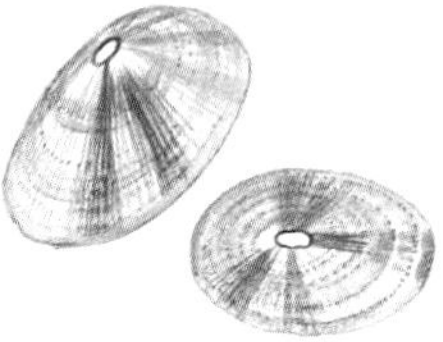

Keyhole Limpet *Shell* length up to $1\frac{1}{2}$ in (4 cm), surface with radiating and fine concentric ridges; hole in apex. *Colour* normally grey, but may be orange, red, or yellow. *Habitat* on rock surfaces, from lower shore down to deep water.

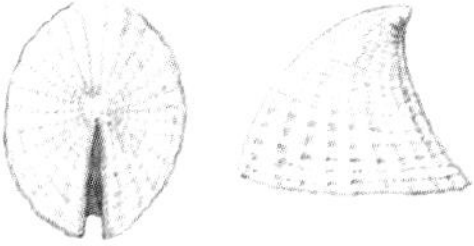

…t Limpet *Shell* length up to $\frac{4}{5}$ in (2 cm), surface net-…e; narrow slit along side; apex bent to one side. …*lour* variable, grey, white, or pale yellow. *Habitat* …rface of boulders on shore, and down to depth of …0 ft (60 m).

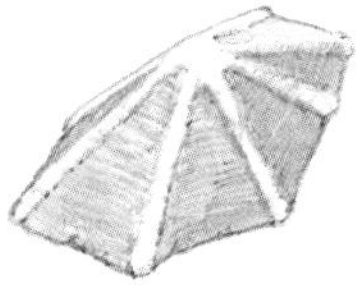

Mediterranean Limpet *Shell* length up to 2 in (5 cm), rather flat and deeply ridged, with irregular margin. *Colour* variable, grey to reddish brown; inside translucent grey; larger than similar Small Limpet. *Habitat* rock surfaces, middle to lower shore.

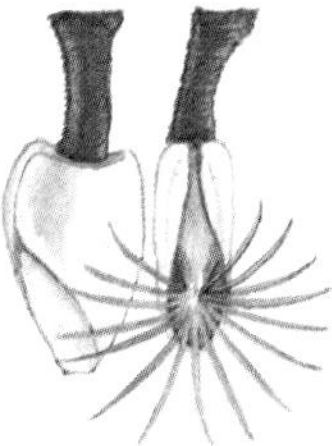

…se Barnacle *Shell* length up to 2 in (5 cm), made up …thin plates; attached to surface by thick muscular …k; shell opens to release 12 legs used to trap prey. …*itat* fixed to slow-moving sailing ships and floating …wood.

Common Ormer *Shell* length up to $2\frac{3}{4}$ in (7 cm), flattened, harp shaped, with folded surface and curved line of conspicuous holes. *Colour* brown to olive green; often coated with algae. *Habitat* rock surfaces among weeds in shallow water.

…k-lipped Dog Whelk *Shell* height up to $\frac{1}{2}$ in (1.5 cm), spire of highly ridged whorls; broad shell lips, lip toothed on inner edge. *Colour* fawn, grey, or …w with stripes. *Habitat* on sand and mud, under …s, in deep water.

Giant Top-shell *Shell* height about 1 in (2.5 cm), width $1\frac{1}{5}$ in (3 cm), spire with prominent stepped whorls. *Colour* white to cream with red or purple markings, but empty shells may be faded. *Habitat* soft bottom down to depth of 33 ft (10 m).

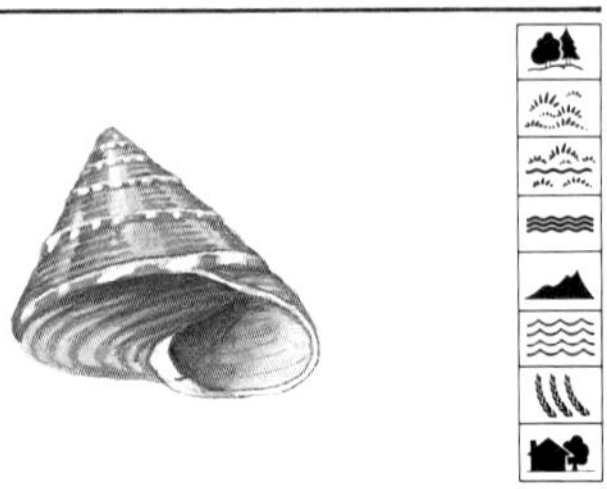

Common Top-shell *Shell* height up to 1⅕ in (3 cm), spire broad, cone shaped, straight sided. *Colour* pink or yellow, with wide red-brown stripes; some forms almost white. *Habitat* on rocks and stones from shore to 330 ft (100 m) depth.

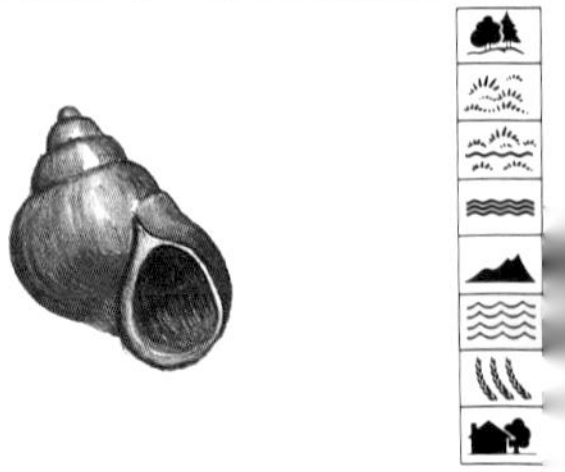

Small Periwinkle *Shell* height up to ⅖ in (1 cm), with 5-whorled, sharply pointed spire; smooth, shiny surface. *Colour* brown to blue-black. *Habitat* on rock surfaces and in crevices on upper and middle shore.

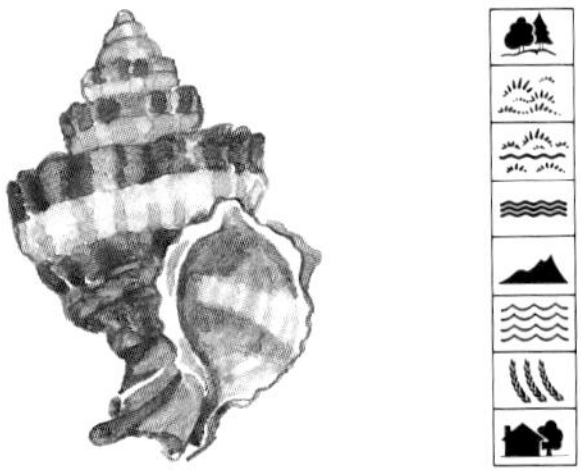

Banded Murex *Shell* height about 2¾ in (7 cm); spire made of about six whorls, with surface of short spines and raised bumps. *Habitat* among rocks on lower shore and to depth of 33 ft (10 m). Shell once highly prized as source of purple dye.

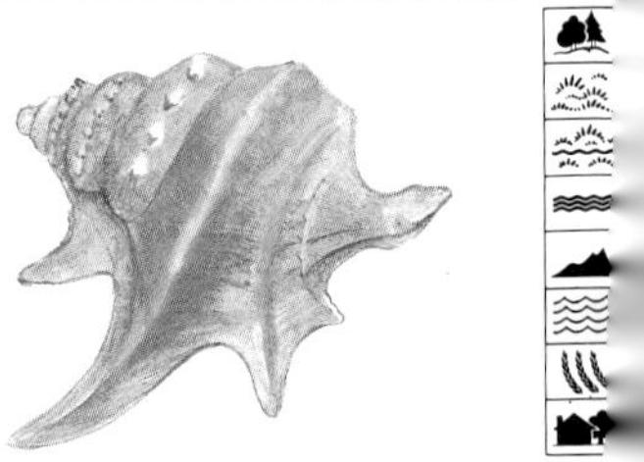

Pelican's Foot Shell *Shell* height 1¾ in (4.5 cm), spire c nine whorls, each with ring of raised bumps; shell lip with four large spreading points, black to yellow insid *Habitat* burrows into soft sea bottom, to depth of 265 ft (80 m).

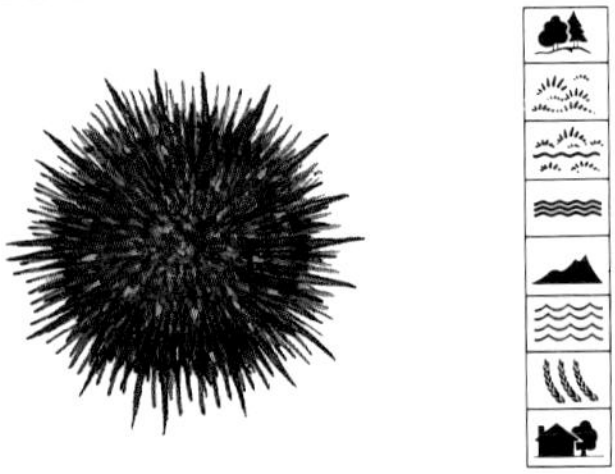

Black Sea-urchin *Size* shell up to 2 in (5 cm) across, spines up to 1⅕ in (3 cm) long; spines very sharp. *Colour* black when alive, but empty shell pink with radiating red lines and large mouth opening. *Habitat* on rocks around shore; SPINES PAINFUL.

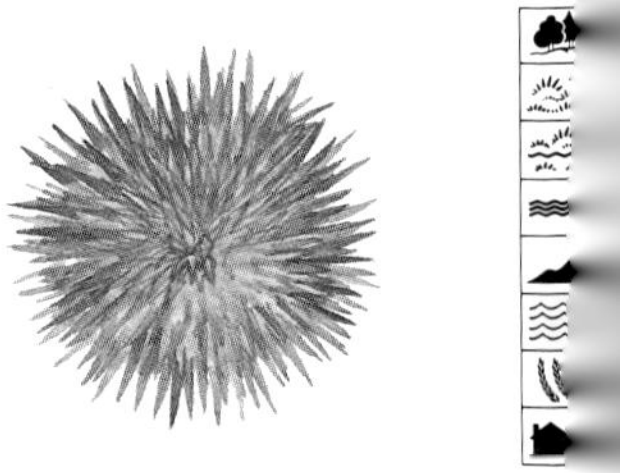

Red Sea-urchin *Size* shell up to 2¼ in (6 cm) across, spines 1⅕ in (3 cm) long. *Colour* variable from green dark brown or red; empty shell pale olive green. *Hab* rockpools on shore and down to 100 ft (30 m) among seaweed.

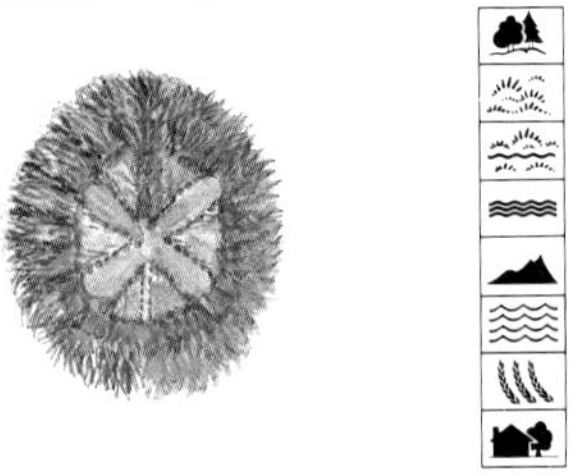

Lyre Urchin *Size* shell up to 2¾ in (7 cm) long, dense felt of short spines. *Colour* red to brown; empty shell pale yellow with characteristic 'lyre' shape below mouth opening. *Habitat* burrows in sand in shallow to deep water.

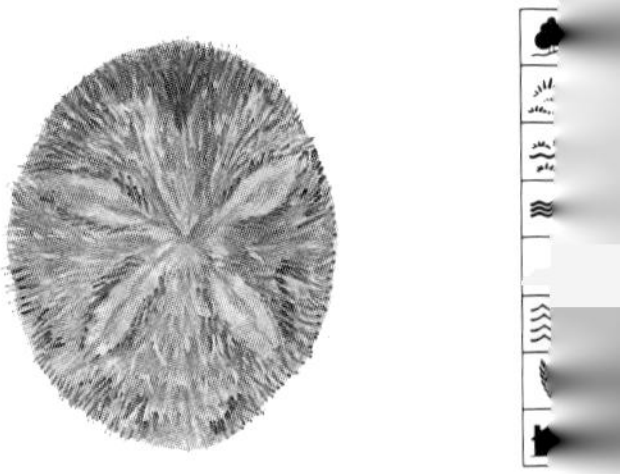

Purple Heart-urchin *Size* up to 4¾ in (12 cm) long; flattened body covered with short spines; some lor more prominent spines on upper surface. *Colour* re purple; empty shell grey with leaf pattern of holes. *Habitat* on sea bottom.

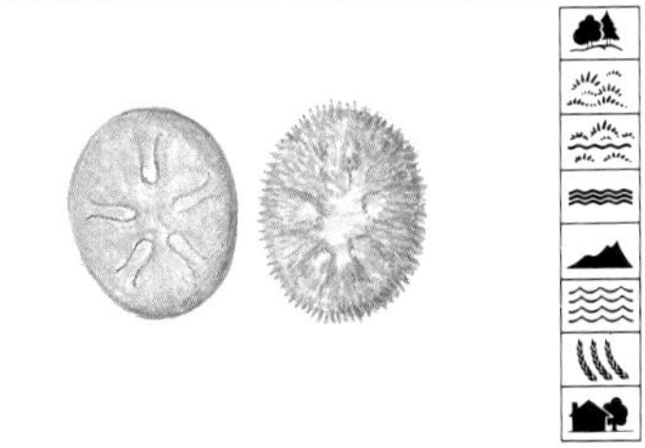

Pea Urchin *Size* shell up to ½ in (1.5 cm) long, spines very short giving felt-like appearance. *Colour* empty shell white with typical pattern of radiating holes. *Habitat* burrows into sand and gravel on lower shore and down to 2650 ft (800 m).

Sea Potato *Size* up to 3½ in (9 cm) long; dense felt of short spines, with few long, curved spines on underside. *Colour* fawn to yellow; empty shell cream coloured. *Habitat* burrows in sand on lower shore and down to 660 ft (200 m).

carlet Starfish *Size* up to 8 in (20 cm) across; upper urface smooth, but underside with rows of short pines. *Colour* purple to red, pale below. *Habitat* on rock urfaces, in warmer waters, shallow to deep.

Spotted Starfish *Size* up to 6 in (15 cm) across; number of arms variable from 6-10, and of different lengths. *Colour* fawn, purple, or white, with blue or brown spots. *Habitat* lower shore to depth of 100 ft (30 m), on rocks.

osefoot Star *Size* up to 6 in (15 cm)across; body flat; ns barely discernible except for thickened area in dline. *Colour* reddish, pale underside; pattern iable. *Habitat* sandy or muddy bottom from shallow deep water.

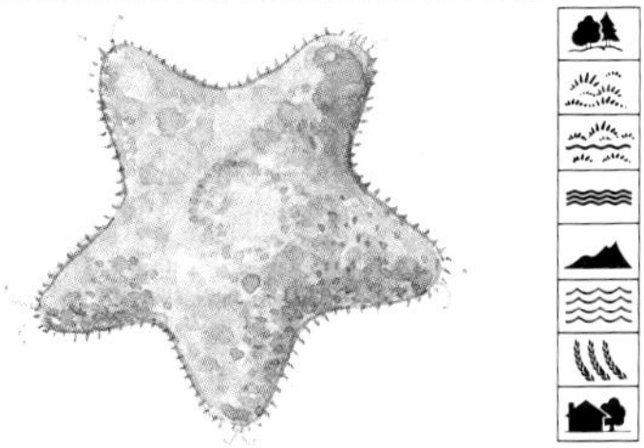

Cushion Star *Size* up to 2¼ in (6 cm) across; rather fat, with short, stubby arms. *Colour* camouflage brown or green with slight pattern; pale underside. *Habitat* under stones and rocks from lower shore to shallow water.

her Star *Diameter* up to 10 in (25 cm); tiny nspicuous body and long feathery arms, very plant- *Colour* red to yellow. *Habitat* on rock surfaces or ched to sea-fans by short, root-like processes.

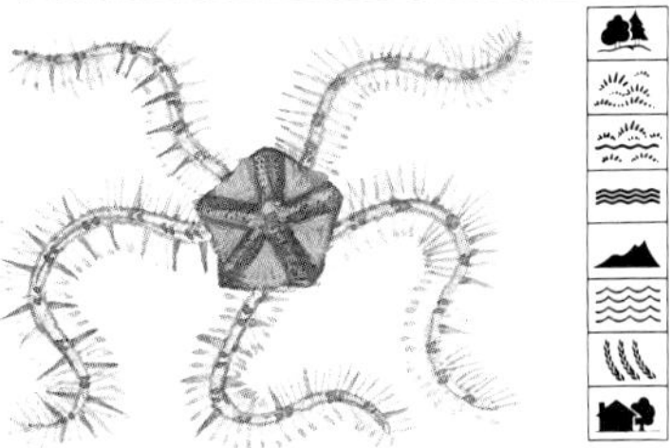

Common Brittle Star *Size* central body disc up to ⅘ in (2 cm) across, arms up to 4 in (10 cm); spiny arms often break off but regenerate. *Colour* variable, brown, purple, red, green. *Habitat* under stones in shallow and deep water.

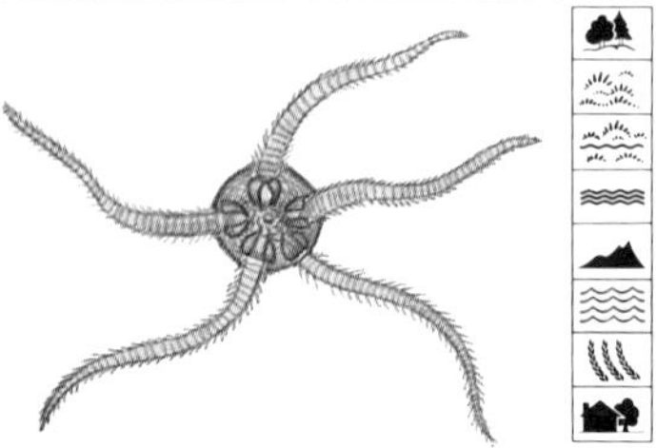

Rough Brittle Star *Size* central body disc up to 1⅕ in (3 cm) across, arms about 4 in (10 cm). *Colour* pale underside, darker above. *Habitat* burrows in sandy bottom down to depth of 660 ft (200 m).

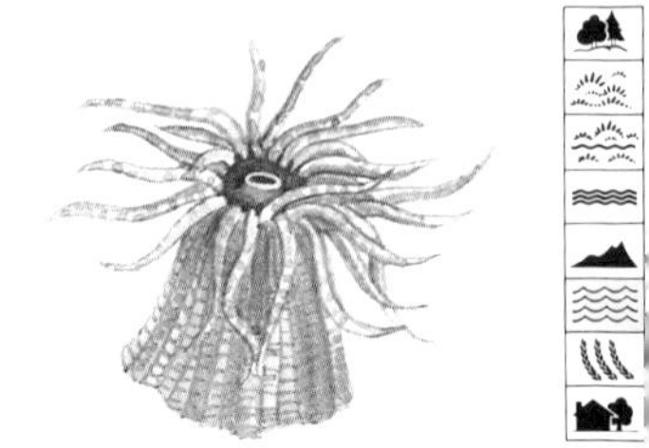

Gem Anemone *Size* up to 1⅕ in (3 cm) across, height 2 in (5 cm); about 48 short striped tentacles. *Colour* pink with grey and white raised warts; tentacles green, grey, or pink. *Habitat* attached to rocks in shallow water in sunny positions.

Snakelocks Anemone *Size* up to 2¾ in (7 cm) across, height 4 in (10 cm); about 170 tentacles which cannot be fully withdrawn into body. *Colour* green, grey, or pale brown. *Habitat* among seaweed on rock surfaces in sunny rock pools and shallow water.

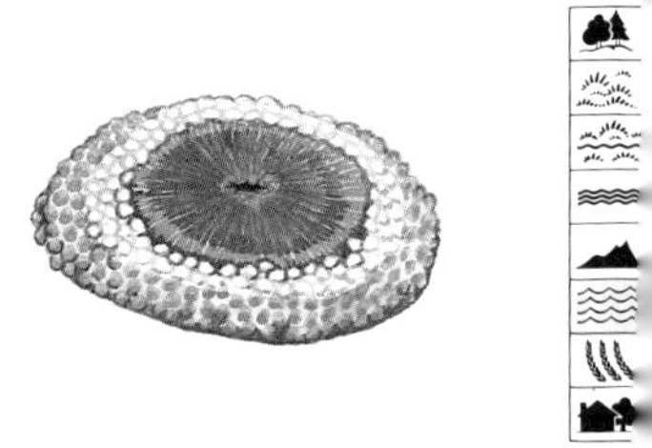

Ringed Anemone *Size* up to 2¾ in (7 cm) across at base; about 150 short, stubby tentacles arranged in 4 rings. *Colour* yellow or reddish with pattern of pale marks; tentacles grey and white. *Habitat* in deep water, on ha surfaces or more mobile.

Daisy Anemone *Size* up to 1½ in (4 cm) across, height 4 in (10 cm); about 750 tentacles arranged in 9 rings. *Colour* camouflage grey-brown with paler splashes. *Habitat* on rocks and other hard surfaces in shallow water and in rock pools.

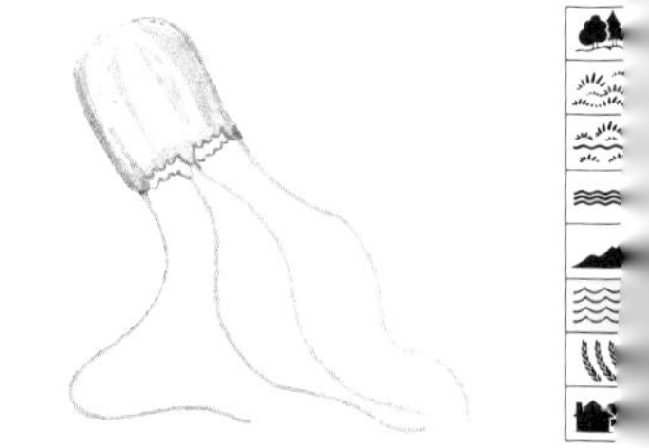

Mediterranean Sea-wasp *Size* 14 in (36 cm) long, including tentacles; umbrella transparent, almost square; TENTACLES CONTAIN STINGING CELLS AND CONTACT CAN BE VERY PAINFUL. *Habitat* surface of op water and washed up on beaches.

Jellyfish *Size* up to 35 in (90 cm) across; umbrella very deep, dome shaped with lobed margin but without tentacles; mouth arms fused into large, central, ornate bunch. *Colour* transparent blue or yellow. *Habitat* open water.

Common Jellyfish *Diameter* up to 10 in (25 cm); transparent, umbrella-shaped mass of jelly with peripheral ring of tiny tentacles; 4 central frilled mou arms. *Habitat* open water, but commonly washed up shore.

By-the-wind-sailor *Length* up to 4 in (10 cm); upper part oval, with curved transparent 'sail'; distinguished from dangerous Portuguese Man-of-war by short tentacles. *Habitat* surface of open water, often in groups.

Portuguese Man-of-war *Length* up to 12 in (30 cm), width 4 in (10 cm); upper part with large 'sail', lower part with very long tentacles used for breeding and feeding. DANGEROUS STING, SHOULD NOT BE TOUCHED. *Habitat* open sea surface.

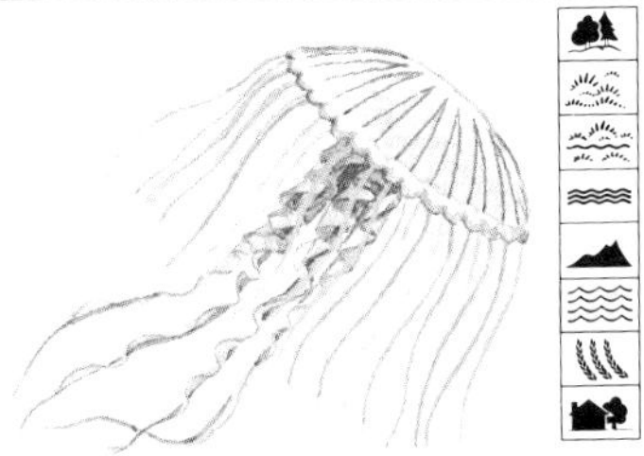

Compass Jelly *Size* up to 12 in (30 cm) long; umbrella margin distinctly lobed and with ring of tentacles; mouth arms very long. *Colour* umbrella surface with pattern of dark, radiating lines like compass. *Habitat* in open water.

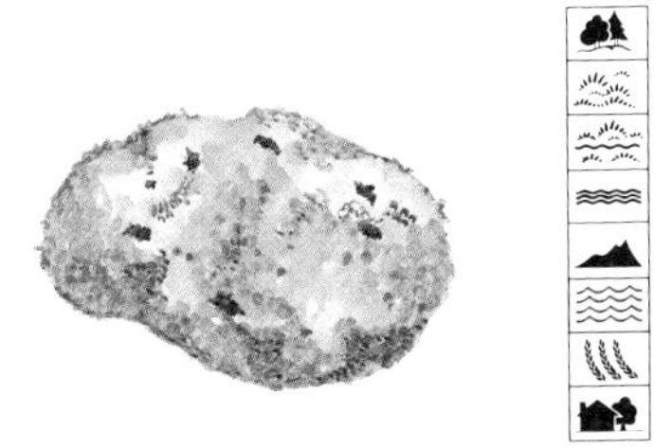

Bath Sponge *Width* up to 12 in (30 cm); large irregular mass with skeleton of spongy fibres and rough, pitted surface. *Habitat* on solid surfaces down to depth of 165 ft (50 m). Harvested commercially and skeletons cleaned for use in bathroom.

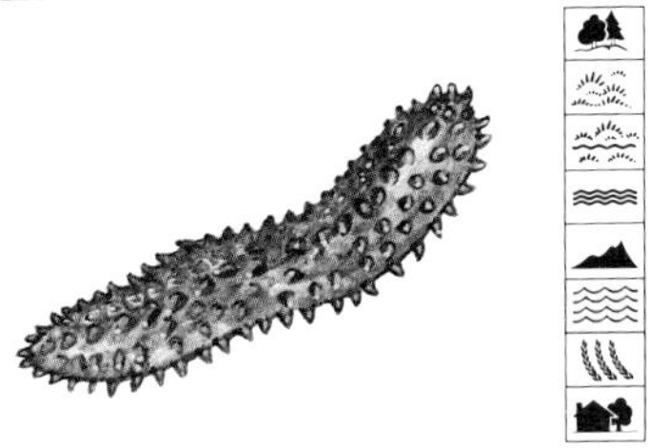

Sea Cucumber *Length* up to 8 in (20 cm); upper body surface sticky, covered with rows of pointed warts. *Colour* dark brown above with yellow and red underside. *Habitat* on sandy or muddy bottoms, among eelgrass; ejects white, sticky threads if upset.

Sea Gooseberry *Length* up to 1⅕ in (3 cm); a combjelly with 8 lengthways combs and a single pair of tentacles, used for catching plankton. *Habitat* form shoals in coastal waters; swim by beating tiny hairs in combs; luminescent.

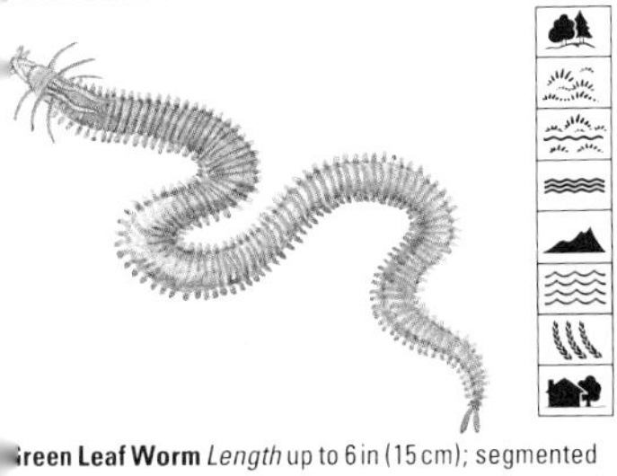

Green Leaf Worm *Length* up to 6 in (15 cm); segmented worm with 8 short 'tentacles' at head end; pair of simple eyes. *Habitat* under stones and in rock crevices; crawling on shore exposed by tide.

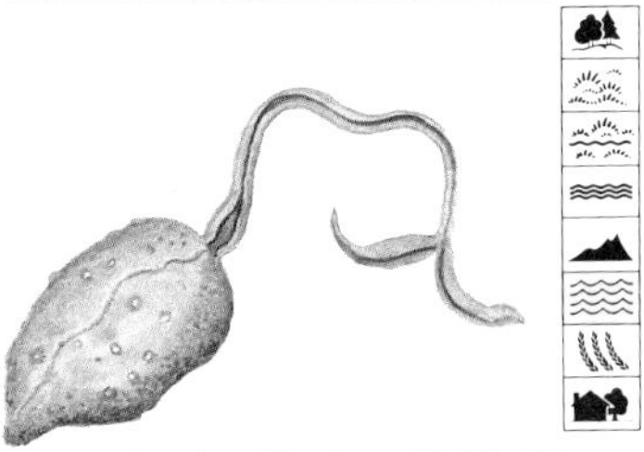

Green Sea Pear *Length* female up to 6 in (15 cm), tiny parasitic male $\frac{1}{10}$ in (2 mm) lives inside female; long tube which projects from crevice traps food particles in mucus and passes it back to mouth. *Habitat* under water in rock crevices.

Lugworm *Length* up to 8 in (20 cm); segmented worm thicker at front end, tapering to rear; 13 of segments carry breathing gills for extracting oxygen from water. *Habitat* forms U-shaped burrows in sand of middle to lower shore.

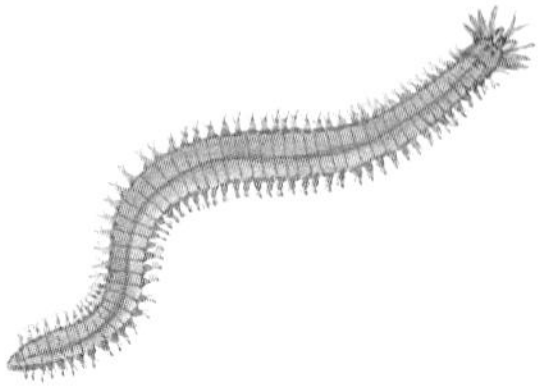

Ragworm *Length* up to 4¾ in (12 cm); each segment has a projection on either side bearing tiny bristles used for movement. *Colour* variable, but usually greenish, with orange or red stripe. *Habitat* burrows in mud on lower shore.

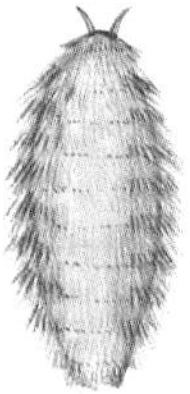

Sea Mouse *Length* up to 6 in (15 cm); segmented worm with segments only visible on hairless underside; upper surface with dense felt of hairs with thick bristles to sides. *Colour* grey with iridescent green sides. *Habitat* mud, sand.

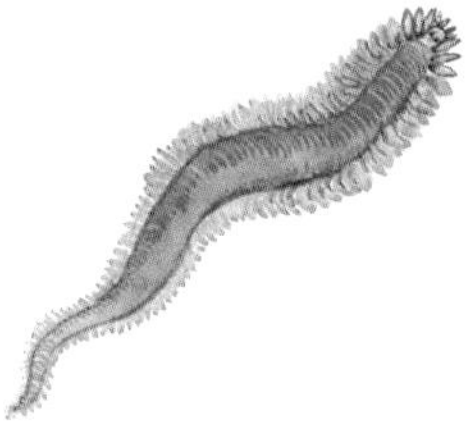

Paddle Worm *Length* up to 12 in (30 cm); body segments with conspicuous paddle-shaped projections at the sides, becoming smaller at tail end; pair of large eyes. *Colour* variable blue to green, yellow splashes. *Habitat* shallow water, under stones.

Peacock Worm *Length* up to 10 in (25 cm); segmented worm with 2 fans of narrow striped gills at head end; in tube made of particles stuck together with mucus; gills withdrawn into tube if disturbed. *Habitat* lower shore and shallow water, in mud.

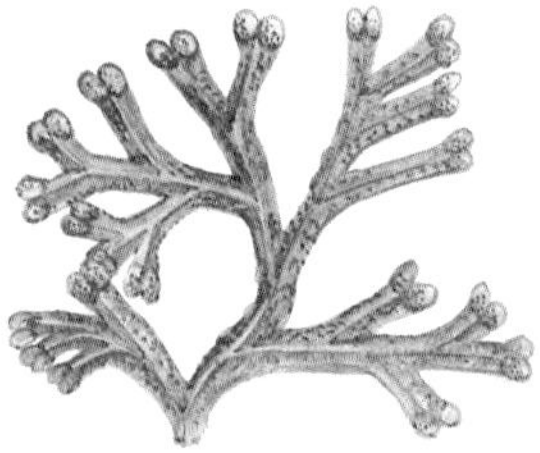

Brown Wrack *Length* up to 8 in (20 cm), broad, leathery fronds with thickened midrib, and fat, oval, breeding structures at tips. *Habitat* on rock surfaces from middle shore down to shallow water.

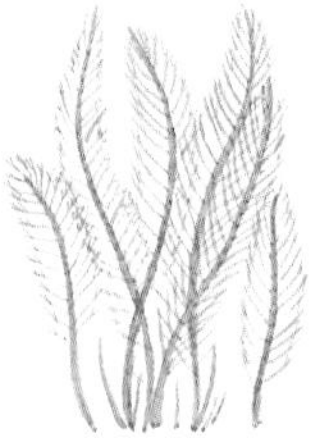

Goose Feathers *Length* up to 4 in (10 cm), frond branched, feather-like. *Colour* female fronds dark shiny green, male fronds more yellowish. *Habitat* on rocks in shallow water and in rock pools.

Mermaid's Cup *Height* up to 3¼ in (8 cm). *Frond* a delicate pale-green stalk bearing many leaf-like structures arranged in a ring. *Habitat* forms dense colonies on rock surfaces in shallow water.

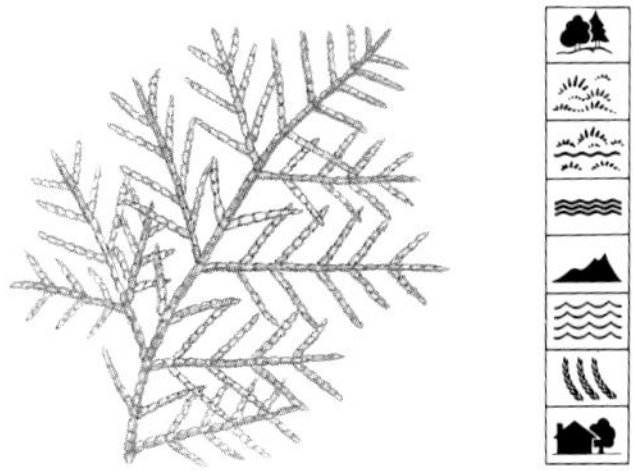

Common Coralweed *Length* up to 4¾ in (12 cm), fronds branched, fern-like, with segmented appearance. *Colour* purple, red, pink; when plant dies, chalky white outer skeleton remains. *Habitat* rocks in pools and on ower shore.

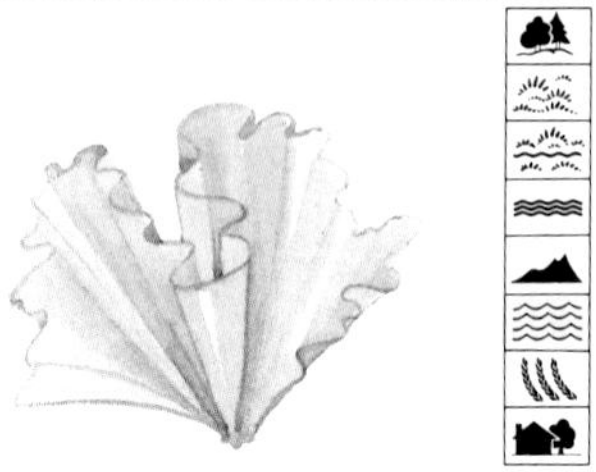

Sea Lettuce *Length* 6-17½ in (15-45 cm), fronds thin, translucent, with irregular shape and wavy margin. *Colour* pale, delicate green, but becoming darker with age. *Habitat* attached by short stalk to rocks in pools and shallow water.

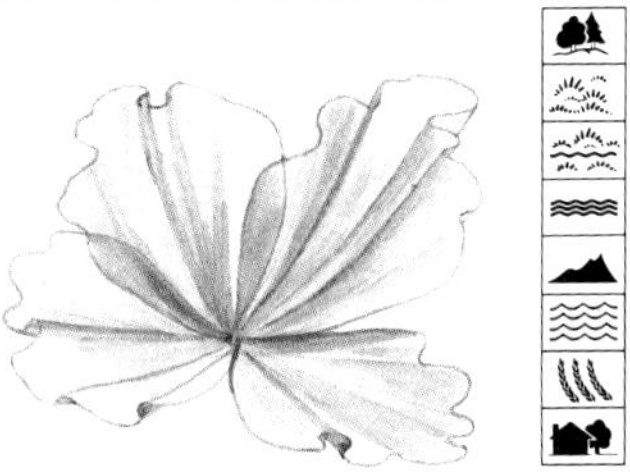

urple Laver *Length* 6-16 in (15-40 cm), fronds thin, road, irregular, without stalks. *Colour* pale purple hen young, becoming brown to green with age. *abitat* attached to rocks on lower shore. Eaten as aver bread' in Wales and Ireland.

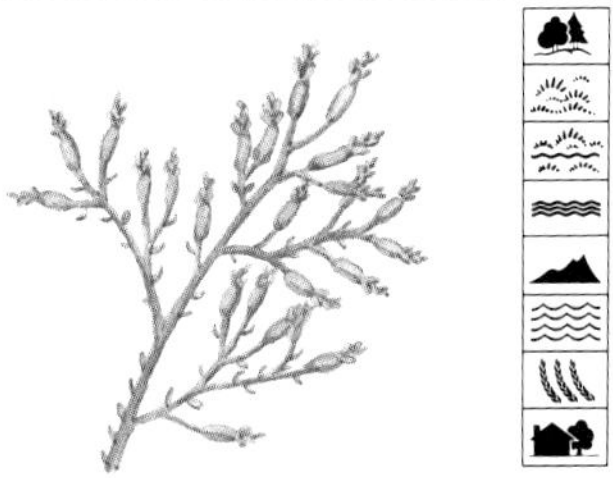

Rainbow Bladderweed *Length* 12-17½ in (30-45 cm), branched, bushy fronds, short spines on stem and air sacs at tips. *Colour* olive green, but changes to iridescent blue-green in water. *Habitat* attached to rocks in shallow water.

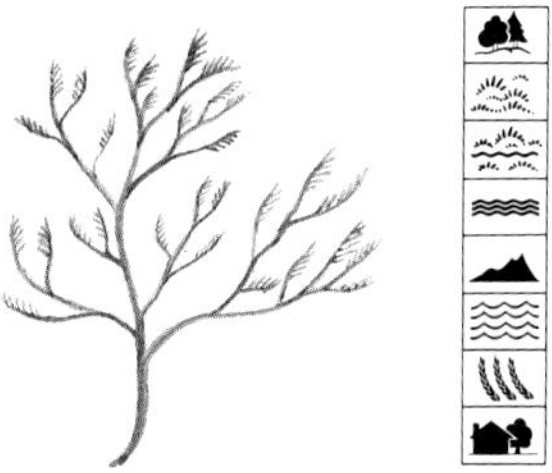

:kscomb *Length* 3¼-8 in (8-20 cm), narrow branches h tooth-like divisions at tips forming 'combs'. *Habitat* ached by tiny holdfast to surfaces of rocks and nes in shallow water and rock pools; often washed by tide.

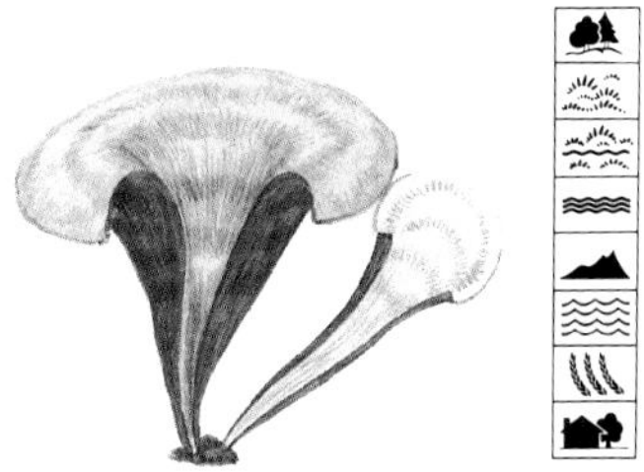

Peacock's Tail *Length* up to 4 in (10 cm), hairy frond flat when small but curves inwards to form funnel shape as it enlarges. *Colour* inner surface green to olive or grey. *Habitat* in shallow water, attached to rocks by slender stalk.

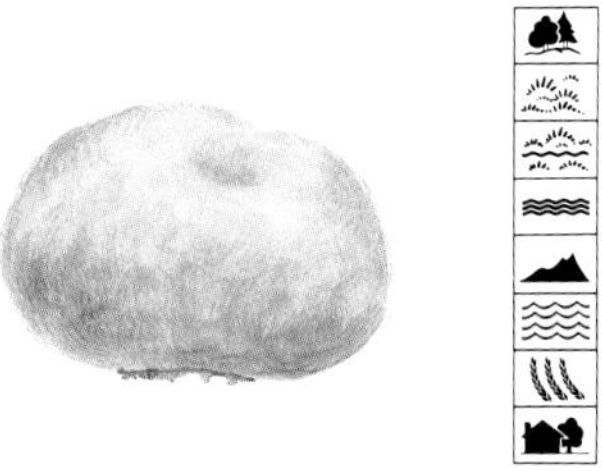

weed *Size* up to 8 in (20 cm) across, frond a round gy mass made of tangled filaments. *Habitat* hed by root-like holdfast to surface of rocks in ow water; often washed up on the shore.

Sea Worms *Length* up to 10 in (25 cm), fronds thick, rubbery and worm-like. *Habitat* attached by tiny round holdfast to rocks on the shore and in shallow water.

Crack Willow *Height* up to 80 ft (25 m); bark grey, rough; leaves hairless, pale underside. *Flowers* April/May; catkins long and dangling. *Habitat* by freshwater streams and ponds; often cut back or pollarded to prevent trunk splitting.

Carob or Locust Tree *Height* up to 33 ft (10 m); leaves leathery. *Flowers* August-October; in clusters with tiny green petals; fruits leathery brown pods used as cattle fodder and as chocolate substitute. *Habitat* often cultivated, also wild in rocky places.

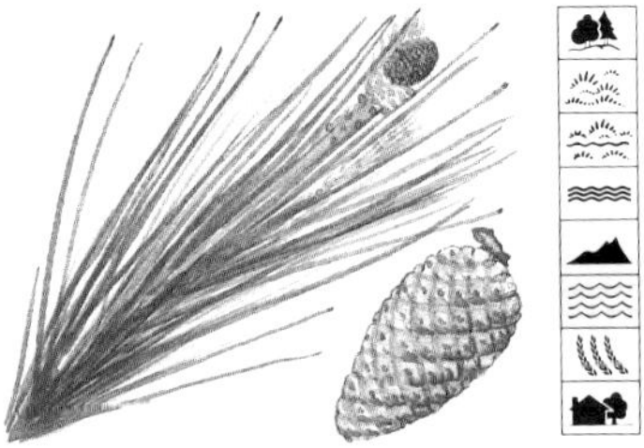

Aleppo Pine *Height* up to 66 ft (20 m), umbrella shaped. *Cones* March-May; dangling, take several years to ripen. *Habitat* rocky ground and coastal limestone hills. Tree once an important source of shipbuilding timber. Resin used in retsina wine.

Stone or Umbrella Pine *Height* up to 100 ft (30 m), crow umbrella shaped. *Cones* April/May; fat, upright, containing large edible seeds. *Habitat* sandy coastal areas; may be grown as ornamental in parks and gardens.

Black Pine *Height* up to 165 ft (50 m), pyramidal. *Cones* May; upright, conical. *Habitat* forms dense forests in mountain areas; also extensively planted for commercial wood.

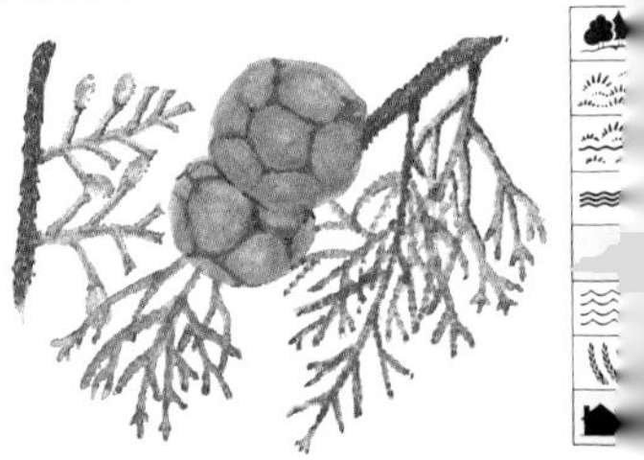

Italian or Funeral Cypress *Height* up to 165 ft (50 m), columnar *Cones* April; tiny, globular. *Habitat* dry hillsides, but the more pyramidal form is commonly planted as an ornamental in gardens and cemeteries

Cork Oak *Height* up to 50 ft (15 m); very thick corky bark which is regularly stripped off and used to make bottle corks. *Flowers* April/May; flowers form long chains; acorn fruit. *Habitat* sandy hills near the coast.

Black Poplar *Height* up to 100 ft (30 m), spreading ha very dark bark. *Flowers* March/April before leaves appear. *Habitat* by water and damp areas. Many varieties, including Lombardy Poplar planted as ornamental in gardens.

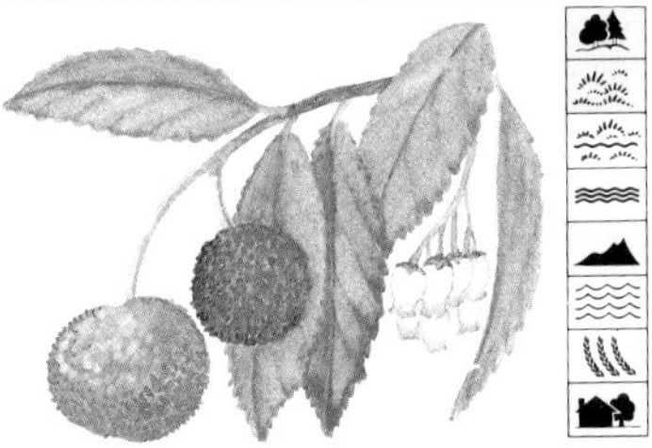

Strawberry Tree *Height* up to 33 ft (10 m); evergreen shrub or small tree. *Flowers* October-April; clusters of delicate waxy pink or white flowers; attractive strawberry-like fruits with rough texture, used to make liqueurs. *Habitat* woodland edges, stony hills.

Fig Tree *Height* up to 13 ft (4 m). *Flowers* June-July; flowers concealed inside fleshy green, pear-shaped fruit; ripe fruit purple with red centre, eaten fresh or dried. *Habitat* on stony hillsides, but widely cultivated.

Olive Tree *Height* up to 30 ft (10 m); old trees with gnarled, twisted trunks. *Flowers* May/June; white flowers in clusters; oval green fruit ripens to black, pressed to extract olive oil used in cooking. *Habitat* stony hillsides, cultivated.

Sweet Bay or Laurel *Height* up to 50 ft (15 m); shrub or small tree with aromatic leaves used in cooking. *Flowers* March/April; tiny yellow flowers in leaf axils; fruit black berry. *Habitat* damp rocky places, often cultivated.

Sweet or Spanish Chestnut *Height* up to 100 ft (30 m); spreading habit. *Flowers* July; yellowish catkins with strong scent; fruit 2 or 3 shiny brown edible nuts in a spiny husk. *Habitat* woodland, in dry soils, often planted in parks.

Walnut *Height* up to 100 ft (30 m); spreading habit, deciduous. *Flowers* April/May; female flower upright green spike, male flowers in catkin; fruit, a hard brown nut in furry green skin. *Habitat* mainly cultivated.

…indle Tree *Height* up to 16 ft (5 m); woody shrub. *…owers* May-June, tiny greenish-white flowers in loose …usters; capsule bright pink, opening to show orange …eds. *Habitat* hedges, scrub, open woodland.

Prickly Pear *Height* 10-13 ft (3-4 m); a spiny cactus composed of large, flat, oval sections. *Flowers* April-July; flowers stalkless; fruit, succulent, edible when spines removed. *Habitat* dry, rocky places; used as hedging.

Ribwort Plantain *Height* 4-16 in (10-40 cm); perennial; strap-shaped leaves with parallel veins. *Flowers* April-October; knobbed cluster of inconspicuous flowers, yellow anthers. *Habitat* waste ground, fields, meadows.

Hop *Length* 6½-13 ft (2-6 m); perennial. *Flowers* July-September; male and female flowers on separate plants; female green, cone-like, used in beer production. *Habitat* climbing hedgerow plant, often cultivated.

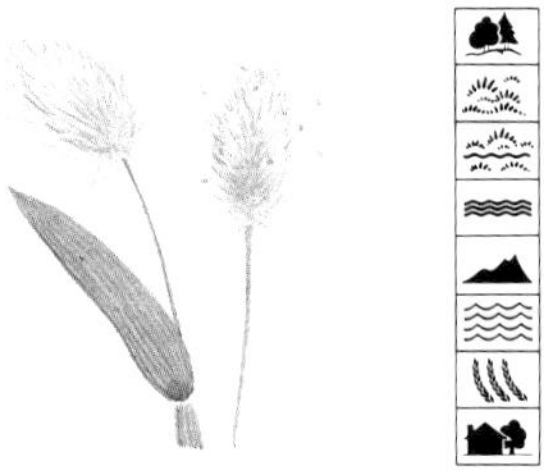

Hare's-tail Grass *Height* 2-20 in (5-50 cm); annual. *Flowers* April-June; inconspicuous flowers in oval silky head which persists when dry; often used natural or dyed in flower arrangements. *Habitat* dry coastal hills.

Great Quaking Grass *Height* 4-24 in (10-60 cm); annual. *Flowers* March-June; inconspicuous, set in broad, silvery head made of overlapping sections which persists when dry. *Habitat* dry hillsides.

Wall Pennywort or Navelwort *Height* 4-16 in (10-40 cm); perennial; smooth fleshy leaves. *Flowers* June-August. *Habitat* cracks in rocks, old walls.

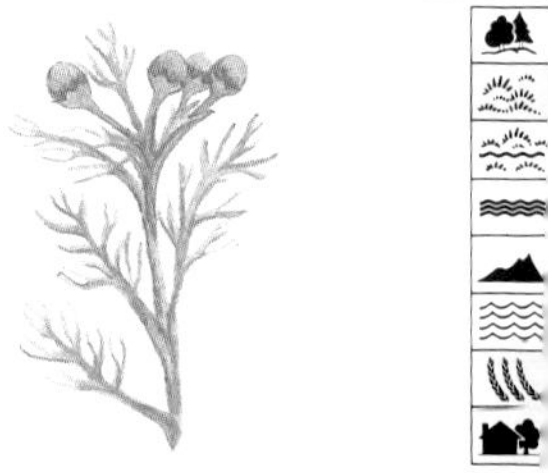

Pineapple Mayweed *Height* 2¾-10 in (7-10 cm); fleshy hairless annual, gives off strong smell of pineapple if crushed. *Flowers* May-November; yellowish-green domes without petals. *Habitat* well-trodden paths, roadsides.

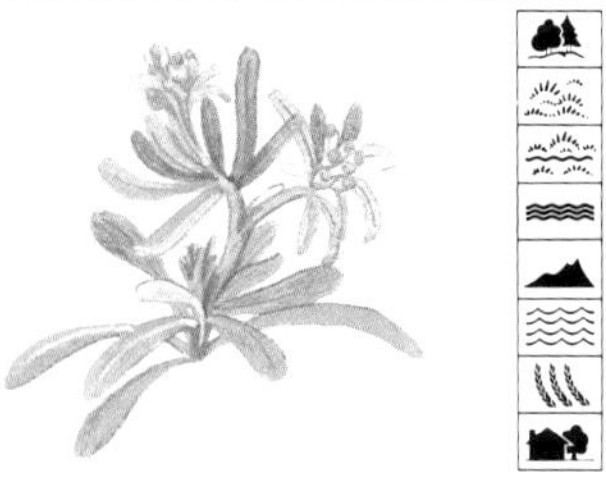

Marsh Cudweed *Height* 4-8 in (10-20 cm); annual with silvery grey leaves, much-branched stem. *Flowers* July-October; bud-like, without outer petals. *Habitat* damp bare places, stream and river banks.

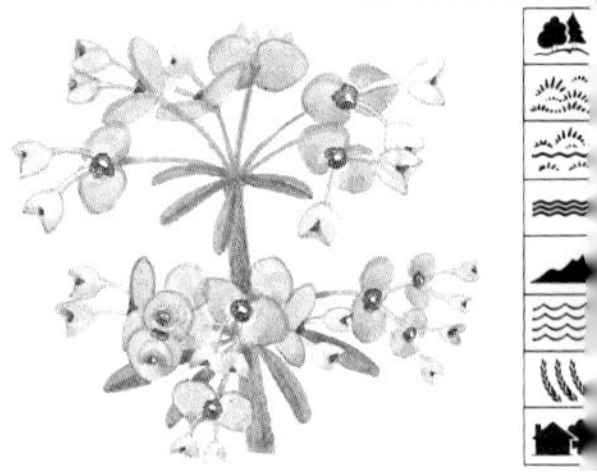

Large Mediterranean Spurge *Height* 31-40 in (80-100 cm); perennial; thick woody stems marked by mar leaf scars. *Flowers* March-May; tiny petal-less flowe inside conspicuous green bracts. *Habitat* dry stony hi in clumps.

Pigweed *Height* 4-32 in (10-80 cm); annual; large shiny leaves, up to 6 in (15 cm) long; hairy stem. *Flowers* July-September, papery white flowers in prickly spike. *Habitat* warm dry fields, paths, waste ground. Originally from North America.

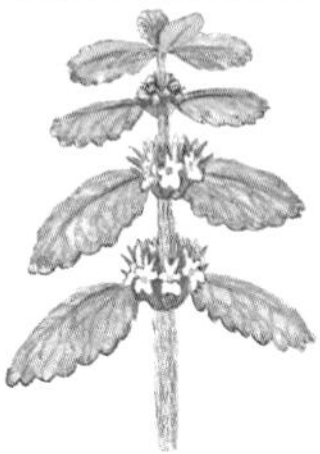

Horehound *Height* up to 24 in (60 cm); woolly leaved, strongly scented perennial. *Flowers* April-September; arranged in tight whorls around stem. *Habitat* dry hillsides, by paths, waste ground. Medicinal herb.

Mediterranean Coriaria *Height* up to 120 in (3 m); shrub vith leathery green leaves. *Flowers* April-July; tiny greenish flowers in upright spike; poisonous black berries. *Habitat* dry hills and woodland.

Shrubby Milkwort *Height* 4-8 in (10-20 cm); woody stemmed perennial with evergreen leaves. *Flowers* April-September; colour white with yellow, occasionally pink to red. *Habitat* mainly in mountains, pinewoods, scrub, grassland.

iarlic Mustard *Height* 8-40 in (20-100 cm); biennial; vrinkled, heart-shaped leaves give off strong smell of arlic when crushed. *Flowers* April-August; seeds in ong pods. *Habitat* hedges, woodland edge, by shaded aths.

White Star-of-Bethlehem *Height* 4-12 in (10-30 cm); bulb perennial with grass-like leaves. *Flowers* April-May. *Habitat* grassy places, vineyards, roadsides.

hite Dead-nettle *Height* 8-20 in (20-50 cm); hairy rennial, spreading by underground roots to form umps. *Flowers* March-November. *Habitat* roadsides, aste places, cultivated ground.

Scentless Mayweed *Height* 4-20 in (10-50 cm); annual; feathery green leaves without aromatic scent of similar plants. *Flowers* April-October. *Habitat* cultivated land, waste ground.

Laurestinus *Height* up to 10 ft (3 m); large shrub with grey bark and leathery, evergreen leaves. *Flowers* February-June; flat clusters of pink or white fragrant flowers; fruits ripening to black. *Habitat* coastal woods, thickets.

Sage-leaved Cistus *Height* up to 40 in (1 m); small spreading shrub; leaves dark green, wrinkled. *Flowers* March-May. *Habitat* on acid soils, stony hillsides, woods, scrub.

Fragrant Clematis *Length* 10-26 ft (3-8 m); woody climbing perennial. *Flowers* May-August; sweet-scented flowers up to 1⅕in (30 mm) across; seeds with short feathery plumes. *Habitat* in hedges, scrubby areas, waste ground.

Traveller's Joy or Old Man's Beard *Length* 10-26 ft (3-8 m); woody climbing perennial. *Flowers* June-September; seeds in clusters with long white feathery plumes. *Habitat* scrambling in hedges, woodland edge.

Hogwood *Height* 32-60 in (80-150 cm); biennial or perennial; stout hollow stem ridged and bristly. *Flowers* April-November; in broad flat clusters up to 8 in (20 cm) across, white to pale pink. *Habitat* meadows, damp woods, paths.

Giant Hogweed *Height* up to 16 ft (5 m); perennial; very thick stems and roughly hairy leaves; HANDLING PLANT CAN CAUSE SERIOUS SKIN RASHES. *Flowers* June/July; in flat heads up to 50 cm across. *Habitat* damp ground.

Ox-eye Daisy *Height* 8-20 in (20-50 cm); coarse-leaved perennial. *Flowers* May-September; up to 2 in (5 cm) across. *Habitat* grassy places, waste ground, roadside verges.

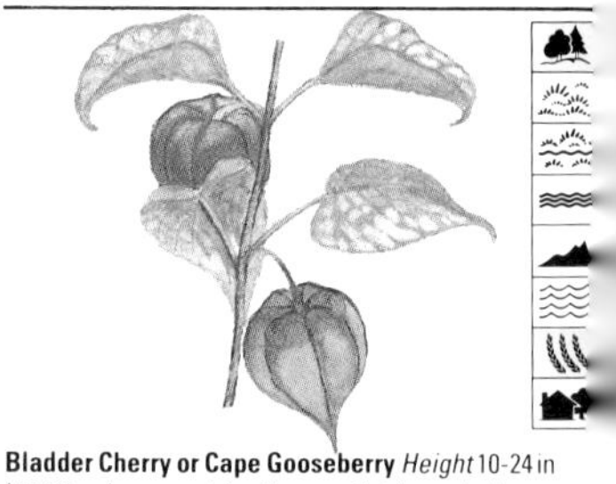

Bladder Cherry or Cape Gooseberry *Height* 10-24 in (25-60 cm); perennial with smooth, triangular leaves. *Flowers* May-October; fruit, a red berry inside orange 'Chinese lantern' which persists. *Habitat* woods, vineyards.

Spiny Bear's Breeches *Height* up to 40 in (1 m) when 'lowering; stiff perennial with very spiny, thistle-like eaves. *Flowers* May-June; flowers set in spiny purple ›racts. *Habitat* dry grassy places and open woods.

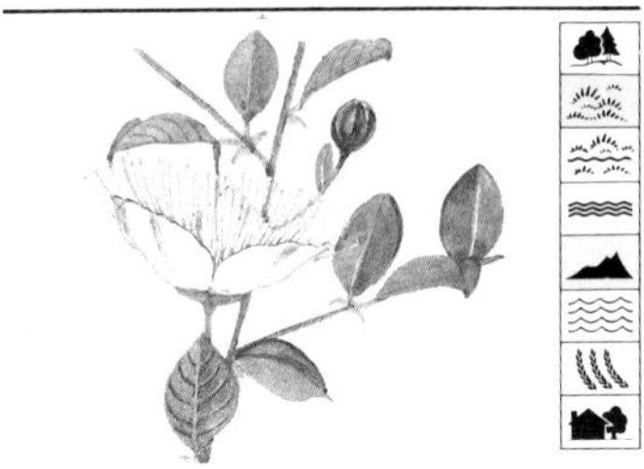

Caper *Height* up to 5 ft (1.5 m); sprawling, spiny shrub. *Flowers* June-September; single, large, and pale with conspicuous stamens; berries split showing red centre. *Habitat* rocky places; unopened buds used in cooking.

esembryanthemum *Height* up to 12 in (30 cm); annual ›th small fleshy leaves forming mat. *Flowers* April- ›ly. *Habitat* salt marshes, cliffs, coastal areas.

Gypsywort *Height* 8-32 in (20-80 cm); perennial with nettle-like leaves. *Flowers* July-September; tiny white flowers arranged in compact whorls in leaf axils. *Habitat* damp places, ditches, marshes, river banks.

er's Greenweed *Height* 12-24 in (30-60 cm); upright nder-stalked perennial. *Flowers* June-August, in tall ke; seeds in long smooth pod. *Habitat* open ciduous woodland, rough grassland, roadside.

Fly Honeysuckle *Height* up to 6 ft 6 in (2 m); deciduous shrub. *Flowers* May/June; pale flowers 1-2 in (2-5 cm), in pairs, not scented; fruits, pairs of red berries, NOT EDIBLE. *Habitat* deciduous woodland, occasionally hedges.

ezewort *Height* 20-100 cm; perennial with shiny gated leaves. *Flowers* July-September. *Habitat* on soils, damp meadows, marshes, river banks, ›es.

Alexanders *Height* up to 60 in (150 cm); biennial. *Flowers* April-June; fruits rounded, ripening to black. *Habitat* open grassy places on the coast; glossy, aromatic leaves used as culinary herb.

Bird's-foot Trefoil *Height* 2-12 in (5-30 cm); low sprawling perennial. *Flowers* May-September; yellow to orange or red; long seed pods arranged like a bird's foot. *Habitat* grassy fields and meadows.

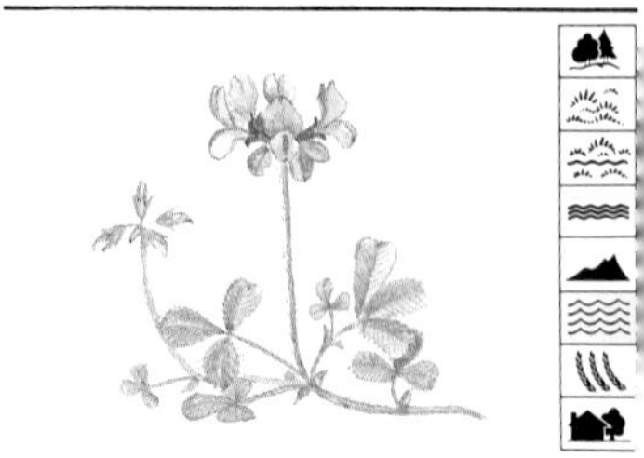

Southern Bird's-foot Trefoil *Length* 4-16 in (10-40 cm); spreading, woody perennial. *Flowers* March-June; seeds in long pod. *Habitat* coastal sand-dunes and cliffs.

Coltsfoot *Height* 2-8 in (5-20 cm); perennial. *Flowers* February-April; flowers appearing before leaves; seeds in a white, feathery 'clock'. *Habitat* on lime-rich soils, waste ground, river banks. Used in cough-medicine.

Black Medick *Length* 4-16 in (10-40 cm); annual. *Flowers* April-October; flowers tiny round head, 3-8 mm; fruit, cluster of bean-shaped pods, becoming black as they ripen. *Habitat* bare and cultivated land, grassy fields, meadows.

Silverweed *Length* up to 32 in (80 cm); low creeping perennial, spreading by runners; leaves with silvery down, especially on underside. *Flowers* May-August. *Habitat* grassy areas by roads, paths, rivers.

Crown Daisy *Height* 20-32 in (50-80 cm); annual, formi thick clump of feathery leaves. *Flowers* April-September; colour usually deep yellow, but form with pale outer ring. *Habitat* stony hillsides and waste ground.

Bellardia *Height* 4-32 in (10-80 cm); hairy annual with narrow toothed leaves. *Flowers* April-July; broad, white lip, arranged in dense pyramidal spike. *Habitat* damp sandy soils, fields.

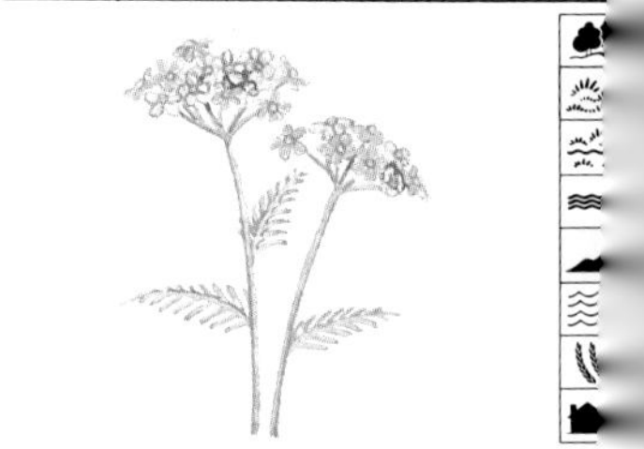

Yellow Milfoil *Height* 2-8 in (5-20 cm); perennial; narrow feathery leaves, covered with silvery down. *Flowers* May-July. *Habitat* poor dry grassland, rocky slopes, in mountain areas.

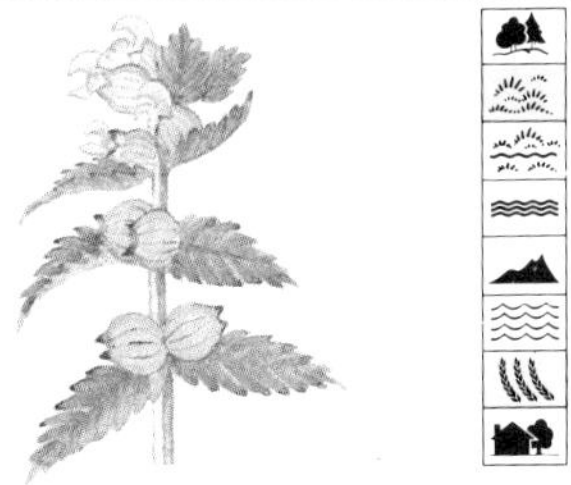

Yellow Rattle *Height* 6-16 in (15-40 cm); semiparasitic annual *Flowers* May-September; set in conspicuous rounded bracts; seeds rattle inside capsule when ripe. *Habitat* grassy meadows, cultivated fields.

Yellow Loosestrife *Height* 20-48 in (50-120 cm); perennial; oval leaves with tiny black dots. *Flowers* July-August; up to ¾ in (2 cm) across, arranged in loose clusters. *Habitat* wet places, ditches, fens, river banks.

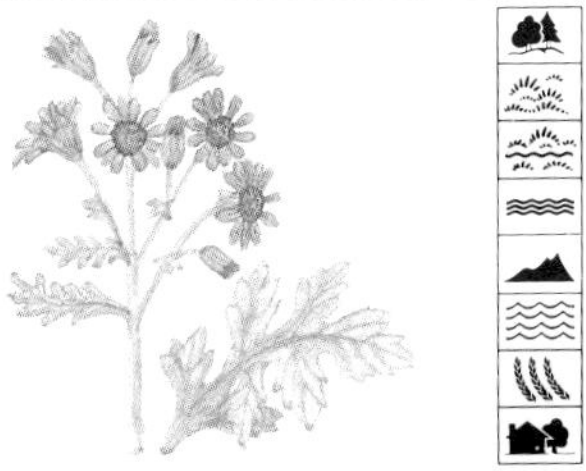

;ommon Ragwort *Height* 12-24 in (30-60 cm); biennial; ƨaves blunt tipped *Flowers* June-November. *Habitat* ›rassy fields and meadows. Poisonous to cattle.

Field Marigold *Height* up to 12 in (30 cm); annual. *Flowers* throughout year; heads ⅖-⅘ in (1-2 cm) across; spiny, c-shaped seeds. *Habitat* dry stony fields, vineyards, waste ground.

ırist's Thorn *Height* up to 6 ft 6 in (2 m); spiny shrub th smooth, oval leaves. *Flowers* small, yellow in ısters; distinctive umbrella-shaped fruits. *Habitat* dry lsides and thickets.

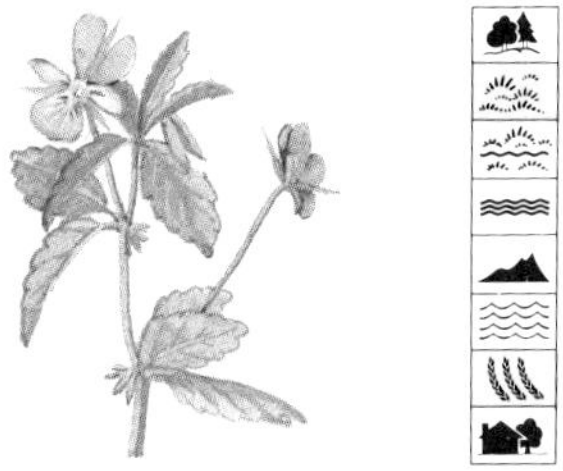

Field Pansy or Heartsease *Height* 2-8 in (5-20 cm); annual. *Flowers* April-November; cream or pale violet; seeds in capsule which splits into 3 lobes. *Habitat* cultivated land, hedgerows, roadsides.

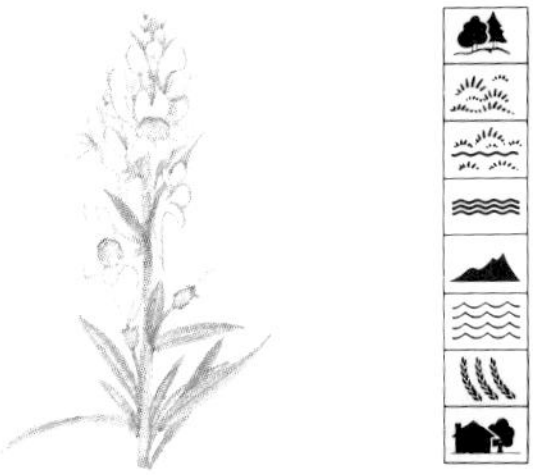

ımon Toadflax *Height* 8-24 in (20-60 cm); perennial; ves smooth, greyish green. *Flowers* June-October; ender spikes. *Habitat* railway embankments, rries, woodland edge, waste ground.

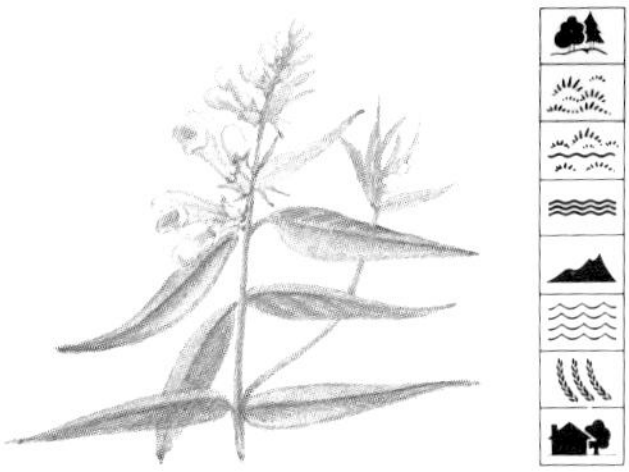

Common Cow-wheat *Height* 4-20 in (10-50 cm); semiparasitic annual. *Flowers* May-September, either pale yellow or white with pink tinge. *Habitat* woodland edge, moorland, heaths.

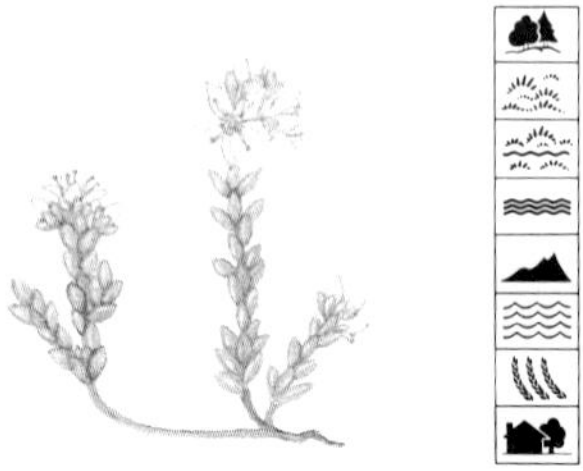

Biting Stonecrop *Height* 2-7½ in (5-15 cm) perennial forming dense, fleshy leaved mat. *Flowers* May-July; flowers ½ in (12 mm) across, at tips of branching stems. *Habitat* dry, stony places, walls, roofs, shingle, rocky cliffs.

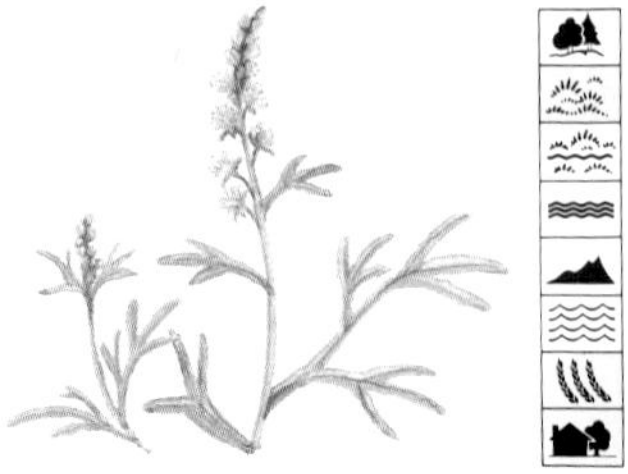

Wild Mignionette *Height* 8-20 in (20-50 cm); perennial; distinguish from similar Weld by toothed leaves and sweet scent. *Flowers* June-September, in tall spike. *Habitat* bare, disturbed ground, quarries, wasteland.

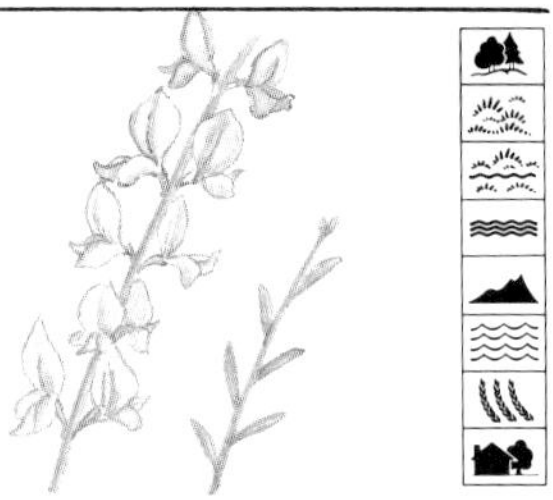

Spanish Broom *Height* up to 8 ft (2.5 m); shrub with relatively few leaves. *Flowers* May-August; large, ⅘ in (2 cm) long, sweet smelling; fruits, long black pods. *Habitat* scrub and woodland on dry, chalky soils.

Great Leopard's-bane *Height* 8-20 in (20-50 cm); upright hairy perennial, spreading by underground stems. *Flowers* May-July; 1⅗-2⅓ in (40-60 mm) across, in clusters. *Habitat* woodland, shady places, in mountain areas.

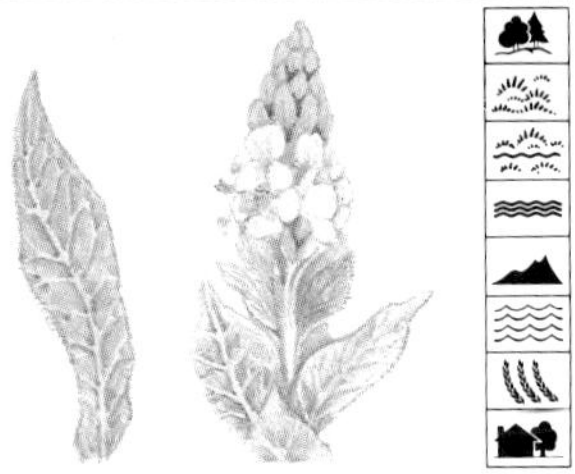

Great Mullein *Height* 8 80 in (20-200 cm); biennial; leaves up to 16 in (40 cm) long, covered with thick grey down. *Flowers* June-August. *Habitat* dry woodland clearings, grassy places. Once used as torches by coating plant with tallow.

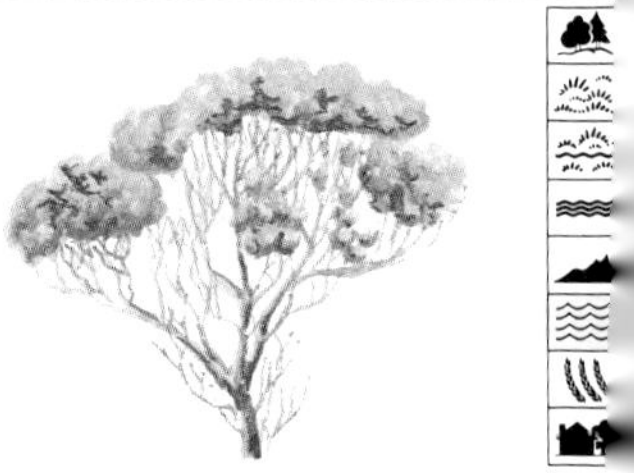

Tree Spurge *Height* 8 ft (2.5 m); woody shrub. *Flowers* April-June; yellow, in dense terminal clusters. *Habitat* as thick clumps on rocky cliffs and hillsides on coast.

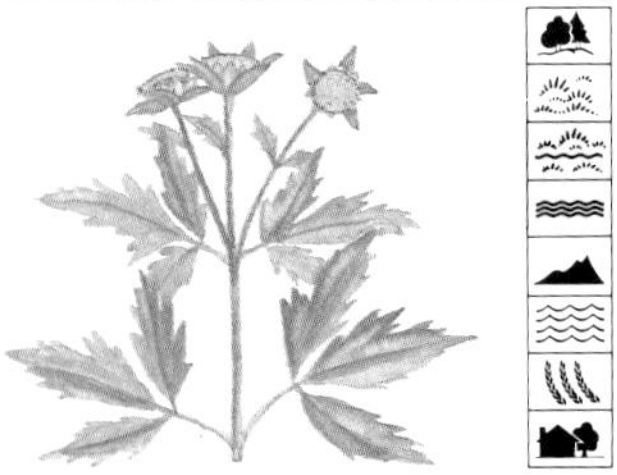

Trifid Bur-marigold *Length* up to 40 in (100 cm); sprawling, hairless annual. *Flowers* July-October; flowers with tiny yellow petals; bristly seeds. *Habitat* damp places, ditches, pond margins.

Autumn Hawkbit *Height* 4-16 in (10-40 cm); branchec annual with smooth leaves. *Flowers* July-Septembe seeds carried by white parachute of hairs. *Habitat* ri grassland, parks, roadside verges.

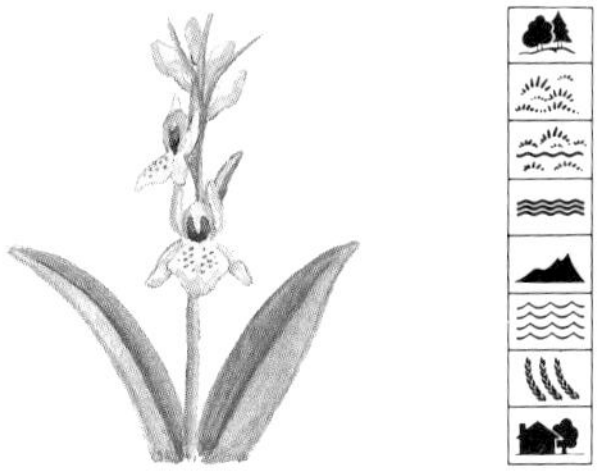

Elder-flowered Orchid *Height* 4-12 in (10-30 cm); perennial. *Flowers* April-July; yellow or red. *Habitat* mountain meadows and clearings; up to 6900 ft (2100 m).

Lesser Spearwort *Height* 4-20 in (10-50 cm); perennial with long narrow leaves. *Flowers* ⅖-⅘ in (10-20 mm) across; June-October. *Habitat* wet soils, ditches, damp meadows, by streams.

'ouch-me-not Balsam *Height* 12-31 in (30-80 cm); mooth-leaved annual. *Flowers* July September; bright ellow, with or without orange spots; seed capsule pens explosively if touched. *Habitat* damp woods, haded places, by rivers.

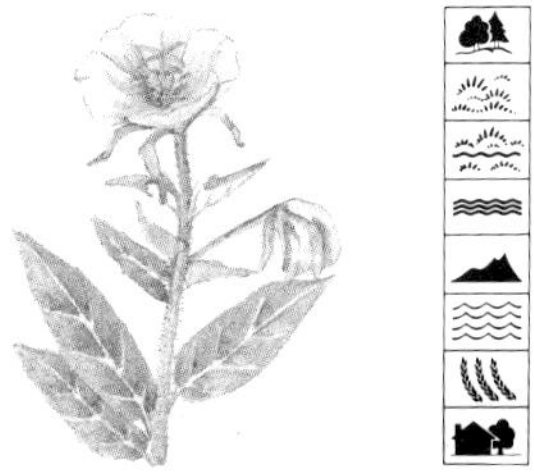

Evening Primrose *Height* 20-47 in (50-120 cm), biennial with deep taproot. *Flowers* June-September; sweetly scented, often opening at dusk. *Habitat* bare ground, roadsides; naturalized garden escape from USA.

neysuckle *Length* up to 16 ft (5 m); woody stemmed nbing shrub. *Flowers* June-October; pinkish, 1½-2 in 5 cm); sweet, heavy scent; cluster of red berries. *bitat* scrambling in hedges, deciduous woodland.

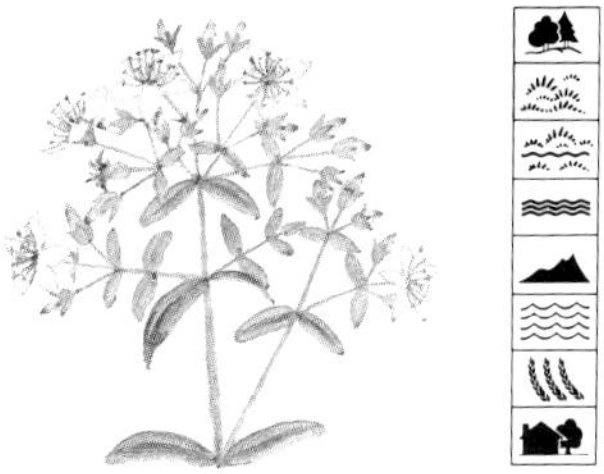

Common or Perforate St John's Wort *Height* 12-24 in (30-60 cm); perennial; separated from similar plants by 2 prominent ridges at sides of stem. *Flowers* July-September; flowers deep yellow with black dots. *Habitat* woodland edge, scrub.

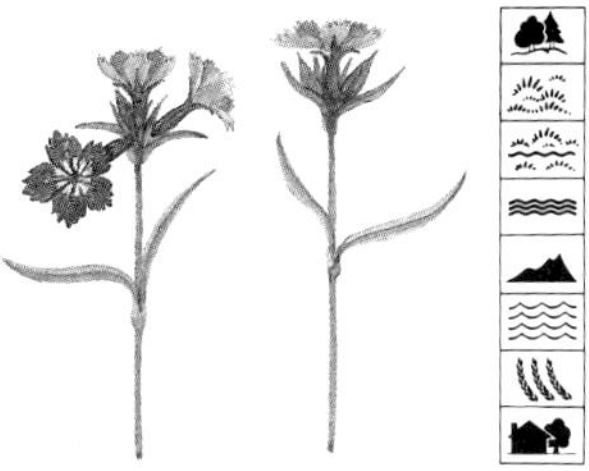

thusian Pink *Height* 6-16 in (15-40 cm); hairless ennial with strap-shaped leaves. *Flowers* May-ust; colour dark pink or red, set in brown bracts. *itat* grassland on chalky soil, woodland edge.

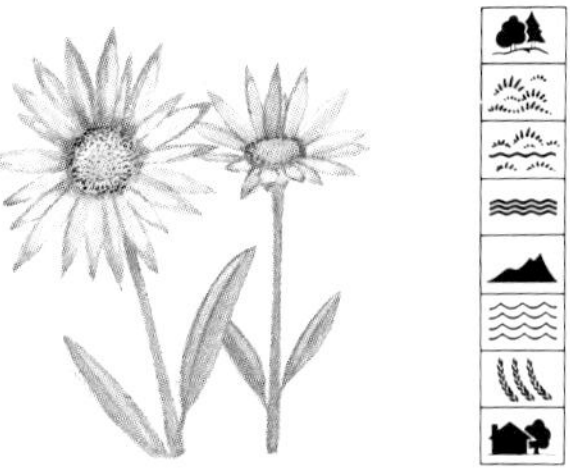

Pink Everlasting *Height* up to 16 in (40 cm); slender, silver-grey annual. *Flowers* June-July; true flower yellow, but pink bracts serve as petals; outer silvery bracts persist when dry. *Habitat* dry, rocky slopes.

Wild Thyme *Height* 2-6 in (5-15 cm); hairy stemmed shrub with creeping, horizontal branches; aromatic leaves. *Flowers* June-September; colour pale pink to purple. *Habitat* dry grassland, open woods, up to 10 000 ft (3000 m).

Tree Mallow *Height* up to 10 ft (3 m); biennial or perennial with woody stem and rounded, downy leaves. *Flowers* April-September; flowers up to 8 in (20 cm) across with black veins. *Habitat* coastal, on bare, rocky ground.

Field Bindweed *Height* up to 6 ft 6 in (2 m); creeping perennial which twists around other plants and solid supports. *Flowers* June-September; colour usually pink, occasionally white. *Habitat* fields, hedges, gardens.

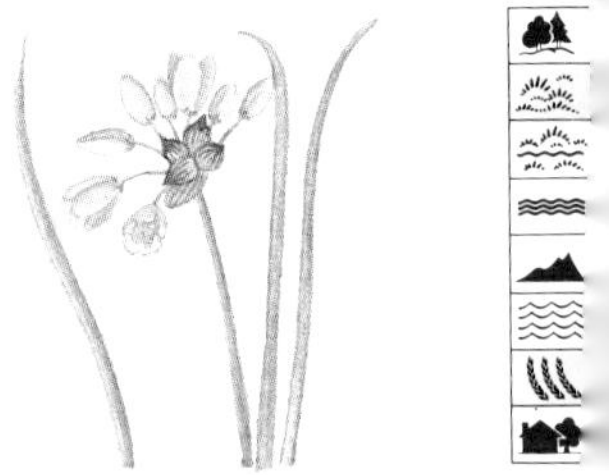

Rose Garlic *Height* 6-16 in (15-40 cm); bulb perennial with grass-like leaves, smelling strongly of garlic. *Flowers* April-June; pale-pink flowers in rounded cluster. *Habitat* rocky hillsides, rough fields.

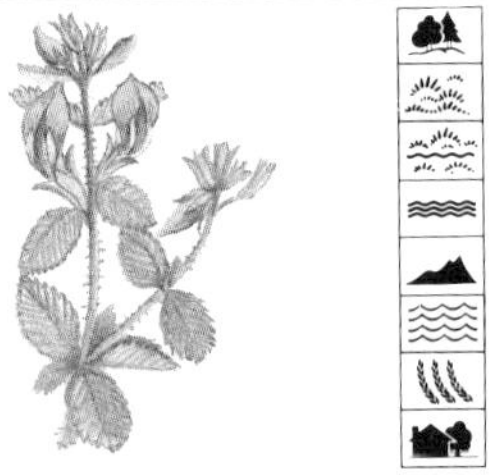

Restharrow *Height* up to 5½ in (14 cm); sprawling hairy perennial with occasional spines. *Flowers* July-September; in short spikes; colour pink to purple. *Habitat* sandy soil by coast, chalky soil inland, grassy places.

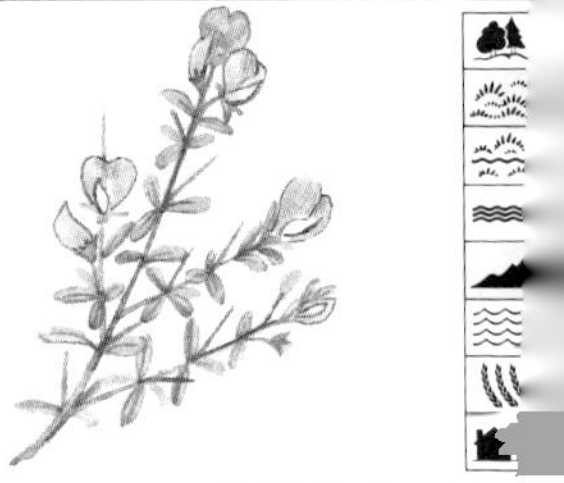

Spiny Restharrow *Height* 8-20 in (20-50 cm), woody shrub with sharp spines. *Flowers* April-June. *Habitat* c chalky soils, dry hillsides and meadows; up to 6000 ft (1800 m).

Greater Knapweed *Height* 12-40 in (30-100 cm); perennial with roughly hairy leaves. *Flowers* June-September; single flowers up to 2 in (5 cm) across; bracts at base green. *Habitat* chalk grassland, on cliffs, roadside verges.

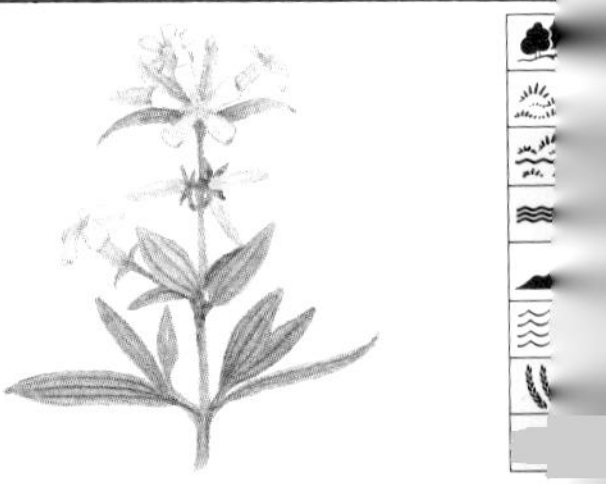

Soapwort *Height* 12-31 in (30-80 cm); smooth-leaved perennial. *Flowers* June-September; colour pink to white. *Habitat* damp fields, hedgerows, river banks, roadsides. Can be boiled to produce a soapy washir liquid.

Common Hemp-nettle *Height* 4-24 in (10-60 cm); hairy nettle-leaved annual. *Flowers* July-September; usually pale pink, occasionally yellow or white. *Habitat* cultivated fields, woodland edge, waste ground, roadsides.

Crow or Wild Garlic *Height* 12-24 in (30-60 cm); bulb perennial. *Flowers* June-August, usually long stalked, in rounded head, pink or white. *Habitat* vineyards, grassy places, fields.

lastic Tree *Height* 3-10 ft (1-3 m); dense evergreen hrub with strongly aromatic scent. *Flowers* April-June; 1 small clusters; fruit pea sized, ripening to black. *'abitat* scrubby hillsides; plant resin used to make arnish.

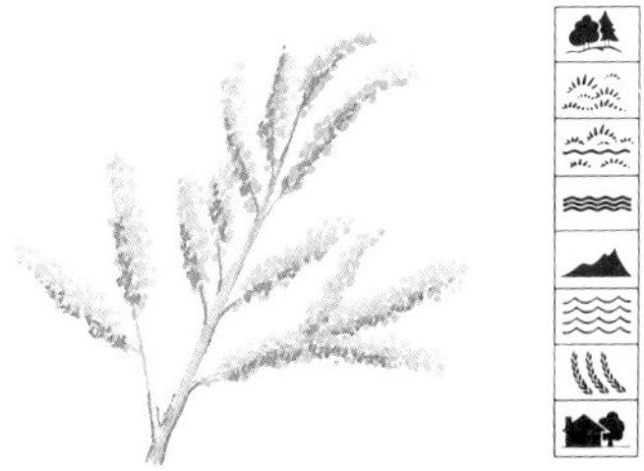

Tamarisk *Height* 6 ft 6 in-33 ft (2-10 m); shrub with long flexible branches bearing feathery leaves. *Flowers* March-July; tiny flowers in long spikes. *Habitat* mainly coastal, but also damp places by freshwater; garden ornamental.

nk Hawksbeard *Height* up to 12 in (30 cm); annual th hairy toothed leaves. *Flowers* April-June; up to ½ in (4 cm) across; seeds in white 'clock'. *Habitat* ickets, on rocky hillsides, Olive groves.

Rosebay Willowherb *Height* 20-60 in (50-150 cm), perennial; hairless stem and leaves, reddish in dry situations. *Flowers* July-September. *Habitat* often colonizes burnt ground, also on walls, waste ground, and woodland clearings.

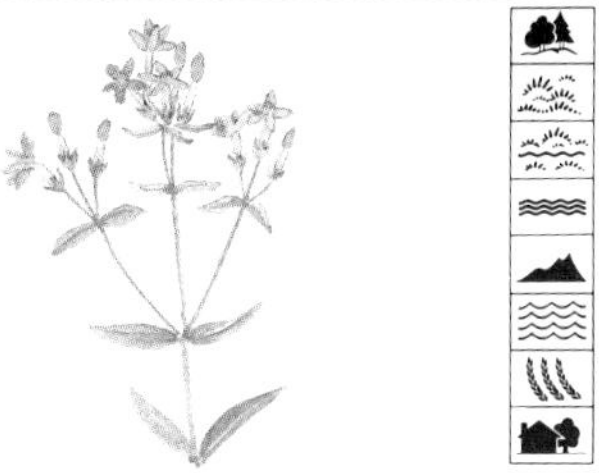

nmon Centaury *Height* 4-12 in (10-30 cm); smooth y-green annual, with leaves in basal rosette. *Flowers* e-September, usually in a terminal cluster. *Habitat* d-dunes, dry woodland, and grassland near coast.

Spear Thistle *Height* 23½-47 in (60-120 cm), biennial; very spiny stems. *Flowers* July-September; usually solitary, up to 1½ in (4 cm) across; seeds arranged in a 'clock'. *Habitat* waste ground, gardens, woodland clearings.

Creeping Thistle *Height* 24-48 in (60-120 cm); deep-rooted perennial with smooth stem and spiny leaf margins. *Flowers* June-September; heads up to 1¼ in (3 cm) across; seeds carried by feathery down. *Habitat* cultivated and waste ground.

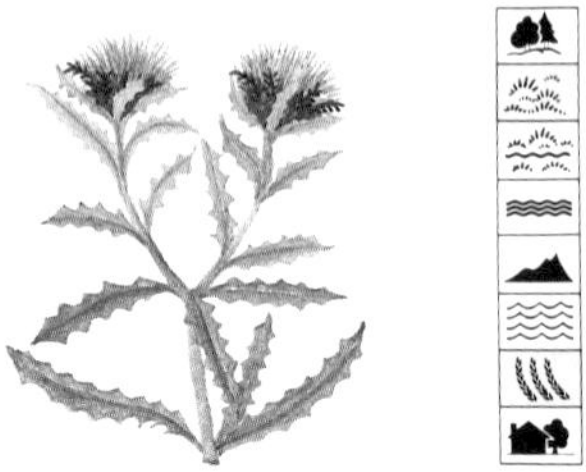

Distaff Thistle *Height* up to 10 in (25 cm); annual; leaves covered with white down, long bristly hairs around the edges. *Flowers* April-July; small flower heads surrounded by curved spiny bracts. *Habitat* dry hillsides, paths.

Oleander *Height* 6 ft 6 in-13 ft (2-4 m); evergreen shrub with stiff, leathery leaves. *Flowers* May-July; up to 5 cm across, pale pink or white, sweet smelling. *Habitat* in damp places, along stream and river beds. POISONOUS SAP.

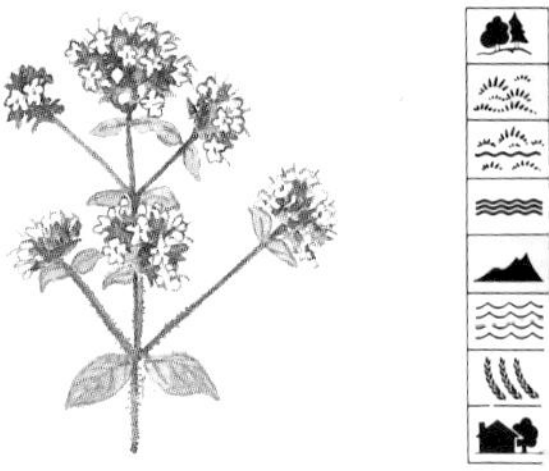

Oregano *Height* up to 31 in (80 cm); aromatic perennial used as culinary herb. *Flowers* July-September; colour pink or white. *Habitat* dry stony hillsides.

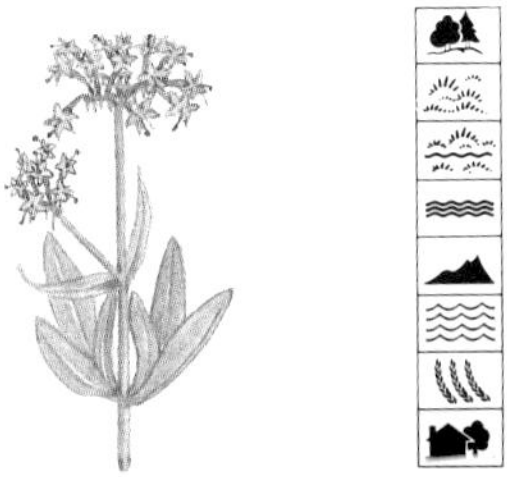

Red Valerian *Height* 12-32 in (30-80 cm), smooth-stemmed fleshy perennial with blue-green leaves. *Flowers* March-September; colour pink or white; *Habitat* rocky cliffs, old walls; often cultivated as ornamental.

Basil Thyme *Height* 4-12 in (10-30 cm); hairy stemmed annual with a faint minty smell. *Flowers* June-September. *Habitat* on chalky soils, dry bare ground, stony fields, and hillsides.

Common Poppy *Height* 8-32 in (20-80 cm); hairy annual; solitary or in dense carpet. *Flowers* 2¾-4 in (7-10 cm) across; April-July; tiny seeds in 'pepperpot' capsule. *Habitat* cornfields, roadsides, gardens.

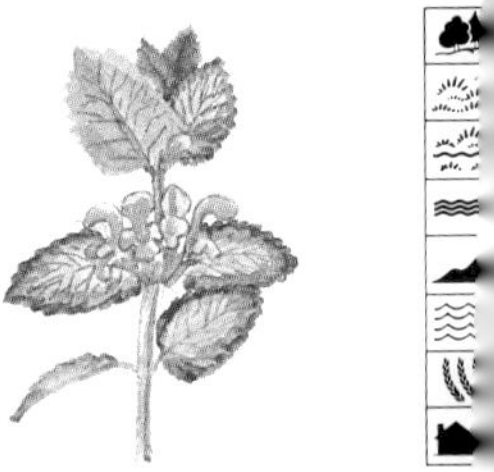

Spotted Dead-nettle *Height* 8-24 in (20-60 cm); hairy strongly scented perennial; leaves with irregular wh blotches. *Flowers* April-September. *Habitat* woodlar edge, hedges, waste ground.

Red Hottentot Fig Low, creeping perennial forming mats covering large areas; thick, fleshy leaves. *Flowers* March-July; up to 4 in (10 cm) across; purple, lilac, yellow, or orange; fruits edible. *Habitat* sea cliffs.

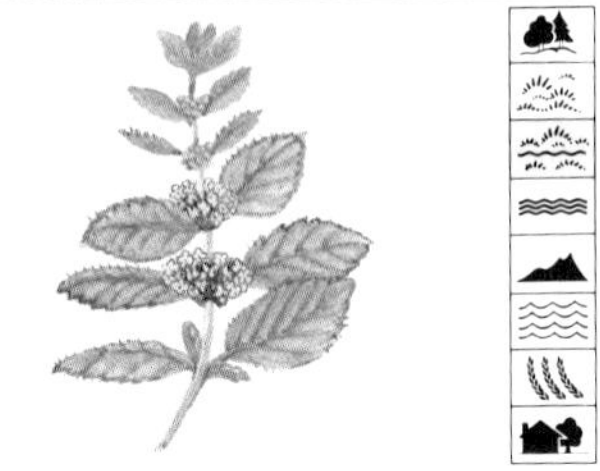

Corn Mint *Height* 4-16 in (10-40 cm); hairy aromatic perennial. *Flowers* July-September; tiny lilac flowers arranged in tight whorls at leaf axils. *Habitat* damp grassy places.

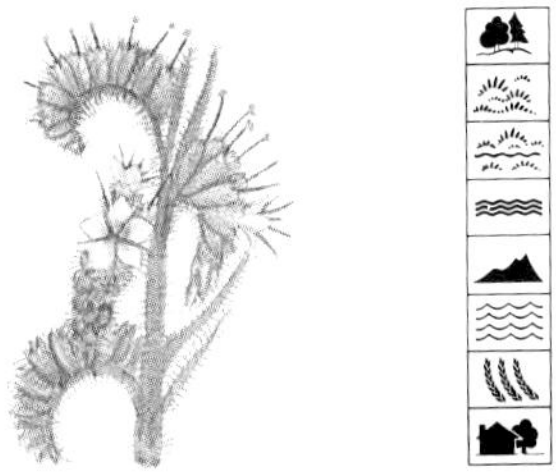

Pale Bugloss *Height* up to 40 in (1 m); biennial with bristly leaves. *Flowers* March-July; small, up to ⅔ in (14 mm) across, white to pale violet. *Habitat* weedy fields, waste ground, roadsides.

Rosemary *Height* up to 60 in (1.5 m); woody shrub with narrow aromatic leaves used as culinary herb. *Flowers* throughout year. *Habitat* on dry coastal hills, often in dense thickets. Rosemary Oil used in perfume industry.

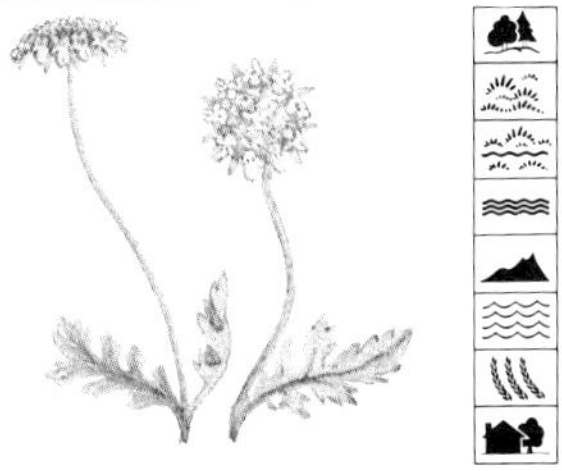

mall Scabious *Height* 8-24 in (20-60 cm); hairy erennial. *Flowers* June-October; distinguished from imilar Field Scabious by smaller flower head ontaining tiny black bristles. *Habitat* dry grassland on ne-rich soil.

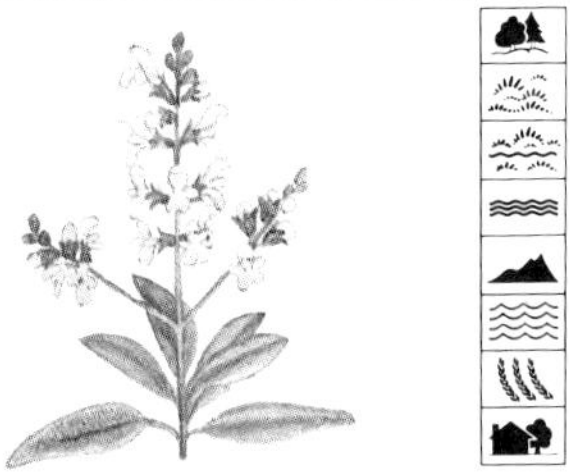

Three-lobed Sage *Height* up to 60 in (1.5 m); woody aromatic shrub with greyish wrinkled leaves. *Flowers* March-June; colour pale lilac. *Habitat* bushy thickets near coast. Fragrant tea made from dried leaves.

mmon Cornsalad *Height* 4-8 in (10-20 cm); branched nual, sparsely hairy. *Flowers* April-August; tiny lilac wers in small terminal clusters. *Habitat* cultivated ds, waste ground, paths, hedgerows, sand-dunes.

Sea Lavender Height 8-20 in (20-50 cm); perennial; much-branched stems. *Flowers* July-September; dead, dried flowers persist. *Habitat* form dense patches in saltmarshes around Atlantic coast.

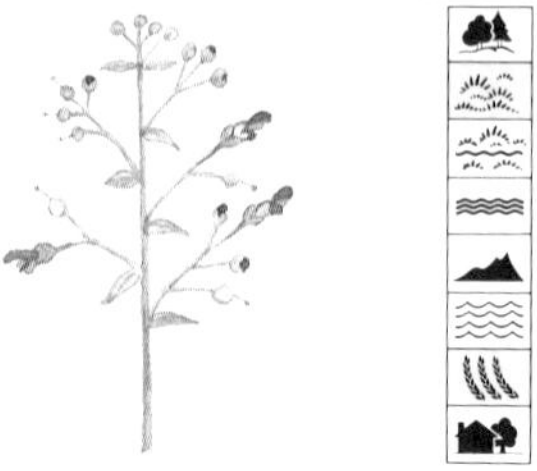

Figwort *Height* up to 24 in (60 cm); perennial; stem much-branched, hairless; leaves divided into lobes. *Flowers* March-July; small flowers, 1/10-1/4 in (3-6 mm) across. *Habitat* bare, rocky ground, waste places.

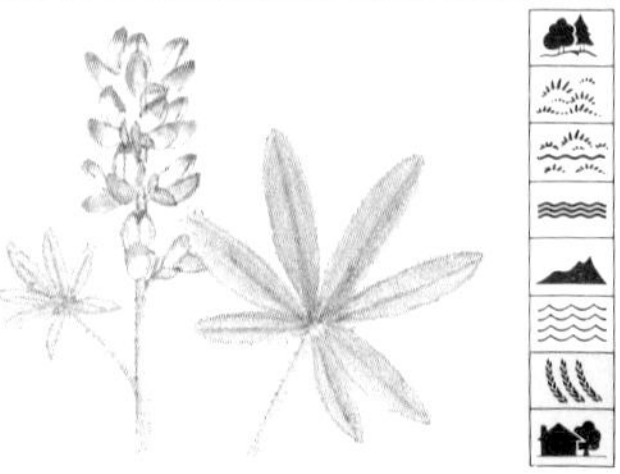

Hairy Lupin *Height* up to 16 in (40 cm); annual with hairy leaves and stem; leaves broad, up to 2 in (5 cm) across. *Flowers* February-April; seeds in hairy pod. *Habitat* cultivated land such as vineyards and Olive groves, roadsides.

Dame's Violet *Height* 16-40 in (40-100 cm); perennial; leaves roughly hairy. *Flowers* May-August; white, violet, or lilac, sweetly scented; seeds in upright pods. *Habitat* damp places, hedgerows, garden escape.

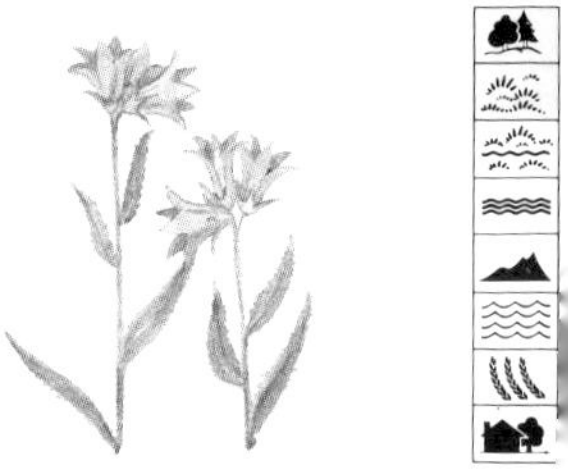

Rampion Bellflower *Height* 20-31 in (50-80 cm); biennial with slender stem and narrow hairy leaves. *Flowers* May-August. *Habitat* dry fields, woodland edge, scrub.

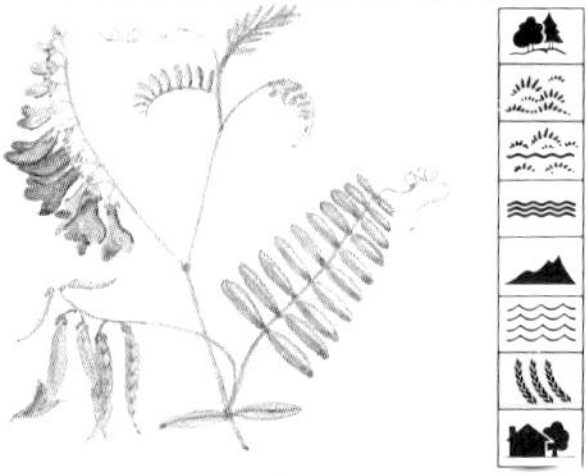

Tufted Vetch *Length* up to 40 in (1 m); prostrate perennial scrambling up other plants using tendrils. *Flowers* June-August; arranged to one side of long-stalked spike. *Habitat* grassy meadows, hedge banks; up to 7250 ft (2200 m).

Common Vetch *Length* 12-32 in (30-80 cm); low creeping annual, holds on to other plants using tendrils. *Flowers* April-September; seeds in tiny brown or black pods. *Habitat* fields and grassy places, hedgebanks.

Salsify *Height* up to 40 in (1 m); biennial; smooth grass-like leaves. *Flowers* April-June; flowers only open for part of day; seeds in large round 'clock'. *Habitat* dry grassy places. Cultivated for edible root.

Borage *Height* 8-24 in (20-60 cm); annual; leaves and stem bristly. *Flowers* May-September. *Habitat* roadsides, vineyards; often cultivated as medicinal herb to lower fevers and relieve coughs.

Viper's Bugloss *Height* 12-24 in (30-60 cm); stiff bristly perennial. *Flowers* May-August; buds pink, opening to blue. *Habitat* dry open places, quarries, stony fields, beside paths, sand-dunes.

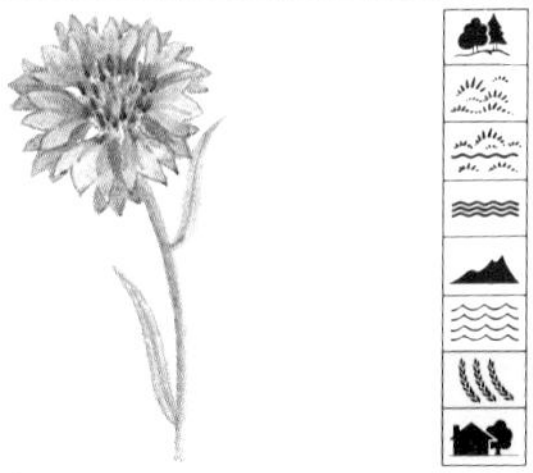

Cornflower *Height* 12-31 in (30-80 cm); annual; narrow leaves and stem with white downy covering. *Flowers* June-August; up to 1¼ in (3 cm) across. *Habitat* waste ground, field margins, increasingly uncommon in cornfields.

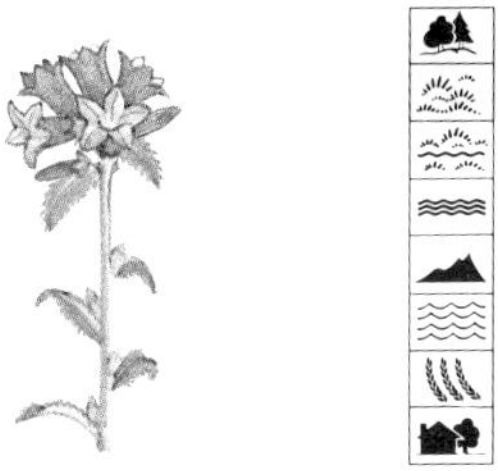

Clustered Bellflower *Height* 8-24 in (20-60 cm); perennial; lower leaves heart shaped, stalked, upper leaves narrow, unstalked. *Flowers* June-October; most flowers in dense terminal cluster. *Habitat* chalk grassland, woods.

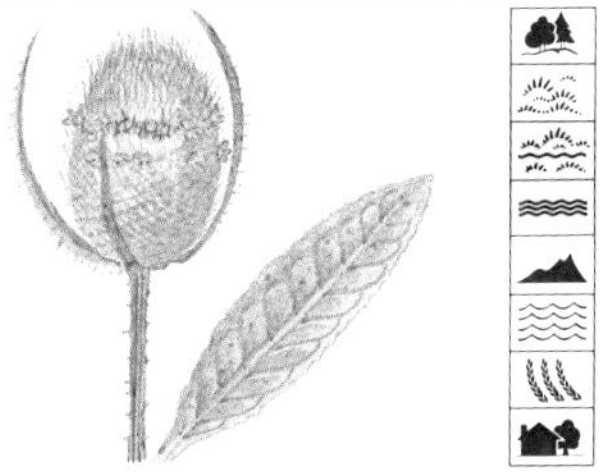

Teasel *Height* 27½-60 in (70-150 cm), perennial; stem very prickly. *Flowers* July-August, flowers set into green spiky head which dries and persists; head once used as brush in cloth making. *Habitat* river banks, damp ditches.

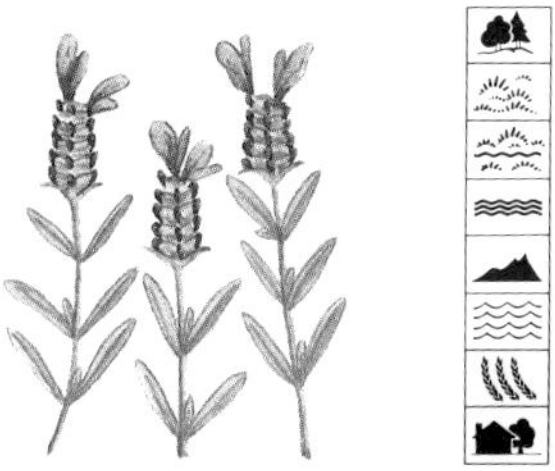

hicory *Height* 12-48 in (30-120 cm); stiff hairy perennial ith narrow upright leaves. *Flowers* May-September; ually blue, occasionally pink or white. *Habitat* adsides, waste ground. Leaves and roots eaten.

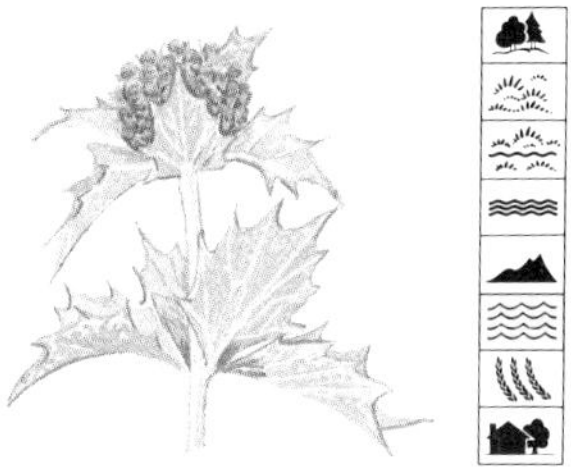

Sea Holly *Height* 8-24 in (20-60 cm), perennial; hairless leaves with very spiny margins. *Flowers* June-September; fruits oval, covered with tiny hooks. *Habitat* sand-dunes and coastal regions.

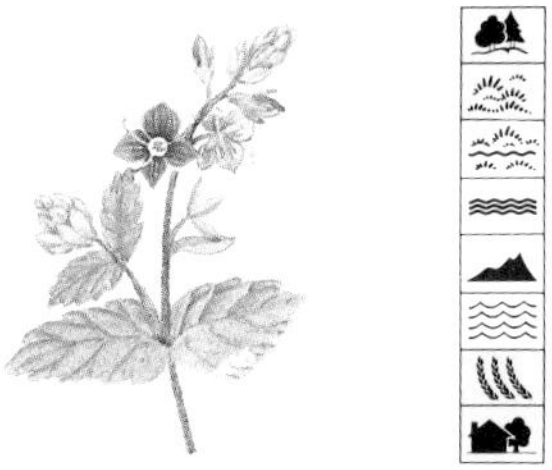

mander Speedwell *Height* 4-12 in (10-30 cm); ual. *Flowers* April-June; flowers much brighter blue n similar Field Speedwell. *Habitat* damp woods, ges, grassy places, gardens.

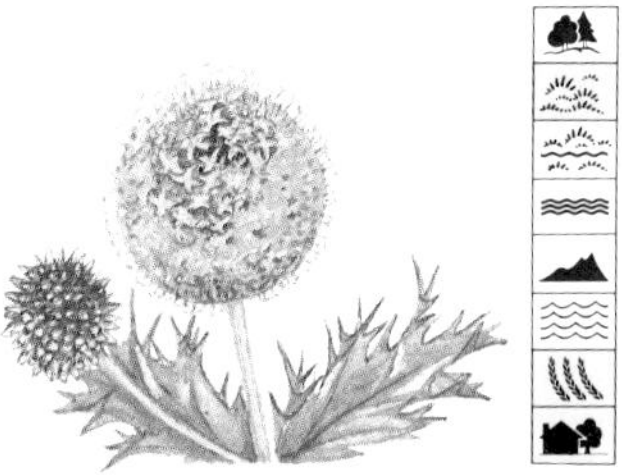

Globe Thistle *Height* up to 40 in (1 m); perennial; undersides of leaves and stem covered in woolly down; upper surface shiny, with very spiny margin. *Flowers* July-September. *Habitat* open stony hillsides, waste ground.

GLOSSARY

We have kept technical terms to a minimum, but a few are unavoidable and are defined here. A very few are also defined in the text, but are repeated here for ease of reference. Words used in a definition which are themselves defined in this glossary are printed in small capitals.

annual any flowering plant that completes its life cycle and then dies within a single growing season.
antenna one of a pair of sense organs or 'feelers' on the head of an insect, millipede, or centipede, richly endowed with scent and touch detectors.
anther the male, pollen-producing structures of a flower.
aromatic of plants which secrete scented oils that evaporate readily; includes most culinary herbs.
axil the upper angle between a small stem or branch and a larger one, or where a leaf stalk joins a stem.
biennial a flowering plant that takes two years to complete its life cycle and die; typically, food is stored in the first year, and flowering and seed production occur in the second year.
bract a leaf, usually small or modified, which grows in the AXIL of a flower or INFLORESCENCE.
calcareous rock a rock, such as chalk or limestone, often formed from the laying down and compression of vast millions of skeletons of prehistoric microscopic marine creatures, largely composed of calcium carbonate.
capsule a dry fruit which splits open to release seeds.
climax vegetation the final, self-perpetuating stage in a succession through time of plant communities which have reached a balance with the environment.
crystalline rock rock which has been formed by crystallization from a liquid, molten state or under great pressure.
deciduous of trees which shed their leaves seasonally, usually autumn, and spend at least part of the year in a leafless state.
elytron(a) the horny wing case of earwigs, beetles, and some bugs, formed of modified forewings and which protect the hindwings when at rest.
endemic of a plant or animal whose geographical distribution is restricted to the region under discussion.
evergreen tree with persistent leaves which are not shed seasonally.
garrigue low-growing vegetation, derived from primary Mediterranean forest and replacing it over much of the region as a result of several millennia of human interference, especially grazing by goats; dwarf, prickly shrubs and aromatic herbs with drought-resistant foliage dominate.
gastropod literally, 'stomach foot', referring to those molluscs, such as snails and slugs, which move along by means of a single, large, mucus-secreting muscular foot on the underside of the body.
inflorescence the particular pattern of arrangement of flowers of a

given kind of plant.
invertebrate of animals, such as worms, snails, and insects, which have no vertebrae or backbone.
maquis a dense, evergreen community of shrubs, between 1 and 3 metres high which develops in Mediterranean areas after forest clearance.
passage migrant of birds which migrate between a wintering area in southern, warm countries and a summer breeding area in northern countries.
perennial a flowering plant which normally lives for two or more growing seasons and flowers annually, perhaps after an initial period of one to several years without flowering.
primitively social of wasps and bees, where there is no clear-cut distinction between an exclusively egg-laying queen and a worker caste, and social organization is poorly developed.
proboscis the tubular sucking mouthparts of many kinds of insect.
scree coarse rock debris that accumulates at the base of an inland cliff, being continually added to by the weathering and fragmentation of the cliff face.
sepal one of the outer floral leaves in a flower.
siphon in sea squirts, a pair of hollow tubes lined with waving microscopic hairs that generate water currents which carry in food particles; in water bugs and the aquatic larvae of some flies, a hollow breathing tube which pierces the surface film of water.
social living together in colonies, as in ants, wasps, and bees.
solitary of wasps and bees, where each female lives alone and builds her own nest, with no co-operation with other individuals.
succulent a plant with swollen, fleshy leaves which are juicy and retain water; succulent structures (stems and/or leaves) are an adaptation for survival in dry conditions.
tap root a large, central root descending into the soil much deeper than the other roots on a plant, an adaptation to reach soil water at depth; often found in plants in well-drained or arid soils.
tendril part of a stem, leaf, or leaf stalk which is modified as a thread-like, twisted climbing structure; found in plants such as sweet peas.
whorl a complete coil of a marine or land snail's shell.

FURTHER READING

General

Harris, T. 1982. *The Natural History of the Mediterranean.* Pelham Books, London.
Polunin, O and Walters, M. 1985. *A Guide to the Vegetation of Britain and Europe.* Oxford University Press, Oxford.

Seashore

Barnes, R. 1979. *The Natural History of Britain and Northern Europe: Coasts and Estuaries.* Hodder and Stoughton, London.
Campbell, A C. 1976. *The Country Life Guide to the Seashore and Shallow Seas of Britain and Europe.* Hamlyn Publishing Group, London.